Pearson

THE ENCYCLOPEDISTS
AS CRITICS OF MUSIC

THE

ENCYCLOPEDISTS

AS

CRITICS of MUSIC

⚜ ⚜ ⚜

⚜ ⚜

⚜

By *Alfred Richard Oliver*

COLUMBIA
UNIVERSITY PRESS
NEW YORK
1947

780.072
O 48

TO

HORATIO SMITH

FRIEND, TEACHER,

AND HUMANIST

FOREWORD

THE AIM of the present work is to bring before the public a definitive study of the Encyclopedists' relations to eighteenth-century French music, based upon an examination of the references to music in their several works, together with an analysis of the articles on music and related arts in the *Encyclopedia* proper. The earliest students of this subject, Jullien, Tourneux, and Carlez, saw the need of an *œuvre d'ensemble* on music and the *Encyclopedia,* but it was not until Hirschberg published his doctoral dissertation that such a work became available. However, Hirschberg failed to study the very important writings on music of Cahusac and Marmontel, and did not consider the articles on music in the *Encyclopedia*. Like his predecessors, Hirschberg was more interested in the history of the opera in France than in the Encyclopedists' criticism of music, with the result that his study may be called a fragmentary history of the eighteenth-century French opera with occasional references to Encyclopedist comment on that art. He did not study the Encyclopedists' relations to the traditions of musical criticism set up by the late seventeenth-century classical writers and furthered by the generation of critics immediately preceding the *Encyclopedia*. The Encyclopedists' stand in the Bouffons' Quarrel, their controversy with Rameau, and their role in preparing the Gluck reform-opera were rather inadequately treated. Hirschberg's conclusion was that the Encyclopedists' work was mainly negative.

In the present study the history of musical criticism in France will be traced from the classical authors of the late seventeenth century to the Revolution. It will be seen that the Encyclopedists are the outstanding exponents of this new literary effort. Their position in this century of musical criticism in France will be found laid deep in French traditions, traditions which the Encyclopedists modified, but did not essentially disturb. The lacunae with reference to Cahusac and Marmontel will be filled, the articles on music in the *Encyclopedia* will be analyzed, and the Encyclopedists' relations to the Bouffons' Quarrel, Rameau, and the reform-opera will be restated in the light of the new material afforded by the music articles of the *Encyclopedia,* as well as of the Supplement. The present work is concluded with a *vue d'ensemble* of the critical reaction to the work of the Encyclopedists. It will be seen that this criticism was on the whole superficial and unsympathetic.

It is indeed with great pleasure that I acknowledge here my indebtedness to the late Professor Paul Hazard for furnishing me with inspiring directives in the early stages of this work. I wish especially to express my deepest gratitude to Professor Norman Torrey, of the Department of French, for his patient guidance and understanding supervision, and to Professor Paul H. Láng, of the Department of Music, for his invaluable suggestions as regards the musicological framework of this dissertation. I should also like to thank the International Institute of Education for granting me an American Field Service Fellowship which afforded me the opportunity of consulting the incomparable treasures of the Bibliothèque Nationale in Paris.

A. R. Oliver

New York
June 16, 1947

CONTENTS

PART I: CRITICISM OF MUSIC IN THE
            ENCYCLOPEDIA

    I. Introduction: Musical Criticism before the *Encyclopedia*   3

   II. Historical Considerations of the Opera   21

  III. Criticism of the Opera   32

  IV. Suggested Reforms of the Opera   57

    V. Instrumental Music   61

  VI. The Dance   74

PART II: POLEMICS AND REFORMS

  VII. The Bouffons' Quarrel   89

VIII. The Rameau Controversy   101

  IX. Gluck's Reform-Opera   113

PART III: THE INFLUENCE OF THE *ENCYCLOPEDIA*
              ON THE CRITICISM OF MUSIC

   X. The Influence of the *Encyclopedia* Abroad   127

  XI. The Influence of the *Encyclopedia* in France   140

 XII. Post-Encyclopedist Criticism of Music in France   149

XIII. Conclusion   155

Appendix A: Index of Articles on Music in the *Encyclopedia*   171

Appendix B: Authorities on Music Quoted in the
            Encyclopedia   189

Bibliography   197

Index   211

PART I

CRITICISM OF MUSIC
IN THE *ENCYCLOPEDIA*

" . . . let poets sing and musicians compose, but it is the philosophers' due to discourse intelligently concerning both arts of poetry and music."——ROUSSEAU

CHAPTER I

INTRODUCTION: MUSICAL CRITICISM
BEFORE THE *ENCYCLOPEDIA*

*This wonderful art of music, so full of charm, not only
pleases the ear and stirs the passions, but through the magic
of its sheer beauty captures reason itself.*—PERRAULT

THE GRADUAL DEVELOPMENT of opera in France owes its first impetus to
Mazarin's introduction of Italian operas, largely through the inter-
mediary of the Barberinis, who fled Rome after the death of Pope
Urban VIII (1644) and brought to Paris singers and composers of
great talent, such as the soprano Leonora Baroni, the composers Rossi,
Caproli, and Cavalli, and the very important operator of stage machinery, Torelli. Although these attempts were short-lived, because the
French did not take interest in an opera sung in a foreign tongue,
they neverthless created a desire for an opera in French. Accordingly
Corneille did an *Andromède* in 1650, with music by D'Assoucy. If we
are to believe the criticism Corneille wrote of this opera, success was
due to Torelli's machines. Perrin and Cambert exploited the possibilities of creating a national opera, and in 1669 they were accorded a
license to this end. After three years of mismanagement the opera again
foundered, when Perrin was thrown into prison for debt. Meanwhile
Lulli had been composing music for Molière's comedy ballets, eying
skeptically the fortunes of the national opera. The shrewd Italian perceived that although Perrin and Cambert were not equal to their task
they nevertheless secured a considerable following. Lulli visited Perrin
in jail and bought the rights to the establishment of the opera. Thus
the year 1672 marks the beginning of French operatic history.[1]

In France the decay of tragedy, or rather its transformation into

[1] Rolland, *Les Origines du théâtre lyrique moderne;* Prunières, *L'Opéra italien en France
avant Lulli.*

opera,[2] is symptomatic of the disintegration of French classicism. After the first performances of Lulli's and Quinault's operas, Boileau, La Bruyère, Fénelon, St. Evremond—to mention only the most forceful critics of the opera—protested against this new mixed genre, which foreshadowed the loosening of the tenets of the classical tragedy. This opera, this hybrid they would say, composed of machines, florid decorations, dances, music, and mythology, had the effrontery to advertise itself as tragedy. In the name of everything beautiful they scoffed at the idea that this monster could take the place of staid Corneille and nobly passionate Racine. This opera was only a sensual thing fit for the vulgar ear; what else, they asked, is this continual noise that accompanies the action on the stage but an appeal to the senses? But these classical critics reckoned without their audience; the tragedy in a musical setting was eminently suited to the sensual tastes of the new generation.[3] It was principally in their underestimation of the qualifier "musical setting" that the first critics of music misunderstood, and therefore condemned, the opera.[4]

For these writers were criticizing opera as literature. The tragic and poetic aspirations of the new art form drew their fire.[5] Even a superficial comparison of the verse of Quinault's operas with that of Corneille's and Racine's plays convinced them of a considerable falling off in quality. They failed to see that Quinault's verses were a challenge to the actor. Through his declamation alone the latter could instill melody into these lines, and that without changing their meaning. As a matter of fact, their meaning is only half expressed without this exaltation into music. These early critics failed to see that Quinault's dramatic verse thirsted for musical interpretation. The essentially French conception of the opera as a literary form stood in direct opposition to

[2] For studies of the opera in France as a result of dramatic evolution see Rolland's thesis, *op. cit.,* and his *Musiciens d'autrefois;* Prunières, *Lully;* and Brunetière, *Etudes critiques, septième série.*

[3] "L'opéra français tel qu'on le forma dans sa nouveauté fut reçu de la nation avec un applaudissement presque unanime." Cahusac, *La Danse ancienne et moderne; ou, Traité de la danse,* III, 98.

[4] Cahusac observes that Quinault made a grievous error in terming his operas, *tragédies en musique,* and that the poet would have avoided much adverse criticism had he simply used the word *opéra* in reference to his works. *Ibid.,* pp. 95–97.

[5] ". . . les opéras sont . . . les grotesques de la poésie, et grotesques d'autant plus insupportables qu'on prétend les faire passer pour des ouvrages réguliers." André Dacier, *Poétique d'Aristote,* p. 82.

the Italian attitude which rejected all literary implications in the art.

To classical critics of the late seventeenth century the works of Quinault and Lulli were just another form of tragedy. Possibly if the opera had been introduced into France and had been taken over entirely as an Italian genre, the outcry would not have been so violent.[6] For in these accounts Lulli is spared, and when his name is mentioned he is more often commended than attacked. But the genius of the French almost immediately transformed the opera from a musical to a literary effort.[7] Thus, Quinault was singled out for abuse.[8] Although this poet was at best a worthy librettist for Lulli's music, all the vices of the new opera were laid at his door: the perversion of popular taste by an insidious insistence on love scenes; the seduction of the contemporary imagination by the vulgar and fantastic *merveilleux,* and the corruption of classical French tragedy into opera by a wanton appeal to the senses.

Boileau was Quinault's harshest critic; reiterated attacks upon the successful opera poet became almost a mania with him. The following selection from the "Satire X" aptly sums up his attitude toward Quinault and the opera.

The lady you marry may be beyond reproach. They tell me she was formed at Port-Royal in maidenly virtue and taught to regulate her desires according to the dictates of her duty.

But what assurance have you that in your house, where she will be at liberty to do as she please, she will conserve her pristine innocence and remain adamant to the seduction of reigning amusements?

Soon you will take her to the opera. With what eyes, do you think, will your chosen one view this florid spectacle? How will she react to the seductive strains of soft music, to the suggestive dances, to the heroes' sweet enchanting voices? To discourses that treat only of love, spoken in the

[6] According to the contemporary critic La Laurencie, Lulli's job was not so much to impose Italian opera as it was "to introduce vocal and instrumental music into the classical tragedy in such a manner as to please the *amateurs* of the ballets and spectacle without alienating the interest of the literati who came for the play." De la Laurencie, *Le Goût musical en France,* p. 135.

[7] In England the opera was transformed into oratorio, while in Germany a rather awkward Biblical music drama resulted. See Láng, *Music in Western Civilization.*

[8] Dacier, the learned commentator of Aristotle, offers a specimen of this attitude: ". . . car s'il y a rien au monde qui paraisse étrange et contraire même à une action tragique, c'est le chant. N'en déplaise aux inventeurs des tragédies en musique, poèmes aussi ridicules que nouveaux, et que l'on ne pourrait souffrir, si l'on avait le moindre goût pour les pièces de théâtre, ou que l'on n'eût pas été enchanté et séduit par un des plus grands musiciens qui ait jamais été." Dacier, *op. cit.,* p. 82.

sugary tones of sweet Rinaldo or sighed by some mad Roland? Telling her that to Love and Love alone, like some supreme deity, she must sacrifice all, even unto her most carefully guarded virtue? That never too soon can she be fired with passion, that she has been given a tender heart solely that it may be sacrificed on the altar of Love, and other such commonplaces of moral lubricity that Lulli's music instilled with life?

Boileau's invective is aimed chiefly against Quinault. The verse referring to Lulli is meant as praise rather than censure; Lulli breathed life into Quinault's commonplace verse, and Quinault's immoral plays because of their mediocrity would have gone unnoticed had not Lulli's music given them currency by rendering them charming and seductive.

If the opera poem was immoral, then the music was corrupt. The argument advanced by critics of the age of reason was that music could express only the sentiments indicated in the opera text. Music was conceived at this time as enhanced declamation; music had no significance aside from words. Since the poems were of an immoral bent, therefore the music was an agent of vice.[9] It was in this sense that Fénelon classed harmony as an amusement for weak-minded and lazy people, and joined Plato in contending that music was unworthy of a well-policed republic. However, music may be good when it expresses or enhances the significance of the text, provided that the text inspires virtuous sentiments, which of course the opera text did not do.[10] Thus, rationalist critics objected to music because it could not express positive ideas; yet they were extremely disturbed by the sensuous charm which emanated from the opera.

But the opera was answerable to a much more serious charge: that it was ruining the classical tragedy. The touchstone of St. Evremond's violent criticism of the opera is to be found in this indictment: "What annoys me most about the present stubborn fad for the opera is that it will soon ruin the tragedy, which is the most beautiful thing that we have." [11] This is a remarkable statement, correctly presaging the course

[9] Jules Ecorcheville tells us that the Church was quick to oppose the opera as a source of vice, and he quotes the position of the Sorbonne in 1693: ". . . l'opéra est d'autant plus dangereux, qu'à la faveur de la musique, dont tous les tons sont recherchés et disposés exprès pour toucher, l'âme est bien plus susceptible de passion." Ecorcheville, *De Lulli à Rameau*, p. 57.

[10] Fénelon, *Lettre sur les occupations de l'Académie Française,* chap. vi, "Projet d'un traité sur la tragédie," in his *Œuvres*, III, 236.

[11] St. Evremond, "Sur les opéras," in his *Œuvres*, III, 182.

of events. He traces the source of the opera's popularity to the French imitation of Spanish comedy and the desire to witness love scenes exclusively. The French packed the plays they took over from Spain with amorous discourses and exercised their talents chiefly upon the delicate expression of tender sentiments. As for French comedy, it too soon became little more than a vehicle for *la galanterie;* as if the types portrayed by Molière had all passed out of existence or had been engulfed by the *galants*.[12]

Boileau, too, looked down upon the opera as a disgusting love feast. When Racine found difficulty in completing the request opera *Phaëton,* he called in the critic for help. In vain Boileau tried to resist, saying that he had no experience in writing love lyrics. However, he finally condescended to write the prologue, not without a profound feeling of revulsion. The opera *Phaëton* was not to be found among Racine's papers at his death; Boileau suggests that the poet had destroyed it "out of nicety of conscience, and because it spoke of love." [13]

Love, then, was the mainstay of the opera.[14] Just as the novels catered to the popular taste for love scenes, Fénelon tells us, tragedy also gave in to the reigning mode and became corrupt.

Our poets have rendered the tragedy as silly and sugary as the long-winded novel. In it they speak only of passions, love-bonds, and unrequited love.

The reigning fad caused love to be introduced everywhere. Authors believed that it was impossible to escape being tiresome in a two-hour performance without the aid of a gallant intrigue.[15]

He goes on to say that the ancients did not introduce profane love into the tragedy, and he compares the *Oedipus* of Sophocles with that of Corneille to show to how great an extent the latter made concessions to this passion in his plays. Thus the evil was already present in the works of Corneille and Racine. This vogue noticed by Fénelon weakened the classical tragedy first by introducing love scenes; then by insisting more and more on the love interest transformed the classical

[12] St. Evremond, "Sur nos comédies," in his *Œuvres,* III, 150–151.
[13] Boileau, "Prologue," "La Poésie," "La Musique," "Avertissement au lecteur," in his *Œuvres,* II, 479.
[14] For the love thesis in the opera see Lindemann, *Die Operntexte Quinaults vom Literarischen Standpunkte aus Betrachtet;* also Gros, *Philippe Quinault.*
[15] Fénelon, *loc. cit.*

tragedy into opera, where it found full satisfaction, opera arias being built primarily around love motives.[16]

If Corneille and Racine were willing to give in only occasionally to the reigning mode, Quinault subscribed to it completely. The career of this poet shows how the fashion grew. His was one of those strange cases in which popular judgment undergoes a complete reversal almost overnight. Having failed as a dramatist, he turned to the opera libretto and captivated Paris by making the tragedy a long love duet.[17] He retained the Alexandrian couplets of the classical tragedy for the recitative which takes care of the main dramatic action. For his airs he imitated the meter of the love songs from the *divertissements* of Molière's comedy ballets. Lulli, who had collaborated with Molière in the production of these comedy ballets, most probably introduced Quinault to the technique of song writing.[18] But the big asset of Quinault's operas was love; and that is all he ever wrote about. Riccoboni wonders why people do not cry out at last, "No more love, no more love!" [19] However, the classicists finally weakened. St. Evremond, the most austere and in many ways the most intelligent critic of the early opera, in his old age turned to the composition of both the words and music of an "Idylle en musique." Here is the final chorus, a tribute to Quinault.

> Love, love, let us all follow love,
> Let yourselves be fired with passion,
> Let Tircis live for love
> And Lysis love so she may live.[20]

---

[16] Brunetière points out that Quinault's successes awakened Racine's jealousy and emulation and claims that the love treatment in *Phèdre* indicates that Racine did not disdain to compete with Quinault. Brunetière, "Les commencements de l'opéra français," in *Manuel de l'histoire de la littérature française, deuxième édition, sixième époque,* p. 219.

[17] "Le phénix de la poésie *chantante* renaît de ses cendres; il a vu mourir et renaître sa réputation en un même jour. Ce juge même si infaillible et si ferme dans ses jugements, le public, a varié sur son sujet; ou il se trompe, ou il s'est trompé. Celui qui prononcerait aujourd'hui que Quinault en un certain genre, est mauvais poète, parlerait presque aussi mal que s'il eût dit, il y a quelque temps; *Il est bon poète.*" La Bruyère *"Des jugements"* in *Les Caractères,* chap. xii.

[18] A close study of *Cadmus et Hermione* shows an almost slavish imitation of Molière's *comédies-ballets,* not only in the meter of the verse and in the subject of the songs but also in the manner in which these songs are swung into the dramatic action.

[19] Riccoboni, *Traité de la réformation des théâtres* 1743, p. 34; quoted in Ecorcheville, *op. cit.,* p. 65.

[20] St. Evremond, *Œuvres,* III, 312.

Quinault realized clearly the demands of an opera libretto and sup-
plied Lulli with excellent specimens. He recognized that literary and
operatic dramaturgy are not identical, a fact overlooked by later French
librettists and not definitely pointed out until nearly a century later
by Jean Jacques Rousseau.[21]

The attitude toward the music of the opera at the end of the
seventeenth century was similar to our own reaction in the middle
of the twentieth to the music of the cinema. How many of us realize
that an extensive musical score has been prepared for most films, offer-
ing original music that claims to be of a high order? Still fewer of us
would be prepared to give an appreciation of the music of the film we
have just witnessed. We praise or condemn a film on the basis of drama
or spectacle, as the case may be; almost never on the basis of music.
We realize that the music is present, and indeed we should notice its
absence; but we never make a point of praising a film because of its
musical excellence. This was precisely the reaction of classical critics
to opera. Their criticism of the opera was based chiefly on literary and
dramatic grounds.

"You can never make a good opera," says Boileau in the *avertissement*
just quoted, "because music cannot relate." [22] He is saying with
Fontenelle, "Sonata, what are you saying to me?" Both critics are
obviously distressed by the fact that music does not express positive
ideas. In the following century the Encyclopedists were able to grasp
the significance of musical dramaturgy. However, as they approached
concrete musical examples, that is, sonatas, symphonies, and concertos,
rationalist critics were again confronted with the same dilemma.
Boileau's next objection is that the opera does not offer a large enough
canvas for the depiction of passions. What composer would ever set
pen to paper if he thought this criticism just? Boileau missed the direct
and deeper power of music to express passion. He wanted a clear, verbal
exposition perceptible to *la raison raisonnante*.

A less harsh and a much more disinterested critic of the opera was

[21] Jansen, "Schreiben an Grimm über das französische und italienische Musik-Drama,"
in *Jean Jacques Rousseau als Musiker*, Anhang I, p. 456. Rousseau aptly observes in this
leaflet that if Aristotle or Horace could have formulated the rules of operatic composition,
Boileau, La Bruyère, and the rest would not have attacked the opera.

[22] Boileau, *op. cit.*, II, 479.

La Bruyère. He decries the cabal whose adherents, rank amateurs and
would-be connoisseurs, discourage poets and musicians from adding to
man's artistic store.[23] Yet he admits that the opera, in his day at least,
is very unsatisfactory. His own objection is that the opera does not hold
his attention; evidently music was not considered by him to be at all
interesting. In any case, La Bruyère made an attempt to get away from
dramatic criticism and suggested that a new criterion be used.[24] His
own conception of the opera includes for the first time a perfect definition of the role of the *merveilleux,* the spell cast upon the audience by
the elaborately fantastic opera tableaux. The opera should be a spectacle
whose aim is to "hold the mind, the eyes and the ears under the same
spell." [25] To consider opera as spectacle was as far as these critics could
go. Not until the Encyclopedists was the music drama's right to independent aesthetic consideration accepted in France.

St. Evremond found that he was bored at the opera, too; the machines
were pleasing, the music was at times enjoyable, but on the whole the
merveilleux was annoying: "because the mind has so little to occupy it,
of necessity our senses become dull." [26] Like Boileau, his reason revolted
against this spectacle. He tells us further that it is the music that makes
the opera boring, especially the recitative, which is neither song nor
speech.[27] Here again is a classical objection to the opera.

Another aspect of the opera that is difficult for the imagination to grasp,
because it is so unnatural, is the necessity of singing everything from start
to finish, as if the people in the opera had foolishly agreed to set to music
all of life's activities, the humdrum along with the extraordinary. Imagine
a gentleman calling his servant, or giving him orders, in song . . . imagine men locked in combat singing to each other! This factor destroys all

[23] La Bruyère, "Des ouvrages de l'esprit," *op. cit.,* chap. i.

[24] "Il ne faut point de vols, ni de chars, ni de changements aux *Bérénices, et à Pénélope;*
il en faut aux opéras." *Ibid.*

[25] *Ibid.* For the use of the *merveilleux* in the early opera see Marsan, *La Pastorale
dramatique en France.*

[26] St. Evremond, "Sur les opéras," in his *Œuvres,* III, 169–170.

[27] *Ibid.* In England Addison voiced a similar objection to the recitative of Italian operas:
"There is nothing that has more startled our English audience than the Italian recitativo
at its first entrance upon the stage. People were wonderfully surprised to hear generals
singing the word of command, and ladies delivering messages in music. Our countrymen
could not forebear laughing when they heard a lover chanting out a billet-doux, and even
the superscription of a letter set to a tune." Addison, "The recitative part of operatic
music; Purcell; Lully," in *The Spectator,* 1711, No. 29. The Germans were also opposed
to the recitative, the most typical product of the Italian musical theater. See Láng, *Music
in Western Civilization,* p. 393.

sense of theater, which is more important in the play than the music. The great masters of drama added the music as a sort of agreeable accompaniment not really necessary to the play after they had dealt with the more important elements of subject and dialogue.[28]

This paragraph is a solid denial of the very essence of opera. The critic rejects the through-composed opera of the Italians, preferring the very French play with incidental music. Here St. Evremond is most probably thinking of Corneille, who tells us in his *Examen d'Andromède* that he tried to make the music as inconspicuous as possible. For St. Evremond the important element in the opera is the drama. The trouble with Lulli's operas is that one does not think of Cadmus, Thésée, or whatever hero is on the stage, but of Lulli. This does not mean that music must be banished from the stage altogether, says St. Evremond; prayers, divine services, the expression of passions, and the like are apt material for song. The remainder of the opera he wants to be straight drama instead of recitative. Otherwise, he continues, his definition of the opera as a bizarre combination of poetry and music in which both the poet and the composer are constantly getting in each other's way and are at infinite pains to create a bad work is fully justified.[29] For the opera to be really successful the composer must be under the poet's orders.[30] This contention, later supported by Gluck, was again a direct contradiction of the Italian and Austro-Italian stand. Mozart, for instance, expected the poet to be the composer's servant. What St. Evremond wanted was classical tragedy ornamented with music. In general, he reflects contemporary critical reaction to the opera, which is seen to be hostile, unsympathetic, and entirely anti-operatic.

The one noteworthy exception to the Quinault-baiting tendency of the late seventeenth-century operatic criticism was characteristically enough Charles Perrault, champion of the moderns against the ancients.

[28] St. Evremond, *Œuvres*, III, 172. This paragraph may be taken as one of the most significant statements in the history of musical criticism. To it has been attributed the invention of the peculiarly French *opéra-comique*, a spoken comedy with songs and musical interludes—see Font, *Essai sur Favart, et les origines de la comédie mêlée de chant*—as well as Rousseau's *Devin du village*. The paragraph was taken up by Addison in England, Rousseau in France, Quadrio in Italy, and again in France by the Abbé Arnaud. In the last two cases the excerpts from St. Evremond were repeated verbatim. See Quadrio, *Della storia e della ragione d'ogni poesia*, 1739–1752, Lib. III, Distinzione IV, Capo II, p. 443; and Abbé Arnaud, "Essai sur le mélodrame," in his *Œuvres*, II, 6.

[29] St. Evremond, *Œuvres*, III, 173.   [30] *Ibid.*, p. 174.

In his *Critique de l'opéra; ou, Examen de la tragédie intitulée Alceste, ou le triomphe d'Alcide* (1674) Perrault criticizes the opera on dramatic grounds. Like Fénelon, he compares the opera *Alceste,* by Lulli and Quinault, to the tragedy of the same name by Euripides; but, unlike Fénelon, he finds that the opera does not suffer by comparison with the Greek tragedy. As a matter of fact, he finds the Greek wanting from the point of view of drama. Perrault approves of the introduction of love scenes into the opera. Hercules' love for Alceste gives realism to his harrowing of hell to retrieve her.[31] In the play by Euripides Alceste is already aged. Thus her weeping over the bed in which she lost her virginity and her sacrifice to save Admettus from death are, according to Perrault, not plausible enough. The opera rightly commences with the marriage of Alceste to Admettus; it is much more effective to have a young husband die fighting for his bride when she has been carried off, and it gives greater relevancy to Alceste's sacrifice, for these sentiments of love and tenderness are more suitable in newlyweds than in old people.[32] This statement is an oblique acknowledgment of the fact that music demands a more natural love interest; that is, a lyrico-dramatic outlet.

Perrault tells us that at a time when critics were attacking Quinault on all sides, he was the only man in Paris to come out openly in defense of the poet.[33] Most critics objected to the poet's style; his thought was not "noble" enough and his expressions too ordinary. Moreover, his vocabulary was limited, certain words recurring again and again. These were the old literary standards, and Perrault's rebuttal shows that he was the only serious critic of opera before the turn of the century. He says that these critics of opera must be excused, for their ignorance of music does not permit them to appreciate song. Here is the new criterion.

You know that no matter how clearly a singer enunciates his words he always manages to swallow some of them, and that however familiar the words and thoughts of an air may be a great deal is always lost upon the ear. In singing words of more than one syllable the syllable that is clearly heard should suggest the rest of the word to the listener, and in singing phrases, the words that are heard should suggest those that the ear has

---

[31] Perrault, *Critique de l'opéra,* pp. 42–44.   [32] *Ibid.,* p. 45.

[33] Perrault, "En ce qui regarde la poésie," in his *Parallèle des anciens et des modernes,* 1692, III, 242.

not caught. This cannot be achieved unless the words, thoughts, and expressions are very familiar and current. . . . Those critics who attack Quinault on the score of diction condemn him where he is most praiseworthy, for he was able to work many beautiful opera-poems with a given number of ordinary expressions and commonplaces.[34]

Operatic drama, then, is no longer to be judged by the same tenets as those that govern classical drama. Furthermore, it is to have its own aesthetic, based on the realization that not all words are fit for musical adaptation. Perrault was thus the first critic to see that the words and the music of an opera are to be taken together; that words and music complement rather than hamper each other. He was also the first to see that music, aside from its sensual appeal, was a determining factor in the development of opera, not merely a lyrical appendage to the tragedy. For Perrault song was more than an ornament; it was a major dramatic discovery: "Song is, so to speak, a more marked, and a more emotional (*pathétique*) pronunciation than ordinary speech." [35] This definition of song as exalted speech became the touchstone of French operatic criticism for more than a century. We shall see how sixty years later the Encyclopedists applied it as one of the chief tests of musical dramaturgy.

With the turn of the century French writers began to realize that the opera had come to stay. Instead of decreasing in popularity as according to the predictions of the classical critics, the opera became the rage of Paris, although no composer was to be found who could carry on Lulli's traditions. But besides making the opera, Lulli made the French music-conscious. Of great importance was the reaction of the literati and aestheticians. The French, with their genius for conversation and verve for writing about topics of general interest, were quick to seize upon music as a fertile field for discourse and polemical writing. Thus François Raguenet precipitated the first quarrel over the respective musical merits of the French and Italian operas in his *Parallèle des italiens et des français, en ce qui regarde la musique et les opéras* (1702), soon answered by the French champion Lecerf de la Viéville's *Comparaison de la musique italienne et de la musique française* (1704).[36]

[34] *Ibid.*, pp. 240–241.   [35] *Ibid.*, IV, 9.
[36] For studies of these first attempts at musical criticism see Prunières, "Lecerf de la Viéville et l'esthétique musicale classique au dix-septième siècle," also Masson, "Musique italienne et musique française, la première querelle."

If musical criticism of the eighteenth century is at times of a high order, if it is keen and subtle in analysis, it is because the French began to take a sincere interest in contemporary operatic music.

Some of the descendents of the classical writers still violently opposed the opera.[37] One of the chief points that came up for discussion was: Is music a science or an art? Malebranche was the first writer before the *Encyclopedia* to make a successful effort to separate music from geometry, a relationship that had persisted since the days of the medieval quadrivium. He argues very well that geometry is a pure science whose demonstrations must hold universally, whereas a taste for music is very relative—some prefer the Italian, others the French, and the same man may receive vastly different impressions of the same composition at different hearings.[38] Later he goes on to say that geometry is an extremely useful science in aiding the mind to discover the relations of things in the abstract. But geometry may easily lead us astray, since we are so preoccupied in following the evident demonstrations of this science that we do not take the trouble to ascertain whether they correspond to actual natural phenomena. Thus the musical composition in which the proportions of consonances are most rigidly observed is not always the most agreeable music. Geometry is an abstract science; music an art. To use geometry as a basis for musical composition is to belie the fundamental principal of art as an imitation of nature, for nature is never abstract.[39]

In clarifying this first point Malebranche touches on a second of deep aesthetic significance. If music is an art, then like other arts music must imitate nature. Art successfully imitated nature for the classical writers when it followed reason and had certain evident relations to life. This consideration led aestheticians such as Du Bos, André, Batteux, Estève, and others to measure music in terms of classical standards. Du Bos, the first of these aestheticians to give considerable space to music, confines his observations exclusively to the opera. He continues the tradition established by Lulli and explained by Perrault whereby

---

[37] Cf. Montesquieu, "Vomitif: Prenez . . . un recueil de nouveaux opéras." *Lettres persanes*, Lettre CXLIII.

[38] Malebranche, *Recherche de la vérité*, I, 109.

[39] *Ibid.*, II, 288–289. The Encyclopedists were at great pains to convince Rameau that music was not a science. The composer insisted that his theory of harmony, as well as his musical compositions, were based on geometry.

music is taken to have the power of accentuating the force of poetry.[40]
Du Bos argues further that it is natural for poetic sentiments to tend
toward musical expression.[41] Nature supplies the songs proper to the
expression of sentiments: in reading verses which contain tender sentiments, it is difficult for us to avoid sighing, emphasizing, and using
a sort of appoggiatura; this is the material of musical interpretation.[42]
For Du Bos, then, music was integrated into the art-as-an-imitation-of-
nature thesis, since he considered music as a subdivision of poetry.

In 1741 Yves Marie André made an ambitious attempt to restate
aesthetic values. For him beauty falls naturally and classically into
three categories: essential beauty, natural beauty, and artificial or
arbitrary beauty.[43] He defines the essential beauty of art as truth, order,
honesty, and suitability.[44] Natural beauty, whose elements are images,
sentiments, and emotional situations,[45] must always be based on essential beauty; thus images and sentiments must serve truth and virtue.[46] Arbitrary beauty is the style, expression,[47] or personal interpretation of truth.[48] The beautiful in music is defined in terms of these
standards. The essential beauty of music is composed of justness, order,
"the rule of tonal proportions and harmonic progressions," [49] and
"suitability, the sacred law which prescribes for each section its proper
place, the ultimate goal of the work and how it is to be attained." [50]
Natural beauty in music exists eternally in nature, it is God-given,
therefore superhuman and immutable.[51] Each passion or sentiment has
its musical equivalent.[52] Both essential and natural beauty in music
exist independent of the will of man.[53] It is only in the third classification, that is, in the artificial beauty of music, that the composer can
exercise his personality. Artificial beauty consists in the "beauty of
genius, of taste, and of caprice; 1. figures, images, emotional climaxes,
fugues; 2. fine and delicate subjects, artistic employment of tonal grada-
tions, 3. the trifling, the comical, and burlesque." [54] This meticulous
system led André to catalogue musical expression with the uncom-

---

[40] Abbé Du Bos, *Réflexions critiques sur la poésie et la peinture*, I, 637.

[41] *Ibid.*, I, 637–638.   [42] *Ibid.*, I, 673–674.   [43] André, *Essai sur le beau*, p. 61.

[44] *Ibid.*, p. 145.   [45] *Ibid.*, p. 153.   [46] *Ibid.*, p. 163.   [47] *Ibid.*, p. 169.

[48] *Ibid.*, pp. 173–174.

[49] A theory given currency by Euler, *Tentamen novae theoriae musicae*, 1739, and later adopted by Diderot, *Principes généraux d'acoustique*, 1748, *Œuvres*, IX, 85, 105–106.

[50] André, *Essai sur le beau*, p. 249.   [51] *Ibid.*, p. 265.   [52] *Ibid.*, p. 259.

[53] *Ibid.*, p. 266.   [54] *Ibid.*, pp. 276–279.

promising eye of the rhetorician.[55] However, André considers music a
major art, for the chapter on "The Beautiful in Music" is the longest
of the work. In a comparison of music and painting he gives the palm
to the former as being much more expressive.[56]

Diderot called Batteux's book *Les Beaux-Arts réduits à un même
principe* (1746) [57] "une œuvre acéphale," because the author does not
define *la belle nature,* his dominant principle. The *abbé* argues himself
into a vicious circle: the rules of taste are to be drawn from the principle
of imitation; since art imitates nature, good taste in art is essentially
synonymous with good taste in nature.[58] Batteux defines good taste as
the ability to distinguish with certainty the good, the mediocre, and
the bad in art.[59] Good taste, i. e., the knowledge of the beautiful in
nature, not only indicates to the artist what he must imitate, but also
serves the spectator in ascertaining whether nature has been well or
badly imitated.[60] Specifically the principal object of music and dancing
is to express passions and sentiments. In this way the opera libretto is
nothing more than a vehicle for musical expression.[61] Like André,
Batteux sees in music a major art; but he goes a bold step farther in
giving music the upper hand in the opera. Thus, although the *abbé*
never tells us what the beautiful in nature is that music must imitate,
he gives a wide range for musical creation and enjoyment. Music has
meaning which must have a direct appeal. The artist has corrupted
nature if he does not render this meaning manifest.[62]

Pierre Estève, in *L'Esprit des beaux-arts* (1753), says that the purpose
of art is to develop the principles of the truest expression of feelings.[63]
The artist must study human nature and draw out by his art those
sensations which are at once most pleasing and most conducive to
virtue.[64] Estève agrees with Batteux that good taste will indicate what
the artist must imitate and whether his imitation is a true one; but
the origins of this faculty lie in the mechanical pleasures of the senses.[65]
Art degenerates in proportion as the artist gets away from the guidance
of unalloyed "mechanical" sensations.[66] Such a theory of art, based
exclusively on sensations and instincts, was eminently fitted to clarify

---

[55] *Ibid.,* pp. 285–286. *Vide infra,* chap. v, concerning the theory of temperaments
and affections.

[56] *Ibid.,* p. 299.   [57] Diderot, "Plan d'une université," in his *Œuvres,* III, 486.

[58] Abbé Batteux, Les Beaux-Arts réduits, *avant-propos,* p. xii.   [59] *Ibid.,* p. 57.

[60] *Ibid.,* p. 59.   [61] *Ibid.,* pp. 258–259.   [62] *Ibid.,* pp. 262–263.

[63] Estève, *L'Esprit des beaux-arts,* I, 2.   [64] *Ibid.,* I, 8.   [65] *Ibid.,* I, 4.   [66] *Ibid.,* I, 6.

the appeal of music. Accordingly, music being an art that deals with the liveliest and the least inevitable emotions, must at the same time be the art of presenting the deepest and most typical feelings.[67]

Aestheticians thus attempted to integrate music, and we must understand them to mean "operatic music," into the field of artistic endeavor. They all agreed that music must imitate nature. Some (Estève, Batteux) saw that music makes a direct appeal to the emotions; others (Du Bos, André) believed that music resulted on the one hand from enhanced declamation, on the other, from strict artistic obedience to natural laws. Estève may be taken as a link between the work of the aestheticians and of music critics at large. In the work just quoted he gives considerable attention to Lulli's operas. Much of this composer's success, says Estève, was due to his close study of theatrical declamation. This sort of declamation led to a form of musical expression that Estève terms "natural music"; "natural" in that it seemed to derive exactly from the traditional classical manner of declaiming Quinault's verse.[68] Estève's neat analysis of the interdependence of the words and music of Lulli's operas shows clearly why Corneille and Racine—or indeed any great poet—could never successfully be set to music.[69] Lulli set himself the task of interpreting the whole of a scene or tableau. His music was intended to create the atmosphere of the action being represented, not to underline or emphasize certain words. When a particular word was given relevancy by the composer, it was taken as a key to the dramatic or emotional situation. For this reason Lulli required poetry filled with images: "a type of poetry whose diction was not too powerful, else the sounds would have hindered the soft and tranquil motion which he wished to impart in expressing the general mood." [70] Great poetry, in other words, was sufficient unto itself and contained its own music.

There were those in France who believed that the opera had sup-

---

[67] *Ibid.*, I, 145.   [68] *Ibid.*, I, 134–135.

[69] It is noteworthy that most of the great classical French poets of the seventeenth century turned their hands to operatic composition. With the exception of Molière's comedy ballets, all these attempts resulted in failure. This explains in part at least the animosity of Boileau, Racine, Corneille, and La Fontaine—see his "Epître à M. Nyert," 1677—to the opera. Lulli's greatness was enhanced by the fact that although he could have chosen any one of these poets as a collaborator, he preferred Quinault. Consult Ecorcheville, *Corneille et la musique*, Racine, *Poésies, avec une étude sur Racine et la musique* par Samazeuilh; Prunières, "La Fontaine et Lulli."

[70] Estève, *L'Esprit des beaux-arts*, II, 17–18.

planted the tragedy because the former was a higher species of dramatic art. Rémond de Saint-Mard was of the opinion that words could
never adequately express feelings and passions; of necessity, therefore,
music had to be called in to supply this lack.[71] The opera is a tragedy
set to music, which must be played, declaimed, and sung. It will be
apparent that when these three essential elements are observed it is
much more difficult to compose opera than straight drama. For this
reason successful operas are extremely rare. Composers place special
emphasis on singing to the detriment of the other two factors—acting
and declaiming.[72] In joining the Perrault tradition that song is enhanced declamation, Rémond de Saint-Mard explains that whereas in
tragedy all words are acceptable, the opera poem must limit itself to
a scant vocabulary of from twelve to fifteen hundred words; not all
words being fit for musical adaptation. The conception of the opera
differs from the ordinary rhetoric of tragedy in that interest must begin
with the first scene and continue unabated to the end of the work.
Music can express only the most stirring emotional phases of drama;
action therefore must proceed at a feverish pitch.[73] The opera which
is correctly composed with due attention given to its three chief elements offers a spectacle for which "sensitive souls would abandon all
earthly goods." [74]

Critics primarily interested in the theoretical aspects of opera insisted
that the musical tragedy must be distinguished from the classical
tragedy. They differed from the late seventeenth-century critics in that
they accepted the opera as a legitimate spectacle and tried to outline a
new rhetoric for the composition of operatic poetry and drama. From
the point of view of verse, diction, and technique they ascertained that
the opera poem constituted a new genre. They espoused St. Evremond's theory of the fit subject for operatic treatment and accepted
Perrault's definition of song as enhanced declamation. This represented

[71] Rémond de Saint-Mard, *Réflexions sur l'opéra,* pp. 10–11.

[72] *Ibid.,* pp. 69–70, and p. 24.

[73] *Ibid.,* pp. 26–27. St. Evremond realized this, too, when he said that developmental
scenes, intrigues, the discussion of affairs, etc., were not fit for the opera, since music was
powerless to comment them. "Sur les opéras," in his *Œuvres,* III, 172. Cf. Diderot: "Il faut
être clair, laconique et intéressant. Il faut marcher avec rapidité, et suivre cependant la chaîne
des idées et des sentiments." *Miscellanea dramatique; ou, Essai sur un nouveau genre de
spectacle à Florence,* 1769, *Œuvres,* VIII, 462–463.

[74] Rémond de Saint-Mard, *Réflexions sur l'opéra,* p. 100.

the bulk of tradition obtaining in France when the *Encyclopedia* went to press (1750).

Operatic criticism of a journalistic turn was also abundant in France at this time. If Bollioud de Mermet could inveigh against the corruption of French opera,[75] Saunier de Beaumont could champion the local opera with no less ardor; [76] while de Brosses advocated the middle course and suggested that each nation have its own opera, for better or for worse.[77] French opera received a tremendous shock toward the middle of the century. Lulli's works, which had held the stage until 1740, began rapidly to decline at this point. De la Martinière, who had a real appreciation of Lulli's achievements, tells us that one reason for the falling off in popularity of the master's operas was their age. Having created the opera when musical execution was most primitive, Lulli was forced to compose music of an extremely simple nature. This simplicity was retained by his successors when there was no longer any need for it. Because of this Lulli's methods of composition were worn thin by 1750. Objecting to this obsolete manner of composition in France, audiences were revolted not only by the servile imitations by Mouret, Campra, Destouches, and the rest, but by the works of the master himself. They began to desire compositions that were more modern in scope and technique; difficulty soon took the place of beauty: "in a word, they went so far as to put wit into music." [78] This charge of willful complication was aimed at Rameau.

Few composers have been so savagely attacked by their contemporaries as was Jean Philippe Rameau. Although by 1750 he was the outstanding composer of the opera in France, he never enjoyed the popularity of Lulli. We have seen that even the most violent critics of the early opera spared Lulli. Throughout the first half of the eighteenth century music critics held him up as a model; their analyses of his works easily ran into tribute and panegyric. They admired him as the creator of the national opera and loved him as the exponent of French music par excellence. Before the *Encyclopedia*, disparaging criticism of Lulli's music was almost nonexistent. Not so with Rameau.

[75] Bollioud de Mermet, *De la corruption du goût dans la musique française.*
[76] Saunier de Beaumont, *Lettre sur la musique.*
[77] Charles de Brosses, *Lettres familières*, 1739-1740; see also his *Lettres inédites.*
[78] La Martinière, *Introduction générale à l'étude des sciences et des belles-lettres*, p. 347.

From the very first his "complicated" music distressed the French critics. The première of the opera *Dardanus* called forth the following comment: "In general one is struck by the wealth of harmony, but it is so over-burdened with music that for forty-five consecutive minutes the musicians in the orchestra do not even have time to sneeze." [79] Rameau was attacked not only by the critics of the vanguard but also by the followers of Lulli.[80] At the time of Rameau's appearance as opera-composer this meant practically all of musical France.

What the French sought was a modern Lulli. They wanted a composer who respected French dramatic traditions as much as the old master had, but who was capable of writing new music—music that employed the current techniques of composition and instrumentation. They waited so long in vain for this composer that when Rameau appeared with his antiliterary operatic tendencies [81] they were unwilling to champion the cause of the new composer, and, having tired of the old, it is no wonder that the French, and first of all the Encyclopedists, turned to Italy again for guidance. Enthusiasm for music was at a feverish height, whereas operatic composition, except for Rameau, was very dull. Such was the state of affairs when the first volumes of the *Encyclopedia* left the press in 1751.

[79] Bibliothèque de la Ville de Paris, MS 26700, quoted in Emile Dacier, *L'Opéra au dix-huitième siècle, les premières représentations du Dardanus de Rameau, nov.–déc., 1739,* p. 4.

[80] Witness Chabanon's *Eloge de Rameau,* written upon the master's decease in 1764: "Rien n'est si dangereux . . . que ce projet formé de peindre surtout en symphonie." Chabanon, *op. cit.,* pp. 25–26. He adds that it prevented Rameau from grasping the purity of the melodic line, which constitutes the basis of all good music. *Ibid.,* p. 26.

[81] Rameau is reported to have said that he would set the *Gazette de Hollande* to music. Cf. Collé, *Journal Historique,* II, (1760), 211–212. Collé also predicted that *Platée* would no longer be played in 1770; a prediction which came true. See Rolland, *Musiciens d'autrefois,* p. 211. Rameau exactly reversed the proportions of music and drama in the opera, giving two hours and forty-five minutes of *divertissements,* and only forty-five minutes of recitative. M. Masson states that Rameau made music the all-important element in the opera, and that if the composer had desired to retain the excellence of the tragedy, he could have secured the services of competent poets. Masson, "Lullists et Ramistes," p. 207. The Italian opera poet, Metastasio scoffed at the French idea that *anything* could be set to music. Casanova, *Mémoires,* II, 382.

CHAPTER II

HISTORICAL CONSIDERATIONS
OF THE OPERA

THE ARTICLES ON MUSIC in the *Encyclopedia,* of which the first two volumes appeared in 1751–1752, offered a source of history, criticism, and aesthetic theory, from which the Encyclopedists were to draw material for their polemics and reform campaign. Taken as a whole, they represent a consistent body of thought that amply proves the Encyclopedists' interest in music, as well as their sincerity of purpose in the musical wars that followed. Later we shall see how these critics used to advantage the elements contained in these numerous musical articles. The vast richness disclosed in these essays of varying length, in which music is considered from every point of view, shows a considerable advance in this respect over the earlier articles in the Chambers' *Cyclopedia.* Indeed, none of the universal lexicons that the Encyclopedists were able to consult offered anything showing an interest in music equal to their own.

In the articles of the *Encyclopedia* is to be found the best history of the opera in France up to 1750. Practically all the elements that were to make up the opera are here examined by the Encyclopedists. As is to be expected in a work of vast dimensions in which many minds have been engaged in the treatment of the same subject, a connected picture of the origins of opera may be traced with difficulty. Nor can it be expected that these men, lacking the tools of scientific historical criticism and having almost no worthwhile source material upon which to base their claims, could give a definitive study of operatic origins. Yet they did realize that the *fêtes,* or *sacre rappresentazioni,* were prime contributing factors in the development of opera.

The Encyclopedists are not in accord as to exactly where in Italy the opera originated. Jaucourt, in the article "Veroli," places the first opera in Italy as far back as 1480; Sulpitius was said by him to be the creator of this form.

It was Sulpitius who reëstablished the use of music in the theater. Rome, which had in a manner forgotten this practice . . . saw music reappear in the theater about 1480, thanks to the genius and industry of Sulpitius. He began by presenting to the public scenes of operatic composition played upon mobile theaters. Then he appealed to the Pope and the cardinals to support his musical ventures. Finally, his innovations on the lyrical stage achieved public acclaim, as the opera will continue to do for many years to come.[1]

In the article "Fête" Cahusac agrees on fixing the date at 1480, but asserts that Lombardy was the place of origin and that the develop- ment of *fêtes* from that of Bergonce de Botta in 1480 for the Duke Galeazzo of Milan led finally to the opera.

This assembly of acted tableaux having, perhaps, little relation to one an- other were, nevertheless, inspired with wit, imagination, and variety, and caused quite a stir in Italy at that time. They later gave rise to regular scenes set to music, operas, ballets with elaborate machinery, and ingenious *fêtes*.

Cahusac, who was interested in ballets, would naturally tend to stress these *fêtes* in seeking the origins of opera. Jaucourt, a literary scholar, was satisfied that the opera was primarily a dramatic creation. And both in a measure were right. The opera in Italy, begun as a dramatic revival, was soon to take on many of the elements of the *fêtes* here mentioned, in the court shows of Venice, Milan, Florence, and Rome.[2]

The introduction of the opera into France is also variously attributed by the Encyclopedists. Cahusac, in the article "Fête," asserts that Cath-

[1] Cf. Sulzer: "Das erste, gänzliche in Musik gesetzte, oder singend aufgeführte Stück scheint in das Jahr 1480 zu fallen. Johann Sulpitius sagt nähmlich in der Zueignungsschrift seiner Noten zum Vitruvius an den Cardinal Riari: Tu enim primus tragoediae, quam nos juventutem excitandi gratia et agere et *cantare* primi hoc aevo docuimus (nam ejusmodi Actionem jam multis saeculis Roma non viderat) in medio foro pulpitum ad quinque pedem altitudinem erectum pulcherrime exonorasti." Article "Oper"; in *Allgemeine Theorie der schoenen Künste,* 1771–1775, consult Appendix A, Supplement, for the authorship of the articles in this work. Although in general the Supplement represents a later movement of ideas and Diderot would have nothing to do with it—see Le Gras, *Diderot et L'Encyclopédie,* pp. 163–164—the articles on music in it remain faithful to Encyclopedist precepts. See also Abbé Arnaud, "Essai sur le mélodrame," *Variétés Littéraires, Œuvres,* III (1768), 23.

[2] For a good treatment of the early opera see Rolland, *Les origines du théâtre lyrique moderne, histoire de l'Opéra en Europe avant Lulli et Scarlatti,* and his *Musiciens d'autre- fois,* especially the chapter "L'Opéra avant l'opéra."

erine de' Medici brought this Italian spectacle to France, thus hastening the development of the local opera. Jaucourt, who is more precise in his search for operatic origins, states, in the article "Opéra Italien," that the first impetus was given to French opera when Mazarin introduced Italian opera to France in 1646. In the article "Opéra" Jaucourt rightly attributed the first national opera to the attempts of Perrin, who obtained the first license in 1669. And in the article "Florence" Jaucourt states that Lulli was the real creator of French opera and that it was from his compositions that the French were able to claim a national opera, and a taste for music in general:

Lulli's accomplishments in French music equaled Galileo's in astronomy, and his innovations were just as effective: he found a new manner of composing opera, completely unheard of by our other masters; he introduced drums and tympani into our concert halls; he presented us with a great variety of his versatile compositions, exploiting unfamiliar techniques; in a word, he established in this country the reign of harmony, and since Lulli's time we have made progress in the art of musical composition.

An important aspect of the development of French opera was the popularity of *fêtes* at the French court. The term *fête* is taken by Cahusac to cover the *ballet de cour,* or court ballet, as perfected by Benserade, the comedy ballet of Molière and Lulli, and the *divertissements* of Lulli's and Quinault's operas. These last were composed of ballets, scenic display on a large scale, machines, usually a regal chariot or a cloud bearing a divinity or hero, accompanied by chorus and orchestra. This was intended to relieve the opera in progress and to provide a *spectacle*. The articles in the *Encyclopedia* treating this phase of the opera in France were all written by Cahusac, who was an authority on the ballet.[3]

In the article "Ballet" Cahusac gives the history of this art form from the earliest times to its introduction into French opera. The court ballet as conceived by Benserade, says Cahusac, did not observe the unities of time and place. It was a makeshift arrangement of dance —*entrées de ballet*—song, music, and stage sets.

The most important element of the ballet is the plan; next come the set figure dances; third, the dance steps; fourth, the music, which includes the instrumental sections, the songs, and the choruses; fifth, the decorations and

---

[3] See his *La Danse ancienne et moderne; ou, Traité historique de la danse.* Cahusac's significance in the development of the ballet is discussed in Levinson, *Meister des Balletts,* in the chapter on Noverre.

stage sets; and last, the poetry, which is employed merely to explain the action being represented by the ballet.

These ballets are usually divided into five acts, and each act is divided into 3, 6, 9, and sometimes 12 ballet entrances.

A "ballet entrance" is composed of one or more groups of dancers who portray by their dancing the action they are to represent.

Cahusac goes on to show that Molière's comedy ballet supplanted Benserade's court ballet as a court festival and that Quinault followed the form of the comedy ballet for the *divertissements* of his operas.

When the opera was first established in France, its authors used the general plan of an elaborate ballet as a guide, though changing its form somewhat. Quinault invented a mixed genre, in which the spoken lines take care of the dramatic action. In these works the dance played a secondary role. In 1671 [1672] the *Fêtes de Bacchus et de l'amour* was performed and immediately scored a success [4] . . . from that day forward the ballets we have been discussing passed from the stage as a self-sufficient art form; they were subsequently used between the acts as *intermèdes,* as in *Psyché,* the *Mariage forcé,* the *Fâcheux* . . . and the *Bourgeois gentilhomme.*

Cahusac criticized the court ballet of Benserade as lacking unity and coherence. Quinault's operas he attacks because they do not make sufficient use of the ballet. The imitators of the Quinault opera emphasized this shortcoming, and thus the ballet was reduced to a minor role in the French opera.

Quinault, who created the opera in France and had justly appreciated the most telling elements in its composition . . . underestimated the ballet. All those authors who later worked for the lyrical theater unfortunately inherited this blind spot. . . .

After Quinault's death authors used his plan of opera, but failed to animate it with his particular charm and style. . . . He was more easily imitated in his use of the ballet, which was just short of being mediocre. Thus, it may be said that Quinault's successors adequately copied their master only in the least interesting aspect of his art. It was not until 1697 that la Mothe earned the right of being imitated in turn by creating an entirely new genre.[5]

It is evident that Cahusac is here speaking of the ballet and of the opera in the same breath. According to him, the opera in France

---

[4] See the Despois and Mesnard edition of Molière's *Œuvres,* especially the notes to *Georges Dandin* and *Les Amants magnifiques,* wherein the editors show that *Les Fêtes* was in great part composed of scenes from Molière's comedy ballets.

[5] La Motte-Houdard (1672–1731) created *L'Europe galante,* 1697, music by Campra.

should have evolved from the local ballet, rather than from the Italian opera. The order of progression from ballet to opera is seen by Cahusac to begin with the comedy ballet of Molière, to pass through the lyric ballet of La Motte–Houdard, and to reach its climax in the operas of Rameau, popularly known as *opéra-ballet*. Cahusac tells us that the principle elements of this genre are a prologue and three or four *entrées*. In the *tragédie lyrique,* or Quinault opera, the drama prepares an occasional *divertissement* to relieve and ornament the main action of the opera, whereas in the lyric ballet, or the Molière–La Motte–Rameau interpretation of this art form, the dramatic action must be only a vehicle for introducing *divertissements* of songs and dances.

The lyrical ballet consists in three or four ballet-entrances preceded by a prologue.

The prologue and each of the entrances form a separate entity comprising one or two *divertissements* interspersed with singing and dancing.

In the lyrical tragedy the *divertissements* of singing and dancing are marshalled in to support the main dramatic action of the opera. In the lyrical ballet, on the other hand, these *divertissements* are considered an end in themselves, and whatever action is being represented is used merely as an excuse to sing and to dance.

Cahusac deplores the fact that this line of ballet compositions was not more closely developed by the French. Molière, La Motte–Houdard, and Rameau are its only exponents, says Cahusac, and of these three La Motte alone made the *ballet lyrique* his principal claim to dramatic fame. La Motte exploited but thinly the *merveilleux* element of the Quinault opera to create his first successful ballet *L'Europe galante* (1697). But this work was not immediately followed by other successful ballets. Cahusac suggests that La Motte thought little of the ballet genre, and believed that the Quinault opera was the only form really worthwhile.

Quinault had felt that the *merveilleux* was the main prop of the opera. Why not make this same element the mainstay of the ballet? La Mothe did not exclude the *merveilleux,* he merely did without it in his lyrical ballet. Moreover, it is interesting to note that La Mothe did not compose more works in the agreeable vein that he had discovered. We have only his *Europe galante* which has managed to stay on the boards all this time. Did la Mothe come to the conclusion that after all the only form of the art worthy of consideration was the *grand opéra?* [6]

---

[6] This is the earliest use of the term *grand opéra* that we have seen. It is not to be confused of course with the nineteenth-century use of this term.

The main defect in the La Motte version of the ballet, says Cahusac, was the lack of dramatic action. Rameau remedied this shortcoming in his opera ballet, which allied all the elements of opera to pantomimic dancing. Yet Cahusac states that even this vastly improved ballet is uncertain of success. The French, who seem to love the ballet better than any other stage production, have as yet to decide whether in the ballet as in the opera music is to be the all-important element. Upon this decision rests the fate of Rameau's opera ballet.

Of all the elements that go to make up the lyrical theater the French seem to like the ballet best. . . .
However, when we consider the number of celebrated authors who have tried writing ballets, we must admit that very few have succeeded in pleasing us. We have fewer good ballets than good operas, always excepting, of course, the works [opera ballets] of M. Rameau, concerning whose fortunes we would not venture to speak, unless it be to say that in proportion as the French love of music deepens or weakens these works will maintain or lose their superiority.

Cahusac insisted so strongly on the dance as a major influence in the formation of French opera, because he was familiar with the early history of court shows. In these productions the regents invariably turned to some form of the ballet for their amusement. In the article "Fêtes de la cour de France" Cahusac examines in detail these royal spectacles and enthusiastically points out in them such elements as *merveilleux, machines,* and *entrées,* which were to play so important a role in the development of the local opera.[7] Thus, one aspect of the history of the opera in France, the evolution of the court *fêtes* into court ballet, comedy ballet, lyrical ballet, and opera ballet, including the growing importance of the *divertissements* in the opera proper, received exhaustive treatment in the articles of the *Encyclopedia.*

Of historical import also is Cahusac's statement, in the article "Couper," that *danseuses* did not appear on the operatic stage in France until 1681, in the Lulli-Quinault opera *Le Triomphe de l'amour.* Prior to this production the creators of French opera had had to be satisfied with four to six *danseurs.* Cahusac suggests that because of

[7] For the history of the early court *fêtes* see Prunières, *Le Ballet de cour en France avant Benserade et Lulli.* For the ballet's influence on French opera, consult Riemann, *Dictionnaire,* French edition, articles "Ballet" and "Ballet de cour." Silin states that this form of the ballet paved the way for the opera. See his *Benserade and his Ballets de cour,* p. 171.

the lack of dancers Quinault was forced to curtail the role of the dance in the opera.[8] Thus, the late appearance of the dance as a major element of opera, the sparing use of the ballet in the operas of Quinault's imitators, Campra, Lalande, Destouches, Mouret, Mondonville, would be, ironically enough, Quinault's fault. Cahusac is convinced that if he had had at his disposal the great number of dancers that flourished in 1750 in France, he would have created from the very start the Rameau type of opera; that is, more *divertissement* than drama. Cahusac thus concludes that there then would have been no question of Italian influence in the French opera, Rameau's opera ballet being in direct line of descent from the old French court *fêtes*.

We have seen in the foregoing pages that Lulli's contemporaries gave the composer full credit for the creation of the opera in France. Although the Encyclopedists appreciated the work of Lulli in the establishment of the national opera, they tended rather to emphasize the role of Quinault's poems as a determining factor. Thus, in the article "Ballet" Cahusac states that Quinault created the opera in France. The reason for this turn about on the part of contributors to the *Encyclopedia* is due in part to the growing popularity of Quinault as a poet, culminating in Voltaire's vindication of Quinault at the expense of Boileau. In the article "Coupe" Cahusac, in blaming Boileau for this slight upon Quinault's merits, takes the critic to task for misjudging the opera and for comparing such widely different works as the operas of Quinault and the tragedies of Racine with the intention of manifesting the opera poet's inadequacy:

During Quinault's lifetime Lulli was given all the credit for the operas they had produced in collaboration. It is only in the past twenty years that we have realized that Quinault was a poet of rare genius. Despite this belated awakening we are still more likely to say, "*Armide* is Lulli's masterwork," instead of saying, "*Armide* is one of Quinault's masterpieces." How can we persuade ourselves that the type of art work practiced by Quinault, with which we have not as yet entirely familiarized ourselves, is a difficult genre? Boileau affected to scorn this kind of writing. The facile comparison he used to make, on the basis of reading only, between a play of Racine's and a Quinault opera was colored by his friendship for the former and

---

[8] Molière found a similar dearth of dancers. In the "Préface au lecteur" to *Les Fâcheux,* the poet tells us that this lack of dancers eventually led to the invention of the comedy ballet. Nevertheless, Lulli and Quinault had a well-conceived operatic dramaturgy wherein the use of ballets on a large scale had no place.

frank dislike of the latter. Moreover, Boileau's antipathy toward the opera, coupled with a sort of classical severity that outlawed anything so frivolous as an opera-poem from the field of literature, nurtured a highly prejudiced viewpoint that found expression in his writings, which are studied by all our young people at college.

The Encyclopedists believed that music was to take the upper hand in the opera. But they participated in the drive to rehabilitate Quinault, because they realized the importance of his poems in the Lulli opera. They believed that Lulli's *déclamation notée* was derived from Quinault's verses, and, since declamation was the basis of Lulli's operas, to the extent of occupying two and one-half out of three and one-quarter hours of spectacle, the Encyclopedists were loath to minimize the importance of Quinault's text. In the article "Couper" Cahusac states that in preparing tragedies for musical adaptation Quinault had no alternative but to follow classical declamation. Being ignorant of the Rameau or *divertissement* type of opera because of the primitive stage of the dance at this time and of the Italian *recitativo* and aria, Quinault was forced to use the elements of the French classical tragedy in preparing his operas.

Quinault prepared all of his opera poems in strict accordance with the precepts of classical declamation. He could hardly have done otherwise, since all his subjects were suited to this type of treatment and the possibilities of the dance or the ballet as we know it were unexplored in his day. . . . Lulli was satisfied if his *divertissements* were composed of two or three *airs de violon,* taking up in all about forty-five minutes time. But the requirements of the representation had to be met, and to accomplish this Quinault so disposed his opera poem that the declamation scenes alone could have taken up the entire performance time.

In the article "Exécution" Cahusac points out again Lulli's debt to Quinault, the invention of his *déclamation notée* as a result of a close study of Quinault's text. Here again, says Cahusac, the composer was limited by the weakness of his musicians' performance, so that a sort of singing recitative, or *déclamation chantante,* was the only form of opera that could suit prevailing conditions.

That part of French opera improperly termed recitative was the only section which Lulli brought to perfection. The composer immediately seized upon a sort of singing declamation that was suitable to the occasion and in conformity with the French tongue. . . . Lulli perceived that he could not implement the arias, duos, trios, and grand choruses of the Italian operas, not only because of the exigencies of the French language but also because of the professional inadequacy of his singers. . . . Quinault drew up his immortal opera poems on the familiar classical style of declamation. Lulli set his music to this and everyone was satisfied; the French did not and could not have any other taste in opera.

Because of the primitive orchestra and the inadequate capacity of his singers, and because of the lack of good dancers, Lulli had to focus all his attention on Quinault's verse.

These arguments marshalled up to account for the physiognomy of the early *tragédie lyrique* are not altogether corroborated by the facts. The situation was not as bad as Cahusac would have us believe. Lulli's orchestra and singers were adequate; it was rather his recognition of the literary orientation of the French and his own conception of tragedy in music which drove him toward Quinault. By inventing a musical commentary peculiar to himself and based on these verses, Lulli created a *déclamation notée* that was to determine the form of French opera for more than half a century.

Cahusac notes, in the article "Couper," that as orchestras improved, singers became more musicianly, and the dance gained in importance as a major element of opera. This evolution led the opera away from the Lulli-Quinault invention based on good verse declamation and set the stage for the Rameau type, wherein more emphasis was given to the music than to the text, and *divertissement,* because of the extensive use of the ballet, became a more proper appellative for the opera than *tragédie.* Cahusac points out that whereas in the Lulli-Quinault opera the text or *déclamation* provided two and one-half hours and the *divertissement* only forty-five minutes of entertainment, in the Rameau opera the figures were reversed; two and one-half hours were taken up by *divertissement* and dances, and the remaining forty-five minutes were recitative which took care of the dramatic action.

Jaucourt, in the article "Opéra Italien," has an interesting note to the effect that it would be difficult to imagine the Lulli-Quinault opera without the works of Racine and Corneille.

But the first writers for the operatic stage in France did not realize the possibilities of this type of poem until the plays of Corneille and Racine had elevated French dramatic taste. Today we cannot help reading with a certain amount of contempt Gilbert's opera poem and the *Pomone* [1671] by the Abbé Perrin.[9] These opera poems, written about ninety years ago, seem to us today quite Gothic in style. Finally, Quinault, who wrote for our operatic stage later than the authors I have just cited, excelled in this style of writing. Lulli, who created a type of song suited to our language, endowed immortality upon the poems of Quinault with his music—an immortality that Lulli's music had already received from Quinault's verse.

All the elements that were to make the opera in France a distinct genre are explained in the *Encyclopedia*. Cahusac and Jaucourt, who wrote most of the articles referring to the history of the opera in France, consider in turn the evolution of the ballet and the drama into opera.

As for Rameau, although he was contemporary, the Encyclopedists are agreed that he made music the all-important element in the French opera (Marmontel: "Récitatif," Supplement, 1765), and that his compositions represent in their way as high an achievement as the works of Lulli and Quinault. (Cahusac: "Couper"; "Exécution"). Nor did they forget that Rameau's performance was possible chiefly because of the high state of perfection in which he found the orchestra, the dance, and the art of song. In this connection Cahusac states, in the article "Chanteur," that Rameau owed much to the voices of Jélyotte and Mlle Fel.[10]

For a résumé of the development of opera in France, Cahusac's article "Exécution" offers, perhaps, the best page of musical history written in France in the eighteenth century.

In 1699 Perrin and Cambert assembled all the musicians they could find in Paris and summoned singers from the Languedoc in order to establish the French national opera. Lulli, who, thanks to Colbert's protection, soon replaced Perrin and Cambert, made use of whatever he found ready. Singing and orchestral playing were in those days as primitive as are all arts in their infancy. The Italian opera had given the idea for a French opera. Lulli, who was a Florentine, was versed in the art of musical composition to the same extent as were the other celebrated Italian composers in his day, no more no less. Had he been more advanced than his contemporaries he could not have found musicians capable of playing his scores. Lulli's compositions were, then, comparable to any of the good scores being created at the time and were playable by the ordinary run of musicians.

[9] Perrin being in prison, the poet Gabriel Gilbert was asked to prepare a *poème;* he wrote *Les Peines et les plaisirs de l'amour,* music by Cambert, 1672.
[10] Both Jélyotte and Mlle Fel were personally acquainted with the Encyclopedists, as they were frequenters of Mme d'Epinay's salon. See Mme d'Epinay, *Mémoires,* and Billy, "Diderot chez ses amis."

As he possessed a great deal of taste and genius, the art of music prospered under Lulli's touch. In measure as the art advanced among musicians and audiences, Lulli's genius made new discoveries and his imagination became bolder. A complete despot in his theater, Lulli was quick to reward unusual effort, but just as quick to punish faulty playing and inattentiveness. On occasion, he would take the violin from the hands of the offender and smash it on his head, without anyone so much as daring to murmur or complain.

Thus the art of opera was advanced in France as much as could be reasonably expected considering existing conditions. Both singing and orchestral playing made giant strides forward under the aegis of Lulli's bâton. . . .

The art of music could not reach its apogee until the art of playing reached a certain point of perfection, and the composer needed the collaboration of a great number of professional musicians, which only time could form. Rameau seized the occasion, when sixty years of hard work and experience at last bore fruit, and carried the art of orchestral playing to a degree of perfection equal to his operatic compositions.

The foregoing paragraphs may be open to much criticism; the statements regarding the ability of musicians, for instance, are not entirely justified, and Cahusac seems to have his share of eighteenth-century thinkers' delusions with regard to the perfectibility and progress *ad infinitum* of the arts. Yet nowhere else in an eighteenth-century work is such a clear, concise rendering of the inception of French opera to be found. Cahusac seems to have been acquainted with most of the documents relating to the formation of the opera that we now possess. His description of Lulli's rehearsals is exact, and his tribute to Lulli could be reproduced today without suppressing a single word.

CHAPTER III

CRITICISM OF THE OPERA

BEFORE ENTERING UPON an examination of the criticism of the opera in the articles of the *Encyclopedia,* we should consider briefly the state of the opera toward the middle of the eighteenth century. Whereas in Italy the opera had gradually receded from the pure music drama of the Monteverdi type to a melodic feast in the Neapolitan school with the works of Leo, Porpora, Vinci, Scarlatti, and Pergolesi,[1] in France the opera tended to remain faithful to the dramatic traditions of the Lulli-Quinault invention. We may recall that the Encyclopedists pointed out that the principal changes wrought by Rameau consisted in altering the proportions of drama and musical *divertissements.* The ingredients of Rameau's operas are all to be found in the Lulli-Quinault type of lyrico-dramatic compositions. Thus, the *déclamation notée* of Lulli's operas, although its importance declines in Rameau's works, remains essentially unchanged. Of most significance is the fact that in both Italy and France music took the upper hand. The Italian composers sacrificed the libretto to the singer, thus making the aria or melody the mainstay of the opera, while in France Rameau sacrificed the *poème* to the music, thus emphasizing the orchestra or harmony as the principal feature of operatic composition.

It was precisely this tendency of the French opera to remain fixed that drew the Encyclopedists' fire. They did not oppose the operas of Lulli and Quinault because they felt them to be inferior creations. On the whole the Encyclopedists' attitude is favorable to these compositions, which they regarded as sufficient and even wonderful for the period in which they first appeared. But the Encyclopedists knew that this early opera had served its time and that it was now, in 1750, obsolete.

[1] See Láng, *Music in Western Civilization.*

When they considered the sweeping changes that had obtained in Italian opera, the Encyclopedists could not help being a little impatient with the slow progress of the local opéra, and particularly with the reactionary elements in Rameau's works.

Thus, the Encyclopedists razed the venerable though crumbling works of Lulli. These masterworks had cast a shadow upon upwards of sixty years of operatic composition in France. D'Alembert suggests, in the article "Echo," that one reason for the tenacity of the old opera is to be found in the tendency on the part of Frenchmen to be traditional in their artistic tastes and to like only the sort of music they already know:[2] "In France, good music means for many people that which resembles what they have already heard." Foreigners who have not been habituated to appreciate French opera, says Cahusac in the article "Débiter," remark with surprise upon its many shortcomings.

When foreigners arrive we take them to the opera. In vain do they keep their eyes and ears open; they neither see nor hear the marvels we seem to see and hear there. They view us askance, talk in hushed voices about us, and guess that prejudice and pride have formed our operatic taste. Actually, it is merely habit, indifference for the progress of art, or perhaps a good-natured desire to be grateful to those who put themselves out to amuse us that causes the French to cling to their opera.

The Encyclopedists were asking the French to awaken from their musical lethargy.

Just as these men were the first group of critics to look at opera from the point of view of music, they also preceded all others in setting forth an aesthetic theory of operatic composition based upon a close examination of French works. The *philosophes,* who rationalized all natural phenomena, used the penetrating tool of reason to advantage in probing the origins of the local opera. They were quick to see that the opera in France came as the result of a dramatic transformation and that therefore the principal element of the new *tragédie lyrique* was declamation. Upon this item all contributors of musical articles agree. (Cahusac, "Déclamation," "Expression"; Marmontel, "Déclamation," "Chant"; Grimm, "Motif," "Poème lyrique"; Alembert, "Genre"; Castillon, "Musique," Supplement.) Declamation was

[2] D'Alembert's references to music have been studied by Jullien, *La Musique et les philosophes au dix-huitième siècle,* and by Hirschberg, *Die Encyklopädisten und die französische Oper im 18. Jahrhundert.*

the basis of the recitative, which was the principal prop of the opera. (Marmontel: "Déclamation"). By following the declamation of the verse in the classical tragedy, the composer created the recitative sections of his opera. He accentuated by musical notation the actor's declamation and thus arrived at a *déclamation notée:*

Although we know that what we improperly term recitative should give an added expression to the words of an opera text . . . it should, nevertheless, always remain simple and as true to the spirit of classical declamation as possible. The composer should study the declamation of a first rank tragedian, and shape his music along the lines suggested by the actor's delivery. As it is certain that the actor adds considerably to the dramatist's lines by his delivery, so, too, the composer must heighten the expression of the verse by means of the recitative, which thus becomes a permanently scored declamation. (Cahusac, "Expression.")

D'Alembert gives an example of the precise application of this principle; that is, that recitative, or *déclamation notée,* evolved from natural or theatrical declamation.

The composer used the ascending notes of the chromatic scale in this recitative with all the more justice since it seems natural to us. A good actor would certainly deliver the second and third verses as they are scored, that is, in ascending semi-tones. Let us note further that if this section were sung as the recitative in the Italian opera, without unduly stressing each sound but by delivering the words as though they were being read or spoken and paying attention to proper intonation, one would hardly notice the difference between this type of recitative and good theatrical declamation; that is the model of a good recitative. (Alembert, "Genre.")

The Encyclopedists saw theatrical declamation as a basis for recitative only. Recitative formed the connection between opera and drama, and musical contributors to the *Encyclopedia* felt that since French recitative had been derived from stage declamation, it had best be composed along dramatic lines. But here the influence of the drama, albeit very important, was at an end. In no case did the Encyclopedists suggest that melody is equally a product of theatrical declamation. They saw that melody was primarily a branch of music and that the type of declamation that was to be used in writing it was far different from theatrical declamation.[3] In the article "Expression" Rousseau

[3] For Diderot's position on this subject, see his *Entretiens sur le Fils Naturel* and *Le Neveu de Rameau,* in his *Œuvres,* VII, 162–164; V, 466.

states flatly that theatrical declamation cannot serve as a basis for melody. Grimm,[4] in the article "Poème lyrique," claims that the composer must find two types of declamation—one for the recitative and one for the melody.

The composer's first task must have been to find two entirely different kinds of declamation; the first to render ordinary conversation, and the second to portray the expression of passions in all its vigor, truth, and disorder. The latter type of declamation is called the air, or aria, the former is the recitative.

Melody, or aria, the mainstay of Italian opera, was of secondary importance in France, recitative based on a *déclamation notée* having been the chief element of French opera.

When opera is considered solely as a dramatic phenomenon, as it was by the French up to the advent of the *Encyclopedia,* melody is not likely to receive very extensive treatment. Whereas with the Italians melody rapidly settled into the *da capo* aria form, which soon became the all-important feature of their opera, in France no great distinction existed between recitative and melody. Lulli preferred to use a type of melody that grew out of the same declamation as the recitative. It was a slow, measured song that may be called tuneful recitative, in the sense that although its musical qualities cannot be denied, the influence of the words does not fail to make itself felt even when such a melody is played upon an instrument.[5] To this type of melody the French remained faithful. The *da capo* aria never became popular in France.

The French conception of melody, then, was not very clear. Since the basic distinction between opera and drama resides in the former's use of music, which largely appears in the form of melody, the French might well be concerned as to the vigor of the national opera. It was this state of affairs that led to Rousseau's denial that opera existed in France. He had become acquainted with Italian operas in Venice in 1742, and had penned his share of the articles on music in 1749. Less

---

[4] Grimm's musical criticism in the *Correspondance Littéraire* has been studied by Hirschberg, *op. cit.,* and by Carlez, *Grimm et la musique de son temps.*

[5] The type of melody here used is aptly defined by Riemann as a "courte phrase mélodique survenant dans le cours ou à la fin d'un récitatif. L'arioso diffère de l'air, par le fait qu'il n'a point de structure thématique; on pourrait dire que c'est l'ébauche d'un air, un "moment" lyrique." Riemann, *Dictionnaire,* "Arioso."

irritable critics tried to remedy the situation by studying the elements of melody in Italian operas. The rich melodic strains of Pergolesi, Scarlatti, Vinci, Porpora, and the rest, heard in the performances of the Bouffons' troupe in 1752, engaged the curiosity of the Encyclopedists, and soon an adequate aesthetic of melody was available in numerous *Encyclopedia* articles. Invariably, they pointed out the works in the Bouffons' repertory as an object lesson.

In subscribing to the imitation-of-nature thesis, Grimm, in the article "Poème lyrique," states that joy probably gave rise to the first imitation of nature by means of song. In attempting to enlarge the field of musical imitation, the composer learned that all passions were susceptible to musical interpretation, each passion having, as it were, a type of melody proper to its expression. This melody allied to the power of dramatic expression gave rise to the opera, which Grimm takes to be the very finest type of spectacle. Drama alone could never rise to an adequate expression of these elemental passions. Music can express an intensity of feeling entirely unknown to words and mime. A nation of people who continuously enjoyed an exalted state of being would use song as the natural vehicle of expression. Ordinary people attain to song only when deeply moved. Thus, the opera is by definition, says Grimm, tragedy which is under the constant necessity of presenting scenes of conflict, rejoicing, anger, chagrin, love, and similar profound emotions. From the point of view of the composer, the opera is plainly a vehicle for melody. Drama prepares scenes of a highly emotional character and renders the passion in question more precise.[6] Although music is eminently fitted to express passions, it cannot do so without the aid of text. Like all universal languages, melody is vague. The poet is then brought in to supply a canvas for melodic interpretation. Thus, the opera is vastly different from straight drama. Without music, the opera is a poor play; with music, or melody, the opera is heightened drama.[7] However, melody must be used sparingly in the

[6] Compare Nietzsche, "The word is an analogous example of what the music is trying to say." Cited by Professor Campbell, "Nietzsche-Wagner, to January, 1872." Words are also considered by Schopenhauer as rendering the musical meaning more precise. *Welt als Wille und Vorstellung.* Cf. also Wagner, *Oper und Drama* and *Das Kunstwerk der Zukunft,* wherein the composer develops similar ideas culled from Schopenhauer and Nietzsche.

[7] In the operas of Metastasio, which Grimm has constantly in mind in this article, the

opera; scenes of a deeply passionate nature must be led up to. Just as a dramatic character could not reasonably pass immediately from a scene of anger to one of joy and then to a third scene of great sorrow, the opera could never be composed of a series of uninterrupted melodies. Melody is most effective when thoroughly prepared by recitative, which disposes of the calmer moments of dramatic action. The aria, or melody, represents the high point of passion,[8] the breaking out of all the emotion that words are powerless to express.

In the opera *Artaserse* Metastasio has Arbace explain to Mandane, in recitative, why he must leave the city and her. Torn by anguish and sorrow at parting, Mandane reveals the depth of her suffering in the aria:

> Conservati fedele:
> Pensa ch'io resto e peno;
> E qualche volta almeno
> Ricordati di me.

Grimm observes that these lines are useless without the penetrating power of music to express the emotion behind them. Melody is to be used, then, only when the office of words has been superseded. The composer can admirably express in melody an emotion that a long tirade can only beggar. The opera poet's diction should differ from that of the tragedian: he must write with an eye to melodic adaptation, preferring to use the same precise word many times rather than attempt variety. The energy and the flexibility of the music used to comment this one word will surpass the fine poetic diction of the great Racine himself.

A significant difference exists between the dramatist's art and that of the opera poet. When, for instance, the dramatist finds it necessary to become verbose, the opera poet must become precise and use words sparingly, because the moments of passion belong entirely to the composer. No poetry would be less susceptible to musical commentary than all that sublime and harmonious eloquence with which Racine's Clytemnestra attempts to save

---

text is less susceptible to musical commentary as it gains in straight dramatic qualities. *Artaserse* is an operatic masterpiece that pales when read as a play. *Attilio Regolo* could be acted with success, but no successful opera was composed on this text. It is significant that the opera poet preferred this last-named work to the others, though he admitted that perhaps it was not the best libretto. See Casanova, *Mémoires,* II, 382.

[8] This idea was first expressed by Rousseau in his *Lettre sur la musique française.*

her daughter's life. The opera poet who places his character in a similar situation can allow her only four verses:

> Rendimi il mio figlio . . .
> Ah, mi si spezza il cor:
> Non son più madre, oh dio,
> Non ho più figlio!

But with these four short lines the composer can work more effectively to express the pathos in question than the divine Racine could ever produce with all the magic of his poetry.

The composer will insist on these four lines, says Grimm, repeating them in all possible nuances, exploiting by means of music all the phases of Clytemnestra's passion. The *poète* himself should be a musician, so that he may know how to dispose scenes of recitative and prepare the aria.[9] Not great poetry is required, says Grimm, but lines that will lend themselves to musical adaptation. The fundamental distinction between opera and drama is that the one is in constant need of musical commentary. It is essentially a sketch, a canvas, that does not arrive at its fullest expression until allied to music. Whereas drama stands alone. In writing opera, the poet's style should be governed by the realization that music deploys its powers of expression best upon flexible meters.[10] For the aria the broken line is preferable. The disorder that attends all passions should be reflected in the prosody. In no case is the Alexandrian to be employed, not even for the recitative, because musical declamation abhors long, regular verses.

The double aria, or duet, must be a *double plainte*. This does not mean that the members of the duet should sing ensemble from beginning to end, and then repeat, as in the French opera. The difficulty that attends this manner of presentation is patent. The audience cannot know what the singers are saying.[11] Moreover, the attitude towards all melody in the opera should never be one of merely singing a song. If melody is to have any dramatic effect at all, nuances of feeling

[9] Casanova reports that Metastasio told him he never wrote an aria without at the same time composing the music for it. *Mémoires,* II, 382. See also Rolland, "Métastase, précurseur de Gluck," in *Voyage musical au pays du passé,* chap. vi. Metastasio was a well-trained musician with a collection of printed works to his credit.

[10] The irregularity and the richness of variety of Metastasio's verse rendered him popular as an opera poet. See the Introduction to the Zotti and Faulder edition of his works.

[11] It will be remembered that Metastasio conceived the duet as a musical dialogue; the singers do not come together until each has sung his or her verse separately.

should be expressed. Song is complete in itself. Operatic melody is but an integral part of a whole, and as such must derive poetically and musically from what has preceded and blend easily into what is to follow. The opera aria differs from song in that the latter repeats the same melody without catching any of the nuances of expression that a dramatic situation requires. It was precisely in exploiting these varieties of melodic expression that singers such as Caffarelli and Gabrieli made themselves tyrants of the opera in Europe.

In the article "Motif" Grimm studies at great length the need for repetition of melody, and parts of aria, in the opera. He says in this article that the effect of music is lost unless the motif is repeated. This explains the use of the *da capo* aria. In straight drama or poetry repetition is a dangerous practice, in that it serves only to weaken the effect of a good line. But the needs of music are otherwise. The composer cannot transmit to an audience the deep significance of a theme by simply stating it. The vague character of musical expression renders repetition obligatory. In order to fix the import of a given motif, the composer must constantly return to it.

Since the aria is to be reserved for moments of passionate outburst, and since it is, so to speak, the peroration and recapitulation of the scene being represented, the repetition of the words in the aria is rendered exciting by means of the varied declamation with which the composer seeks to grasp the various accents depicting the same passion. For instance, when Merope, overwhelmed with sorrow, says she will die forlorn, she is not content to sing that line once, but will repeat every word twenty times. Now suppliant, she will beg for pity; now desperate, she will cry out with pain and sorrow; now choked with anguish, she will no longer be able to articulate her words properly, but will gasp forth broken syllables, *ah . . . mo . . . ri . . . rà . . .* During all these varied declamations she will sing only the words *disperata morirà*. Anyone who finds in this delivery nothing but monotonous repetition will never properly understand music.

Repetition of an idea in various ways is, then, the most resourceful tool of melody.

The purpose of melody in the opera is, according to Grimm, to express the high point of an emotional crisis. Since melody is the opera's mainspring, the entire opera should be a representation involving scenes of great pathos. It was in this respect that Metastasio proved to be a great operatic poet. He set the stage for the whole of eighteenth-century Italian opera. Grimm gives the poet credit for much of the success of operas by Pergolesi, Hasse, Leo, and other eighteenth-century composers who set his texts. His style, diction, and versification were perfectly suited to musical adaptation. His neat division of recitative and aria rendered the composer's task pleasant and simple. In the article "Poème lyrique" Grimm tells us that music in Italy, having from the very start taken the right direction, that is, the expression of feeling and passion, the opera poet could not fail to grasp exactly what composers sought from him. By a happy coincidence, Metastasio came into being with a host of great composers who were able to collaborate successfully with him. Between them they produced the eighteenth-century Italian melody opera of the recitative and aria type.

But if this group of men furnished Grimm with his aesthetics of melodic composition, he did not fail to see the evils that the Italian insistence on melody was bound to lead to. Overemphasis on the aria brought the singer into prominence. Soon everything else in the opera was sacrificed to this personage. Interest in the dramatic portion of the opera flagged. So long as the audience could be assured that their favorite was to sing an aria, they were content to sit eating and talking throughout the scenes of recitative. In this way the singer became tyrant, and the object of an opera was fulfilled for the audience if he had his air. To so great an extent did he abuse his prerogative that if the aria he was to sing did not suit his taste, he would substitute one that had formerly won him applause, without regard for aptness or for dramatic or musical unity. Grimm would have the producer say to the opera poet: "the opera can't be bad with a Caffarelli or a Gabrieli singing in it." Worst of all, the opera became fixed to suit the singer's wishes in the following manner. There must be three acts, lasting in all about five hours, including the ballets during the entr'actes, a change of scene in each act, making a total of six scenes; six roles, no less than five, no more than seven, including one leading actor, one leading actress, one second actor, one second actress, one king, governor, or old man; the protagonist must be in love with the leading lady, the second actor with the second actress; each sings twice in each act, except in the third, when the hastening of the opera toward a climax forbids this. There must be a duet between the leading male and female actors in the second act—it may be in the first, but never in the third. Each actor must leave the stage after singing his or her aria.[12] The actors will sing in turn, the last singing a brilliant air which must contain some reflection or maxim or a comparison between his situation and that of the other personages. Before an actor sings his second aria, all the others must have sung one, before his third, all the others must have sung their second. The ranks of the singers must not be confused, nor their rights infringed.

Yet these excesses, that followed in the wake of the splendid operatic achievements of Metastasio, Zeno, Pergolesi, Scarlatti, and Hasse, must not obliterate the fact that good melody could be composed as these men had prescribed. Grimm recalls, in the article "Poème lyrique," that because of the Emperor Charles VI's aversion to tragic endings, Metastasio had to bring all his operas to a happy issue. Despite all these stumbling blocks, the best type of melody, and consequently the best type of opera, was that created in Italy in the eighteenth century.

Grimm's analysis of the aria and his insistence on the importance of melody in the opera were universally subscribed to by the other Encyclopedists. The theory of opera as a vehicle to express passions and feelings is reëchoed in the articles "Ecole," by D'Alembert, "Expression," by Cahusac, "Opéra," by Rousseau, and "Poésie lyrique," by Jaucourt. Sulzer, the German aesthetician, in the article "Aria," for the Supplement, agrees that the aria should represent an emotional crisis, and Marmontel, in the article "Air" (Supplement, 1765), repeats Grimm verbatim. The conception of the duet as dialogue is to be found again in the articles "Duo," by Marmontel (Supplement) and by Rousseau. The latter adds "In explaining what the *duo* should be, I have told you exactly the manner of using it in the Italian opera." In attempting to account for the French opera's lack of melody, as conceived in the Italian opera aria, Marmontel, in the article "Air," states that at the time of the inception of the opera in France, the aria form was unknown in Italy and that consequently neither Lulli nor Corelli were acquainted with the recitative and aria-type opera.[13] In

[12] Grimm is in favor of this item. He says elsewhere in the article "Poème lyrique" that the aria being the peak of the drama, any addition to it on the part of the singer would be in the nature of an anticlimax.

[13] This is, of course, incorrect. There are miniature *da capo* arias already present in Monteverdi's *Orfeo*, technically the first opera in history (1607). See Láng, *Music in Western Civilization*, p. 343.

France, Quinault wrote verses that were poetically harmonious, but did not lend themselves to the aria type of melody. This *chant périodique,* or *période musicale,* was discovered, says Marmontel, by the Italian composer Vinci. The Italians have since abused the aria, while the French have remained faithful to the Lulli-Quinault tradition. In scoring the excesses that the use of aria led to in the Italian opera, Marmontel deplores the fact that the French so obdurately resisted the introduction of the aria form into French opera. As an opera poet, Marmontel insists that the French language is very capable of aria in the Italian manner. When once the French have learned how to compose the aria, the vaunted superiority of the Italian opera will vanish.

The art of molding a symmetrical musical phrase is completely unknown in France to this day. . . . As a result of experiments made by me in collaboration with a well-known composer,[14] I venture to say that our language can be very easily adapted to writing arias in the Italian style. We are just beginning to realize that our opera lacks the aria phrased in the Italian manner. When we do learn how to use this style intelligently, not only in the aria but in the duos and recitatives as well, I predict that French opera will be superior to the Italian.

Marmontel does not doubt that the Italians had found the true type of opera, aria and recitative. Nor does he question the excellence of the aria type of melody. In concluding the article "Opéra" for the Supplement, Marmontel implicitly subscribes to Grimm's dictum that Italian opera was the only opera.

When the correct musical phrasing of the melodious aria, sketched, molded, gracefully arching in its subtle flight is at last known in France, it will thrill the ear at any time and in any place. Never will truncated verses, hacked lines, and mutilated songs satisfy us. The Italians are constantly telling us, and we must end by believing them, that the essence of music is song and melody is the soul of song.

Rousseau alone was more sanguine in championing Italian melody and Italian opera.

As far as Rousseau was concerned, music was melody.[15] Since the

---

[14] Probably Grétry; cf. Marmontel, *Mémoires d'un père,* III, 104–106.

[15] For a thorough, though somewhat biassed, account of Rousseau's relations to music, consult Jansen, *Jean Jacques Rousseau als Musiker.*

object of music was the expression of feelings, dramatic music, or opera, specifically the Italian opera, was the highest expression of the art. Rousseau violently opposed the French basing of *chant* on a *déclamation théâtrale,* as in Lulli, and nothing was more irksome to the *philosophe* than the application of Rameau's theory of harmony, whereby melody was to be derived from harmonic progression. He almost never mentions this notion of Rameau's without stating in some form Tartini's opposite theory that harmony is derived from melody. This is to show that in the composition of melody nothing was as useless as a knowledge of harmony.

Let us consider the Italians, our contemporaries, whose music is the best in the world, according to everybody except the French, who prefer their own. Notice the simple chords Italian composers use in their works, and what choice they exercise in their harmony. They do not judge a composition on the basis of the multiplicity of its parts. The most beautiful chords in the world will never hold our attention as completely as do the well-modulated inflections of a beautiful voice. Any disinterested judge will have to admit that melody is, after all, the soul of music. (Rousseau: "Musique.")

Melody is more stirring than harmony. In the article "Accent" Rousseau states that since music is the language of the senses, the aims of this art are far better served by melody than by harmony.

Any theory of melody based on Rousseauistic tenets involves his theory of opera and, for the most part, his general theory of music. In the article "Sonate" Rousseau tells us that music must paint; it must present images.[16] Now this cannot be done without the aid of words. Words and music paint best in the form of melody; that is, passions and feelings are most satisfactorily expressed in melody. Since melody is the mainstay of the opera, and since situations in which human emotions are involved are most aptly introduced by the opera, Rousseau says that dramatic music, or opera, is the highest form of musical endeavor. (Rousseau: "Harmonie".)

In studying melody as the backbone of dramatic music, Rousseau says, in the article "Imitation," that the composer must awaken in the listener the same mood that is being created by the play, so that even without the stage representation, the melody alone should give rise

---

[16] Alembert, "Contre-sens," and the *Discours préliminaire* support this notion.

to an emotional experience of a more-or-less definite character. The object of the words is to render this emotion precise.[17]

The night, slumber, solitude, silence, all belong in the domain of musical interpretation. . . .
The composer does not directly represent these things, but induces in the listener's imagination a mood similar to that suggested by night, slumber, and silence.

Thus, melody can in no way be derived from theatrical declamation: the former aims at expressing the whole thought or mood of the scene; the latter can stress only words, or fragments of thought and emotional experience.

Melody should grasp the mood of the sentiments being represented by imitating the natural, unaffected intonation of the voice. For this reason melody can never be based on theatrical declamation which is itself already an artistic imitation of nature. The composer should first seek a sort of melody based on an interpretation of the words, always remembering to subordinate this to an interpretation of the thought. The final melody should express the general mood the singer is supposed to represent. (Rousseau: "Expression.") [18]

Melody is derived from a mood or passion in a scene, which in turn it helps to create. Theatrical declamation can depend only upon accent and prosody, and these two tools of operatic poetry must constantly subserve the melody. Theatrical declamation, then, is to melody as the recitative is to the aria: the former must always be a means of arriving at the latter.

In breaking down the elements of accent and prosody, Rousseau arrives at some very definite conclusions regarding French and Italian opera. In the foregoing division between melody and *déclamation théâtrale,* it is evident that he is at once pointing to the Italians as having perfected the art of opera, through successful melodic composition, and condemning the French for having created a type of opera based entirely on theatrical declamation. If aria and recitative are taken as the basic features of opera, it can be observed that the French have developed the recitative only and thus might be said to have but half an opera. That far more important half, the melody, was,

17 See Alembert, *Discours préliminaire,* Grimm, "Poème lyrique," and Marmontel, "Opéra," for a similar idea.
18 Marmontel repeats this thought in the article "Chant." *Vide infra,* Chapter VII, for Diderot's views on the *déclamation naturelle.*

according to Rousseau, completely neglected by French composers. French language may in great part have determined the course of the local opera. In the article "Accent" Rousseau states that much of the musical, and therefore melodic quality of the language depends, and in a measure derives from, accent.

The degree of accent in a language determines its musical adaptibility. If this were not true, then we should have to observe that there is no connection between song and speech and that the singing voice does not in any way imitate the accents of the spoken word. However, we know that lack of accent in a language causes melodies composed in that tongue to be on the whole monotonous and dull.

It is not difficult to see in this excerpt a criticism of the lack of accent in the French language. Rousseau dooms the German to a similar unhappy fate. Only the Italian language possesses the elements of variety of accent required for good melodic diction.

An observable difference in the degree of imaginativeness or sensibility between two peoples introduces an immense difference in the accents of their spoken language. The German, for instance, shouts in a monotone when he is angry; the irate Italian, on the other hand, changes the tone of his voice a thousand times. The latter is transported by the same passion, but what a variety of expression he uses in his accents and in his speech! We maintain that Italian melody owes its energy as well as its grace to this variety of accent in speech successfully imitated in song.

Rousseau offers accent as an index to good melodic composition to the French composer also, for later in the same article he counsels every composer to study d'Olivet's *Traité de la prosodie française.*

The dearth of melody in the French opera was due, Rousseau tells us, first, to an exaggerated preoccupation with stage declamation on the part of French composers; secondly, to the lack of variety of accent in the French language; and thirdly, to a faulty prosody. This fault was largely the result of the weak relationship between words and music in the French opera. The French, wholly taken up with the words at the expense of the music, as in the Lulli *déclamation théâtrale* type of opera, or vice versa, sacrificing the text to harmonic versatility, as in the Rameau *divertissement* variety, never sought to develop both words and music in simultaneous agreement.

Since the prosody of the French language is not as sensitive as was the Greek, and since our composers' heads are so full of musical sounds that they cannot think of anything else, there is as little relation between words and music in French song with reference to number and measure, as there is with reference to meaning and expression. (Rousseau: "Musique.")

The variety of expression that the Italians obtained from accent and prosody, the French tried to acquire by compiling a sort of thesaurus of musically adaptable words, such as *coulez, volez, gloire, murmure, écho,* etc. Rousseau rightly maintains that this lamentable practice tended to stultify rather than to vary musical expression. The only other possible escape from monotony for the French was to use a marked measure or rhythm for characteristic themes, such as, slow for a serious and heavy motif, fast for gaiety, and so forth. And again, this method only served to hurry the sterility of composition in France.[19]

The fundamental distinction between French and Italian operas depended, for Rousseau, upon a definition of melody and recitative. Granting that these were the most important elements of opera, Rousseau would say that the Italians wrote good recitative and excellent melody, whereas the French wrote poor melody and had enlarged and developed the recitative until it was no longer recognizable. Good melody is defined by Rousseau as that which is drawn from and reveals deep passions and feelings.[20] As for the recitative, "it is, properly speaking, a sort of musical declamation, wherein the composer must imitate as closely as possible the voice inflections of the person declaiming." (Rousseau: "Récitatif.") In the same article Rousseau states that Italian recitative approaches more closely to declamation than does the French. The French developed so extensively the recitative to serve all purposes of opera that the original usefulness of declamation miscarried in the recitative proper, and any air that partook of the nature of a *déclamation chantante* could not be very rich in melodic expression. Thus, Italian recitative is simple, and French recitative is complicated and ornamental. To so great an extent is this true, that in the French opera foreigners cannot tell the recitative from the air.

In the article "Vaudeville" Jaucourt quotes Rousseau as saying that French melody is not expressive enough and that therefore it is more proper for vaudeville than for opera. The passionate nature of Italian

---

[19] For the lack of variety of French song thesis see Cahusac, "Débit."

[20] All Encyclopedists agree: Cahusac, "Expression"; Jaucourt, "Poésie"; Marmontel, "Chant," "Opéra"; Alembert, "Contre-sens."

melody, on the other hand, makes it a fit vehicle for opera. In the article "Air" (Supplement) Marmontel, in studying this feature in both French and Italian operas, arrives at the conclusion that whereas the Italians sacrifice everything to melody and take many liberties with their prosody, the French are never willing to abandon a strong sense of prosody in the interest of melodic richness. Taken together, these two statements sum up admirably Rousseau's position. He saw that successful opera involved the solution of two distinct problems: the one, based on stage declamation and verse prosody, led to the creation of recitative; the other, stressing crises in emotion, involving the expression of profound passions, naturally resolved itself into the opera aria. Stated briefly, the opera presented at the same time a dramatic and a musical problem. That the French opera was stunted because of the unwillingness to abandon any of the virtues of drama for an improvement of the music and that the Italians adequately solved both problems by presenting a melodic feast with drama as a handmaid are matters of historical record.

The third major aspect of the opera was *le merveilleux*. Within the pale of this term came scenic effects, decoration, ballets, *divertissements,* and *machines.* The purpose of all this paraphernalia was to create an illusion of splendor and magnificence, fit atmosphere within which the doings of gods and heroes were to be unfolded. Whereas the Italians early abandoned this idea of the opera as a vast spectacular pageant in favor of straight drama with subjects drawn from classical tragedy, the French developed the portrayal of scenes from classical mythology to an unprecedented degree, continuing to lavish tremendous sums on brilliant stage sets and complicated machinery even after the Italians had established the recitative and aria type of opera. As we shall remember, in certain aspects the beginnings of opera were similar in Italy and France and the first efforts at national opera in France inevitably partook of the nature of extensive *fêtes,* so costly in their rigging and appurtenances that only the monarch could afford them. This was the type of spectacle that was developed in Italy in the sixteenth and early seventeenth centuries; it survived as an obscure spectacle after the opera had obtained a definite place. In France the *machines* of the Marquis de Sourdéac rendered these spectacles immensely popular; indeed, the pre-Quinaultian opera depended for its success almost exclusively upon this ornamental aspect.[21] It is not difficult to understand, then, why this use of the spectacular persisted in the later opera in France. The French love of show, which has come down to our own day in the form of parade and pageant as well as romantic grand opera —great numbers of the French opera audience still go to the opera merely for the ballet—was nurtured in these early *fêtes*. Cahusac, in the article "Féerie," asserts that Quinault employed this element of spectacle sparingly and, as it were, against his will. But Rameau reinstated pageant and ballets, immortalizing himself in Cahusac's eyes by turning the opera into a vast *fête* or *divertissement*.[22]

Apologists of the French opera were thus afforded ample material in studying the growth and function of *merveilleux* in the opera. Encyclopedist comment upon this aspect of opera included the references to La Bruyère's qualification of the opera as *enchantement* and to its classification as spectacle by Boileau. In the article "Opéra" Jaucourt actually quotes Boileau's ringing denunciation of the opera as a spectacle wherein "more attention is given to delighting the ears than to satisfying the mind." Cahusac, Jaucourt, and Marmontel agree that the backbone of French opera is and must remain *le merveilleux*. In the article "Décoration" Cahusac defines the opera as the "spectacle du merveilleux," and adds that besides beginning to cast the spell of illusion, the decoration must constantly present elements of surprise and wonder. The *merveilleux* depends for its subjects upon mythology. The creator is to develop the supernatural powers given by the Greeks to their gods. Secondly, there is the element of *féerie et magie*. This includes the giving of occult powers to inanimate objects, and rapid changes or inordinate metamorphoses. The classical example of the latter Cahusac draws from the opera *Amadis,* wherein the hero of that name worships a *magicienne,* whom he mistakes for his beloved. All this is brought about by *enchantement,* necessary to the creation of an acceptable fiction by means of "l'illusion du spectacle du merveilleux." (Cahusac: "Enchantement.")

In defining the *spectacle lyrique,* or opera, Jaucourt states, in the

---

[21] See Cahusac, "Fêtes de la cour de France"; and for a study of the machine plays, Gros, "Les Origines de la tragédie lyrique et la place des tragédies en machines dans l'évolution du théâtre vers l'opéra."

[22] We now know that Cahusac and the reigning mode of the *style galant* practically forced Rameau to compose *divertissements.* See Láng, *Music in Western Civilization,* p. 545.

article "Opéra," that it is primarily the representation of an "action merveilleuse." Whereas the Italians went on to develop opera based on classical Greek tragedy, the French preferred to continue the dramatization of the Greek epic. Thus, French opera is "the dramatization of the most sublime parts of the epic." Since the actors are to represent the gods and heroes of the epic, their actions and language must be in keeping with their roles. Hence they will not act like ordinary mortals or speak the language of men. Their actions will be of a supernatural order and will thus partake of the implausible. They will not speak, but sing concerning their affairs. This rationale of song in the opera was meant to answer the many attacks upon opera for presenting impossible characters using impossible means of communication. The quarrel concerning song in the place of speech begun by classical critics St. Evremond, Boileau, Fénelon, La Bruyère, wherein they claimed that it was not "natural" to die singing, was here given a sharp rebuke by Jaucourt. Since music takes us to an ethereal, unexplored universe, says Jaucourt in effect, it is proper to have, not ordinary human beings, but fictitious creations, such as the Greeks imagined their gods to be, people it, and they would better sing rather than speak about their affairs and move about in an atmosphere of magnificence and divine pomp. Though any single element of the opera would be a violation of nature when measured by human standards, taken as a whole, the spectacle represents a fantastic world we know nothing about. We may therefore be content to witness a spectacle that in transcending human experience can only be adequately unfolded by means of the *merveilleux*. Violation of natural laws in the French opera may be considered one reason for its success as a spectacle; it provided an escape from the severe rationalizing tendency of the age.

In the article "Poème lyrique" Grimm supports Jaucourt's argument for song in the opera and goes a step farther, saying that song would be the most plausible means of expression not only of heroes and gods, but of men as well— Men, that is, who represent a higher order of the species.

Imagine a nation of enthusiasts and zealots living in a constant state of exaltation. These people, although sharing our principles and passions, would be much superior to us in subtlety, finesse, and delicate sensibilities. With more highly developed sensory organs than ours, such a community would sing rather than speak, and music would be their natural language.

Whoever hopes to enjoy the opera must similarly be more subtle, delicate, and better versed in the art of communing by song than most people. The opera goer must be an opera hero in potential. The subjects of mythology, accompanied and aided by all the supernatural attributes of modern sorcery and witchcraft, should provide the soul of the French opera; i.e., the *merveilleux visible,* just as the transformations and magic spells furnished the soul of the Greek epic. But this is as far as Grimm is willing to go. He states that this attitude towards the opera is essentially a fantastic one. The opera hall is not large enough to house these grandiose productions, nor are gods and goddesses, the traditional characters of the epic, fit subjects for opera. Moreover, the *merveilleux* is not really susceptible to theatrical representation.

Now, it was upon this very element of *merveilleux* that Marmontel, as well as Cahusac, in his *Traité de la danse,* based all his claims for the excellence of French opera. In a work entitled *Poétique française* (1763) Marmontel had set forth, in Chapter XIV, his ideas concerning this aspect of the opera. In the article "Lyrique" Marmontel defends his position against Grimm's scathing remarks, insisting that without *merveilleux* the French opera would be nonexistent. As a matter of fact, what made French opera superior to the Italian, says Marmontel in this article for the Supplement, was this very item of the *merveilleux,* which gave to song a plausibility and *raison d'être* it does not have in the Italian opera. The opera being the representation of *la nature dans l'enchantement,* it is natural to sustain this illusion by means of the *merveilleux.* Marmontel concludes his defense by stating that this discovery of Quinault's was the greatest poetic invention since Homer and Aeschylus.

But what Grimm objected to most strongly in the *merveilleux* was its complete lack of relationship to everyday life. How could the doings of Greek gods, about which the French knew little or nothing, have any interest for an eighteenth-century Parisian? What bearing could this fantastic spectacle have upon the life of reasoning, enlightened human beings? We have seen that Grimm admitted that the soul of French opera resided in the *merveilleux.* Any attack upon this aspect of the opera in France was tantamount to a proscription of French opera in general. Grimm was entirely aware of this danger, but he did not let this realization deter him from his purpose. The portion of the article "Poème lyrique" which treats of the *merveilleux* is a sustained diatribe against French opera.

First of all, says Grimm in this article, why must an eighteenth-century French composer turn to the gods of ancient Greece for an operatic subject? If the opera did require a religious subject, it would seem natural for a people to prefer the dramatization of its own cult. The opera would then become a religious festival, as, in great part, Greek drama had become. But though it may be said that Greek drama was in a sense a religious art, Greek dramatists used the apparition of gods upon the stage with great discretion. The French, who did not exercise similar caution, found that gods tended to lose their divine character when they appeared for three hours together on an opera stage "under the beard and talent of M. Muguet." The Greek Gods are objectionable enough, but how about those ridiculous creatures of fancy, "un génie aérien, un jeu, un ris, un plaisir, une heure, une constellation, and all those bizarre allegorical beings . . . is there no limit to this sort of nonsense?" Marmontel, in the article "Merveilleux," had pointed to the *épisode de la Haine,* from *Armide,* as the model of the genre termed *merveilleux,* employing as it did all the above phenomena. Grimm analyzes this scene in detail, in the manner of a wide-awake critic of opera; i.e., reading a lesson from its manifold shortcomings.[23]

What is the upshot of this lesson on the *merveilleux?* From the point of view of drama, says Grimm, this element is hopeless. These fantastical creatures do not interest us, because they can change the course of a hero's life in the twinkling of an eye, thus impairing the dramatic unity of the opera. Dramatic ineptitude led to a stunted musical growth. How could a drama devoid of all interest and truth, how could these fanciful creations lead to a rich musical development? Grimm blames the monotony of French melody on the *merveilleux,* as well as the tendency to fix musical expression, cookbook wise, in a tacitly accepted thesaurus of appropriate themes. Thus, French music could only be

---

[23] This long analysis, far too long to quote here, is one of those masterful attacks that only the Encyclopedists, and Voltaire, seem to have been capable of marshalling. I am thinking especially of *Le Neveu de Rameau.*

mediocre, for to prefer thunder and brilliance to dramatic power, says Grimm, is to prefer mediocrity to sublimity. Any composer can represent musically an earthquake, a tempest, a Sabbath, and the like, but the composer who can really portray human passions in a good dramatic situation must remain rare. The French composers failed to seize the fundamental distinction between *aria* and *recitativo* because of the *merveilleux*. They made the recitative slow and boring, basing it upon false ideas of declamation, and what there is of aria so called in the French opera can only properly be applied to the *air de danses,* wherein the *danse* or *merveilleux* element is given much more attention than the song. Haphazard *ariettes* were thrown into the local opera, but these, aside from having no connection with the dramatic and musical thought of the opera in question, waste all their efforts upon such words as *larme, murmure, voltige, enchaîne,* and *triomphe,* terms singled out for their musical adaptability. Finally, insistence on the *merveilleux* led the decorators astray, preoccupied as they became with fairy palaces and enchanted gardens.

We have already seen that Grimm felt that the recitative and aria, or Italian type opera, was the natural vehicle for the portrayal of human emotions. He therefore scores the influence of the *merveilleux,* because it rendered everything in the opera unnatural and *invraisemblable.* Thus, it was unnatural for the French to treat Greek gods in an eighteenth-century spectacle. Transformations, magic spells, and the animation of *jeux, ris, heures, constellations,* not to mention other bizarre allegorical creations, were all beyond human experience. It was not natural to introduce dance upon any and all occasions, nor are there any examples in nature of enchanted palaces.

As may be expected, Rousseau did not withhold comment upon the *merveilleux* in the opera. Indeed, the article "Opéra" in the Supplement, borrowed from his *Dictionnaire de musique,* may be taken as an addenda or complement to Grimm's attack. Rousseau believed that the *vols* and *machines* were indispensable adjuncts of the opera before this spectacle came of age. He points out that in Italy Apostolo Zeno was the first to introduce historical characters into the libretto and that Vinci and Pergolesi completed the break with the old fables, transforming the spectacle into a veritable concert. It was only when the element of *merveilleux* had been excised from the opera that this spectacle became worthy of being called a work of art: "When the opera was finally rid of the cloying *merveilleux,* it became at once a majestic and moving spectacle worthy of appealing to people of taste and to sensitive souls." Rousseau did not fail to track down any element of the opera that was particularly dear to the French and to proscribe it.

Thus, with the *Encyclopedia* itself opinion was divided concerning the *merveilleux.* Typically enough, those who swore by the local opera (Jaucourt) and those who saw in the opera no farther than the dances or *divertissements* (Cahusac), favored the use of *merveilleux,* whereas the inveterate enemies of French opera (Rousseau and Grimm) opposed it. However, it would seem that here again Rousseau had the last word, when he claimed that the *merveilleux* served only as a blind to the glaring defects of French opera. Marmontel, an ardent champion of French opera and of the *merveilleux,* who insisted that "music creates an atmosphere in which the *merveilleux* thrives" ("Lyrique," Supplement), and that "Song is the *merveilleux* of the spoken word" ("Opéra," Supplement), admits, in the article "Récitatif," that dances, elaborate decorations, stage effects, *machines,* etc., were all brought in to bolster the sinking local opera in vain. All the glittering train of the *merveilleux* could not keep the French opera alive. Failure succeeded failure.

Of the minor aspects of opera the Encyclopedists were no less meticulous critics. In a later chapter will be found a discussion of the dance, but it is necessary to note that as far as the French opera was concerned, the *divertissement* was conceived as an integral part of the action. These episodic tableaux were composed of dances accompanied by song, and of course, scenic display. In the article "Divertissement" Cahusac is quite specific regarding the function of this element of the *merveilleux.* In general, he is dissatisfied with their use in the French opera; too often they interrupt rather than supplement the main dramatic action. The usual manner of presenting the *divertissement* was as one or several *entrées de ballet.* Cahusac finds that the ideal *divertissement* is one in which the song and dance are indispensable to the general development and progress of the spectacle: "A good ballet entrance is made up of a plot which the singing and dancing serve to develop and unfold in an agreeable manner." (Cahusac: "Divertissement.") Cahusac mentions *Thésée, Amadis,* and *Roland,* all Lulli-

Quinault operas, as containing models of the genre. We have already seen that Cahusac probably saw in the opera only a vehicle for dances. Since both the *merveilleux* and its handmaid the *divertissement* depended upon dance, this critic was their stanchest champion. He initiated more propaganda for the use of dance in the opera than any other Encyclopedist. The articles "Ballet," "Coupe," "Couper," "Divertissement," "Enchantement," "Entrée," "Expression," "Fête," "Féerie," "Figurant," and "Geste" all include either a mention or a lengthy discussion of this subject. And in each of his several articles treating of the *divertissement* Cahusac warns against including the dance in the opera merely as *postiche*.

In the article "Air" Marmontel hints that the French opera was kept alive mainly because of the dances. Though French composers had not yet found the secret of composing recitative and aria, they compensated for this lack by developing *divertissements*. Thus, for him the dance took the place of the aria in the French opera. Marmontel explains, in the article "Opéra," that the dance must carry on the main action of the opera. Dance and *fêtes* can be integrated in the opera during moments of calm. In this way the suspension of opera for the purpose of introducing dances will not be so strongly felt. He agrees with Cahusac that the French have only exceptionally succeeded in making the dance a part of the opera.

In scoring the ballets and *divertissements* of the French opera as *postiches,* Grimm suggests, in the article "Poème lyrique," that Quinault unwillingly followed popular taste in this department of operatic composition. He points to the dances in *Roland* as aptly fitting into the dramatic action, arguing from this example that had Quinault had a free hand, he might have made more extensive use of the *divertissement* as an integral part of the action. However, as we have already seen, Lulli could not have allowed this if he meant to retain intact the fine symmetry of his operas.

Cahusac, Marmontel, and Grimm represented Encyclopedist thought concerning the use of dance in the opera.[24] They were all in agreement that the French had not made the most of the ballet in the opera, that

[24] For Diderot's ideas concerning the *ballet-pantomime,* in which he shows himself to be in full agreement with these men, see his *Plans de divertissements* and the *Entretiens sur le Fils Naturel,* in his *Œuvres,* Vol. VIII, and VII, 156–161.

Quinault had done as well as he dared, and that Noverre represented the highest aims of the opera insofar, at least, as the dance was concerned. Noverre's *ballet en action,* or *poème-ballet,* was all that the Encyclopedists dreamed for the opera. As for Rousseau, he saw no place in the opera for the dance. (Rousseau: "Opéra.")

Encyclopedist comment was extended to even the minutest details of opera. Cahusac states that the music of the entr'acte should continue the illusion of the spectacle. (Cahusac: "Entr'acte.") And the gestures and facial expression of the singer should be those of the consummate actor. (Cahusac: "Geste.") Rousseau tells us, in the article "Acteur," that the French expect the singer to be a finished actor and that his pantomime should synchronize perfectly with the musical commentary. The music itself should be an actor, carrying on a constant duet with the singer, commenting on his thought and enhancing his passion by revealing the unexpressed. Quite specifically, Marmontel sees music as an answer to speech in the *récitatif obligé.* He sums up the varied role of the orchestra in the opera as follows: (1) to play chords; (2) to supplement; and (3) to answer, as in a dialogue, the voice of the singer; (4) to provide the setting for a scene through the imitation of natural sounds. (Marmontel: "Accompagnement.") Marmontel does not seem to have been aware that in Italy the orchestra had long since been an active agent in the thematic unfolding of musical material, aside from its role of sustaining the singer, in the works of Scarlatti and Pergolesi.

In concluding this section, it may be said that the Encyclopedists saw in the opera a perfectly coördinated spectacle of drama, music, dancing, singing, painting, and scenic effects. All agreed that the Italian opera was superior, but the general consensus of Encyclopedist opinion in no way supported Rousseau's statement that the French opera was hopeless and that it had no future. In summing up his wants for the opera, Cahusac holds out a distinct hope for the French opera in particular.

The successful opera writer should be a man of many talents with an infinite capacity to learn. . . . He should know how to make use of contrasting situations, how to introduce *divertissements,* vary them, and fit them into the action; he should know how to plan quickly; he should be a man of ideas, having more than a smattering of painting, mechanics, dancing, and perspective; he should have a feeling for effect, a rare talent, to be found only in men of lively imagination and keen sensitivity. . . . Perhaps some day the French will awaken and cast off the silly prejudices that have done so much harm to the progress of the art of opera in this country. (Cahusac: "Coupe.")

Marmontel felt that perfection had already been achieved in some of the operas of Quinault, actually, insofar as the *poème* was concerned, and potentially, at least, regarding other elements.

If you can imagine that in an opera, music, dance, decoration, machinery, the singers' talent both for singing and acting, could be in the same degree of excellence as the essential portions of the poems for *Atys, Thésée, Armide,* then you have an idea of the opera as I conceive it, or as Quinault himself had wished it. (Marmontel: "Opéra.")

It was in this spirit that Marmontel rewrote Quinault's libretti for the composer Piccini.[25]

The foregoing quotations prove that the Encyclopedists were not willing to be influenced to an inordinate degree by the opinions of their principal contributor to the articles on music. They may have agreed with Rousseau when he scored French singing (Rousseau: "Chanter," "Crier," "Forcer la Voix," "Fort"; Cahusac: "Débit," "Effort") or when he pointed out faults in execution (Rousseau: "Ensemble"; Cahusac: "Exécution") and again when he ridiculed the French tendency to insist upon certain "musical" words in the *poème* (Rousseau: "Musique"; Grimm: "Poème lyrique"), but none of these critics was willing to admit that the French could not and did not have a national opera.

The upshot of Encyclopedist criticism of the opera is that these writers were the first Frenchmen to recognize the difference between literary and musical opera. But the literary orientation of French composers prevented that naïve abandonment which enabled the Italians to create true opera. The French learned too late that the dominant element on the lyric stage must be music; this explains why despite the activity of the *Encyclopedia* on behalf of musical dramaturgy, the messiah of the new French opera had to be a foreigner.

[25] Marmontel, *Mémoires d'un père,* III, 164–165.

CHAPTER IV

SUGGESTED REFORMS OF THE OPERA

GRIMM HAD SHREWDLY OBSERVED that one reason for the quick growth of opera in Italy was the nonexistence of a vigorous drama in that country. Because of this Italian opera was allowed to develop unmolested, while in France, Grimm pointed out, from the very beginning the local opera was in conflict with the strong classical tragedy. (Grimm: "Poème lyrique.") In the light of this remark it is not difficult to understand that any opera growing in the shadow, as it were, of classical French tragedy must of necessity, if only to satisfy public demand, take on for better or for worse many of its aspects. We have already seen how futile were all attempts to break from theatrical declamation on the part of Lulli's successors and that Rameau preferred, or rather was forced, to abandon the problem of integrating recitative and aria in favor of the *divertissement* type. In other words, Rameau developed a type of opera based on a branch of the Lulli-Quinault tradition. *Divertissements* existed in France before the Lulli-Quinault invention, in the comedy ballets of Molière, for example, were incorporated as part and parcel of French opera and continued an existence outside this tradition. Thus, Rameau did not essentially change the Lulli-Quinault legacy. In 1750 French opera was still largely based on classical stage declamation, no traces of the recitative and aria were to be found, and the opera subjects were still preferably drawn from classical mythology. Insofar as progress was concerned, in the French opera there was none; the whole cycle of the history of its rise, development, and decline was to be found written in the works of Lulli and Quinault. The insistence of the *style galant* on *divertissements* only served to disorganize the severe classical order of their works.

Encyclopedist critics, vexed with the stagnant state of French opera and inspired by the achievements of the Italians, cast about in their analyses of the opera for remedies for the glaring defects of the local opera. Uppermost in the minds of these writers was, of course, a deep respect for French dramatic and operatic traditions. They thus sought change, not through revolution, but by patching here and mending there the old Lulli-Quinault creations. What was wrong with the opera? The charge of monotony being the one most often launched against it, Encyclopedist commentators turned their attention to an inquiry into the causes of slowness and the languishing nature of the local spectacle. The most ostensible source of retardation were the long recitative sections. First to come under revision, then, was the declamation. Marmontel found that much of the slack could be taken up by using a *déclamation simple,* based upon a study of the delivery of the actors Baron and Mlle Dumesnil.[1] (Marmontel: "Déclamation.") A study of this department taught Cahusac that opera singers, basing their style and delivery upon those of ordinary tragedians, were inclined to stay too long with each sound and to mouth their lines of recitative, taking as much as five minutes to speak thirty lines. (Cahusac: "Débit.") He counsels, therefore, speeding up a more varied delivery to create more interest in the spectacle. (Cahusac: "Débiter.") A speedy recitative and rapid movement of the opera in general became the slogan of the Encyclopedists.[2] This was probably the result of their experience with the witty, life-like, and rapid texture of the Italian *opera buffa,* in which celerity was the prime requisite.

The singer's conduct on the operatic stage also left much to be desired. Rousseau early saw that the singer needed to act as well as sing. We have seen that the *philosophe* expected the singer to complement and carry out the dramatic significance of the music by means of pantomime. (Rousseau: "Acteur.") [3] Another fault of the singer's rendition in France, and this cried loudest for amendment, was the tendency to shout rather than sing, a habit as annoying as the actor's tendency to

---

[1] Marmontel's *déclamation simple* is strongly reminiscent of Diderot's *déclamation naturelle;* see the latter's *Entretiens,* in his *Œuvres,* VII, 157, and *Le Neveu de Rameau,* V, 461–462.

[2] Cf. Diderot, *Œuvres,* VIII, 462–463, and Marmontel, *Mémoires,* III, 164.

[3] See also Diderot, *Plans* . . . , and the stage directions to *Est-il bon, est-il méchant?* in his *Œuvres,* VIII, 163.

rant. Rousseau took every opportunity to score this failing; no less than four of his articles on music treat this item exclusively. (Rousseau: "Chanter," "Crier," "Forcer la Voix," "Fort.") Rousseau further admonishes singers and musicians to get into the spirit of the production. (Rousseau: "Expression.") Again, referring to the singer's performance, was Cahusac's suggestion that the chorus show more activity upon the stage. (Cahusac: "Les Chœurs.") Another good idea would be to have the understudy for the leading role conduct the chorus. In this way the chorus would improve in unity, and the understudy could benefit by constantly having his protagonist and model before his eyes (Cahusac: "Doubler")—not to mention the fact, adds Cahusac, with the typical French eye for color, that another brilliant costume would be displayed for stage effect.

Some of the Encyclopedists' ideas were extremely modern as well as economical and useful. Such, for instance, was Grimm's proposal, in the article "Poème lyrique," that the action on the stage be portrayed by pantomimic dancing, while the singers sang from the orchestra pit; an idea later used by Noverre in his collaboration with Gluck. The active chorus, as opposed to the static or contemplative and therefore lyric chorus of the *tragédie lyrique,* is also of Italian origin, as may be seen in the operas of Jommelli and Traetta. However, it may be that these Italians reached back, in their turn, to the chorus under French influences.[4]

From the point of view of composition, Cahusac would have an even mixture of recitative and *divertissements.* This was essentially a compromise betweeen the Lulli and the Rameau type operas; the one being, according to Cahusac, too much recitative and not enough *divertissements,* while the other suffered from reverse causes, i.e., extensive *divertissements* with little and negligible scenes of recitative. (Cahusac: "Déclamation.") Cahusac insisted upon the *divertissements* being made a necessary part of the action of the opera. (Cahusac: "Divertissement.")

Not only did writers counsel composers to study language prosody (Rousseau: "Accent"; Castillon: "Compositeur," Supplement), read poetry (Castillon: "Compositeur"), and cultivate closely the Italian operas, but also there were those among the Encyclopedists who pro-

---

[4] Cf., Láng, *Music in Western Civilization,* pp. 558–559.

posed that a new lyrico-dramatic spectacle be composed that would combine the best features of both the Italian and the French operas. (Castillon: "Opéra," Supplement.) Marmontel advocated the composing of new music for Quinault's texts. (Marmontel: "Air.") This amounts to composing Italian music for French libretti. "Let us take from the Italians what we need most," says Marmontel, in the article "Opéra," "but let us beware of renouncing Quinault's excellent *genre;* rather let us encourage our young poets to make his texts adaptable for a style of music that was unknown to him [the Italian], but of which he is most worthy." Marmontel does not want too much emphasis to be placed on the music. The new opera was to show an even distribution of recitative and melody.

These suggestions and hints by Encyclopedist critics are not at all indicative of despair as regards the opera in France nor do these articles reveal anything but the greatest respect for the works of Lulli and Quinault, as well as for the more recent efforts of Rameau. The general upshot of the Encyclopedist campaign is not "let us do away with the past and start writing in the Italian manner" or "when shall we begin to compose opera?" But by and large the Encyclopedists are appealing to the public. They seem to be saying: "Our opera is good, and the present brand of composition is satisfactory; but let us not be too easily satisfied. Let us show more interest in a spectacle that is so dear to us. Our composers are doing what they can, but the quality of our singing and dancing could be vastly improved. It is only by showing the actors and musicians that we desire a more adequately presented spectacle that we can attain to heights of execution and expression already reached in Italy and Germany."

CHAPTER V

INSTRUMENTAL MUSIC

NOTHING WAS SO BADLY MISUNDERSTOOD by these early music critics as the music of instruments. Such distinctions as we make today between dramatic, program, and "absolute" music, were completely unknown to the Encyclopedists. They believed that all music was one and that its principal object was to "paint." Operatic music was to "paint" states of emotional crises; instrumental music was to "paint" natural phenomena. All this thinking grew out of the Encyclopedists' lamentable attempt to force music into the imitation-of-nature thesis. No doubt many of these men really appreciated instrumental music. Diderot's letters, for instance, are a golden repository of his remarks on that art. But with only two notable exceptions, when the music articles came to be written for the *Encyclopedia* the contributors all adhered to the contemporary doctrine of affections, which may be taken as a rationalistic manifestation in music. According to this doctrine, a piece was set in a certain style or mood, and even individual instruments were endowed with human sentiments: one spoke of the "modest flute," the "pompous horn," and the "proud bassoon." Music was thus endowed with anthropopsychical aspects: a piece was lively, gay, somber; a melancholy composition appealed to a bilious person, dance music to a sanguine individual. A sonata exploited one affection, which had to be its basic mood, and did not admit of contrasting themes, as did the later classical sonatas.[1]

For Rousseau, the affections turned to expressiveness. This comprised the ticketing of keys, tempi, and inscriptions with certain moods. Diderot modified the classical imitation-of-nature thesis by shifting the emphasis that had been placed upon nature and truth to artistic

[1] Consult Láng, *Music in Western Civilization,* "The Doctrine of Temperaments and Affections," pp. 434ff.

representation; thus, the artist's conception became a more important source of beauty than natural phenomena. Diderot asserted that life itself was but a poor reflection of the truer image of reality called up by the artist's imagination.[2] This new view was ignored or overlooked by the other Encyclopedists, who subscribed in general to the affections theory.

Since nature could be imitated by direct copy or indirectly by interpretation—whereby the imitation called up an image of the object imitated or a representation of the emotions involved—the Encyclopedists fitted most of the powers of music into the first class, i.e., the imitation of thunder, earthquakes, running water, tempests, and the like, and stuffed whatever was left over into the second, i.e., the representation of fairies, fauns, heroes, and divinities, or the depiction of moods or states of being calling up sentiments of anguish, fury, hate, love, tranquillity, and the like. D'Alembert's *Discours préliminaire* to the *Encyclopedia* included a clear statement of this position. "Music which does not paint is just noise," he says in this masterful essay, and adds that the scope of musical imitation must be considered limited, not because of the poverty of that art, but because of the lack of resourcefulness on the part of composers. He gives music the last place among the arts of imitation, since composers had not as yet exploited the full range of musical expression. This commendable reserve on the part of a critic who in his own writings showed a complete lack of appreciation of the sort of music here being discussed, is highly indicative of the great caution with which Encyclopedists in general approached these knotty problems. Until the art of music had "reached its maturity," D'Alembert was not willing, as was Rousseau, to rush to dangerous conclusions.

The entire section of the *Discours préliminaire* relating to music is a masterpiece of artful dodging and clever sidestepping. To begin with, says the author, music was, perhaps, only intended to represent noise. It has gradually become a discourse or a language by means of which divers sentiments and passions of the soul get expressed. Why should musical expression be limited to passions, asks D'Alembert, and why cannot music be made to express all the affections? A terrifying noise or a frightful object, for example, will always give rise to the same

[2] See Leo, *Diderot als Kunstphilosoph*, p. 27.

reaction in us. Is it not possible for the composer to seek out in nature exactly those sounds which, when properly reproduced, will cause the listener to experience the same fright or terror as if the object were actually present and the noise heard in its original surroundings? At first blush D'Alembert would seem to be counseling direct imitation of natural sounds, but we must extend his statement to include not only the reproduction of obvious sounds but also the depiction of images ("painting") and the creation of states of being or emotional crises (poetic catharses). We know now that such words as painting and representation should be left out of musical criticism altogether. The power of music to "paint" objects or to represent natural phenomena is on the whole negligible. But D'Alembert, at a loss for a definite aesthetic of music other than that it appealed or did not appeal to him, employed the tools of classical rationalistic criticism as best he could to give a tentative critique concerning an art that refuses to yield to analysis and does not easily lend itself to intelligent discussion.

In subscribing to the theory of music as an imitation of nature Cahusac agrees with D'Alembert that music must "paint." A concerto, a sonata must "paint" something in order to imitate successfully. Instrumental music is otherwise nothing more than a series of meaningless, lifeless harmonious sounds. (Cahusac: "Expression.") The first law of musical imitation, then, is to express something definite. Whenever a Lulli-Quinault opera did not succeed, it was due, says Cahusac, to Lulli's failure to grasp and express musically the fine tableaux presented by Quinault. In this way many of Quinault's greatest scenes were ruined by Lulli's unsuccessful musical "painting." Such, for instance, was the *air de violon* in the first act of *Phaëton,* which was supposed to comment the metamorphoses of Protée. The scene was a failure because Lulli's music failed to depict the transformations of Proteus from a lion into a tree, a sea monster, a fountain, and a flame. Cahusac claims that Lulli's air was "cold, monotonous, and without expression." (Cahusac: "Expression.") Furthermore, if music is to imitate nature successfully, it must correctly express the sentiment or mood in question. Cahusac would seem to say—and this was also Rousseau's crotchet—that each sentiment, mood, passion, or state of being had a precise musical corollary. (Cahusac: "Enthousiasme"; Rousseau: "Chromatique," "Ton.") That music could aid in the creation of a mood was no mystery to anyone, then as well as now. But that so many sounds should be taken as the equivalent musical expression of an exact emotional experience represents the carrying *ad absurdum* of the musical thought and speculation of the era of rationalism.

In general, then, it may be said that Encyclopedists favored the theory of music as an imitation of nature, and espoused the view that instrumental music must "paint." Practically all writers on subjects of musical interest in the *Encyclopedia* use the expression "peindre les sentiments" in referring to the function of instrumental music. Just as the painter denotes suffering in the face of a subject by means of a few strokes of the brush, the Encyclopedists believed that the composer could set down a definite sentiment by means of certain notes in certain time. Thus, Cahusac felt that very often Lulli's music played traitor to Quinault's text. (Cahusac: "Expression.") D'Alembert qualified as *contre-sens* music which did not express what the action on the stage represented. (D'Alembert: "Contre-Sens.") Some few Encyclopedists were satisfied to state merely that music must "paint" (Marmontel: "Chant"; Chastellux: "Idéal"), but the great majority were willing to add that a definite picture must be presented. Now how can instrumental music "paint" a picture? The anonymous author of the article "Instrumentale" tells us that before composing any sonata or concerto a definite plan should be made as to what the work is to express. Thus, not only sentiments and images may be presented musically, but character studies as well. So long as the composer remains faithful to his purpose, the music cannot fail to represent objects and people just as surely as the painter's brush. All music that is not composed with a definite idea, image, scene, or person in mind can only be meaningless and boring, "a harmonious murmur." The author of the article would say with Grétry, "You have done enough vague drawing, apply your ideas to a more definite subject." [3] Grétry, a disciple of Encyclopedist thought, expressed here the fundamental doctrine of the *philosophes* with regard to a theory of music; i.e., that music receives its fullest expression only when allied to words.

[3] Grétry, *Mémoires,* III, 377. In the person of Diderot, he counsels Haydn to quit the composition of trios, symphonies, etc., and to turn his talent to the creation of more important works; that is, the opera (III, 377–378).

Thus, instrumental music approaches perfection in proportion as it attains to the power and richness of the human voice.

The human voice is beyond question the instrument that is best equipped to render the accents of passion. From which we can deduce the fundamental principle that musical instruments are to be classified as good or bad in proportion to their similarity to the tonal quality of the human voice in all its variations. ("Instrumentale.")

Instruments were invented merely to imitate the voice of man. (Cahusac: "Chant.") Instrumental music, says Grimm, in the article "Motif," must follow the principles of vocal music in order to be successful, and "the nation which sings best will have the best instrumental music." These considerations lead Rousseau to state that the *symphonie* is no more nor less than instrumental melody. Since music can paint only by means of melody, Rousseau finds that all instrumental music which does not sing has failed in its purpose and cannot be said to imitate nature. (Rousseau: "Mélodie," Supplement.) The creation of a sonata, concerto, and the like must be controlled by the same aesthetics of composition as obtain in the invention of an operatic aria.

It is needless to add that the Encyclopedists believed that instrumental music could never equal the power of expression of the human voice. The author of the article "Instrumentale" finds that the oboe is the most expressive instrument, since it approaches closest to the sound of the voice. On the whole, however, he does not feel that instruments can successfully imitate the voice of man. D'Alembert laughs at the idea of composing a flute sonata, an idea which he calls "une bizarrerie," since the flute was intended only to express sadness and tenderness. (Alembert: "Elégiaque.") But the most eloquent enemy of the music of instruments was undoubtedly Rousseau. The article "Sonate" is a sustained diatribe against the "fad" of absolute music. The author accuses the French of turning to the composition of sonatas only after having failed miserably in the creation of opera. Since the local composers could not equal the efforts of the Italians in the opera, Rousseau says, they attempted to hide their inadequacy in matters musical by producing works that were no better than concerted noise. The aim of music is to comment and enhance a sentiment or object called into being by means of words, and only the musical sounds produced by the human voice can boast of attaining to this power: "Can all the follies of Mondonville's violin move me as deeply as two notes sung by Mlle le Maure?" asks Rousseau. As for sonatas, symphonies, concertos, and the rest, the composer would do well to emulate that inept painter who had to inscribe "this is a horse" below his representation of that animal. Fontenelle was entirely justified, says Rousseau, when, overwhelmed by the interminable, meaningless sounds of a *symphonie*, he cried out in despair, "sonate, que me veux-tu?"

The chief trouble with instrumental music, says Rousseau, is that invariably it serves only to show off the composer's knowledge of harmony. (Rousseau: "Harmonie," "Mélodie.") Listening to two melodies simultaneously, he explains, is somewhat akin to following the conversation of two people speaking at the same time. It is astonishing that Rousseau believed this argument to be conclusive. So wrought up was he with logical concepts adduced merely for purposes of discussion, that he did not even stop to consider that the above statement shows a deplorable lack of appreciation of music. What actually happened was that Rousseau carried his definition of melody as musical discourse to the ridiculous extreme of suppressing the word musical entirely. He goes on to say, in the article "Harmonie," that harmony cannot present images or express sentiments; this is the province of melody alone. In the article "Musique" Rousseau divides music into two categories: harmonic, or "natural," and melodic, or "imitative." Rousseau concluded, then, and most Encyclopedists agreed, that instrumental music is inferior to vocal.

It is not likely, however, that Rousseau's collaborators would have borne with his statement that the composition of instrumental music was a fad indicative of the poor taste of French composers and that like all fads this lamentable desire to be "Gothic" would pass. (Rousseau: "Harmonie," "Sonate.") For there were two notable exceptions to this tendency to condemn all instrumental music per se, at least one of which was a valiant contradiction of all that Rousseau had to say on this subject.

In the article "Idéal" for the Supplement, the Chevalier de Chastellux questions the validity of practically every one of Rousseau's musical doctrines. To begin with, there are arts which imitate nothing, or only by chance have a distant and vague relation to nature. Such are architecture, which cannot be said to find its model in nature, and instrumental music. What exactly in nature does a prelude or a melody imitate? The song of birds, the murmur of a brook? Chastellux scoffs at this idea and asks what in nature might the nightingale or the brook be imitating. To limit man's artistic endeavors to an imitation of nature, says the Chevalier, is to deny him the power of creating for himself works of beauty. By means of his industry and imagination man has the capacity to embellish and, so to speak, to improve upon nature by producing objects of joy and satisfaction; in short, by creating works of art. Compare, for example, the simple airs and rhythms an Iroquois plays upon his *calumet* to the finale of *La buona figliuola*.[4] Where in nature is this vast progress of the European composer over the native indicated? Moreover, the song of birds has no measure, nor do birds ever sing in harmony. It is evident that the beauty of music is entirely ideal, created with great difficulty by man for human consumption only. Works of art are not only imitative, but—and more important—creative as well. They express man's thought; that thought which results from his most ambitious desires and reveals all the ardor with which he seeks his pleasure. Chastellux has a concluding paragraph which is unique in the eighteenth century, both for its vision and its eloquence.

Those who insist that music must be limited to an art of imitation or to the expression of fixed sentiments are not worthy of listening to the melodies that Buranello, Piccini, and Sacchini wrote. These universally acclaimed melodies are submitted in France to a sterile and pedantic criticism which would banish richness from art and outlaw artistic pleasure. A man who is carried away by a real passion utters words in a disorderly manner. The poet counts and arranges these words, the composer prolongs and repeats them. If you deny the artist his privileges, you reduce art to cleverness, the most useless attribute in the world when it is bereft of sensitivity and imaginativeness.

Thus, those who limit art to an imitation of nature reduce great artists to the stature of pygmies. They would deny to genius the masterful control that transforms an inarticulate passion into a thing of beauty.

The foregoing apology for instrumental music was far and away

---

[4] *Opéra-comique* by Piccini; Italian title, *Cecchina nubile,* Rome, 1760. Riemann says of the finale here referred to: "Il [Piccini] imagina, le premier, le final composé sur les motifs de plusieurs scènes, avec changements de mouvement et de tonalité, et il donna de l'extension à la forme du duo, qu'il rendit plus dramatique." Riemann, "Piccini," in *Dictionnaire.*

ahead of Encyclopedist aesthetic theory in general. There were those among the Encyclopedists, however, who would reserve final judgment and seem to betray an appreciation of absolute music. Jaucourt defines music as "the expression of tender sentiments by means of inarticulate sounds." (Jaucourt: "Lyrique.") Marmontel in the article "Art," Supplement, takes Rameau to task for stating that the universal principle of harmony and melody is to be found in nature. He is willing to admit that nature may serve as a guide, but never as a model, for musical composition. Moreover, if it is a fact that all sounds and chords are to be found in nature, it is nonetheless an art to combine these sounds and develop these chords in an agreeable ensemble or composition. This performance, Marmontel holds, is the profoundest secret that man has stolen from nature. Art—specifically musical art—is thus rescued from the tyranny of natural law, and the artist is liberally vindicated. Marmontel joins Diderot [5] and Chastellux, for in good faith he desired to leave the door open to instrumental music.

If instrumental music is merely pleasing to the ear and does not suggest any distinct picture to the imagination or represent any particular mood to the soul, if through a veil of sound this music allows the listener to see and feel what he pleases depending on his individual state of mind at the concert, then it has served its purpose. (Marmontel: "Chant.")

These and similar statements that would seem to include a larger view of musical aesthetics, large enough, that is, for an appreciation of absolute music, show that although in general Encyclopedists were limited in their theories concerning instrumental music, such a vast enterprise as the *Encyclopedia* did not fail to make room for more comprehensive, albeit contradictory, theories of art.

Though the Encyclopedists were perhaps not prepared openly to espouse the cause of "absolute music," they did take considerable interest in the technical progress of instrumental music in France. If they seemed

---

[5] Alongside the articles on instruments in the *Encyclopedia* must be mentioned Diderot's true and universal appreciation of instrumental music. He carefully selected pieces for his daughter to play on the harpsichord, and her repertory included such composers as Muthel, Cramer, Schobert, Fisher, Filtz, C. P. E. Bach, Eckardt, Alberti, Corelli, Scarlatti, Pergolesi, and perhaps even the great Johann Sebastian, who is mentioned once in the *Leçons de clavecin*, in his *Œuvres*, XII, 302. At home as well as abroad, in Holland, Russia, and France, Diderot exposed himself to the widest possible range of instrumental compositions. For his enthusiastic reactions to these concerts, *vide infra*, note 12.

to champion music of the program type, they but followed public taste, as indeed did Rameau in his compositions.[6] The French, then as now, favored a pictorial rather than an acoustical interpretation of music. With this in mind, it is interesting to turn to Encyclopedist accounts of the rise and development of the music of instruments, wherein are to be found many pages of sound criticism.

One of the points that is made again and again in the articles of these critics is that the actual progress of instrumental music is dependent upon a similar advance in the manufacture and in the playing of instruments. (Cahusac: "Exécution"; Diderot: "Instruments"; Rousseau: "Ouverture"; Anonymous: "Instrumentale.") Cahusac, in studying the orchestra used in the time of Lulli, states that despite the primitive nature of that unit and the poor execution of the late seventeenth-century musicians, Lulli managed to give the world orchestral music of wonderful though simple beauty. He adds that this composer could have written far more complicated scores—there are indications in his works that he was far in advance of the scoring and playing of his time—but that he preferred to limit his art and to compose only such music as could easily be played by his musicians. Though as a conductor Lulli was a tyrant who thought nothing of cracking the skulls of faulty violinists, it is known, says Cahusac, that these musicians were under the constant necessity of employing mutes to cover their inability to play certain passages, they needed as many as thirty rehearsals, and their sight reading was painfully slow—even in executing a score that would seem simple, adds Cahusac, to the weakest of contemporary scholars. The greatest praise is due Lulli, then, not only for his thorough drilling of a backward orchestra, but also for his capacity to adapt himself to prevailing conditions in his orchestral compositions.[7]

With the advance in the technique of playing musical instruments came a better understanding of the organization of the orchestra. In 1725 Anne Danican Philidor founded the "Concerts spirituels," which

[6] Lavoix fils, in his *Histoire de l'instrumentation depuis le seizième siècle à nos jours*, tells us that scenes of thunder, the imitation of storms, battles, etc., were the ". . . obligatory elements of all *tragédies lyriques* in the eighteenth century," p. 228, and that "le pittoresque était dans le goût de l'époque." *Ibid.*, p. 230.

[7] Lavoix esteems Lulli as one of the finest orchestrators of all time. *Op. cit.*, p. 31. We have already seen that conditions were not as bad as Cahusac assumes.

Cahusac calls the finest orchestral group in Europe. Outstanding talent in every field of musical endeavor participated in these concerts.

Whenever a famous musician or a renowned singer appears in Paris you will certainly be able to hear him at the Concerts spirituels. The orchestra, which is composed of the best musicians in France, the choruses, which are chosen from the best church choirs in Paris, the best loved voices from the Opéra, and the most brilliant singers from the king's own chapel and chamber make that place a veritable music lover's paradise. (Cahusac: "Concert Spirituel.")

The improved choirs of this orchestra, coupled with the finest singers in the king's pay, could not fail to influence the trend of music in France. Cahusac attributes in great part the high perfection of Mondonville's motets to the interpretation of this unit.[8]

Another direct result of the improvement in instrumental execution was the change wrought in certain forms of orchestral compositions. Rousseau notes that the vast progress in instrumental music since 1725 led to the modern overture, known universally as the Italian type. This form of the overture is divided into three sections—allegro, adagio, allegro—in contrast to the old French-type overture, which ran adagio, allegro, adagio. The reason here given by Rousseau was that the advance in orchestral playing permitted the Italians to begin with a brilliant introduction, which served to fix the attention of the audience from the very first measure. He further reports the Italians as saying that the first *coup d'archet* of the French-type overture only served to prepare ennui rather than interest. Rousseau does admit, however, that Lulli's overtures really set the mood for the opera about to be unfolded, as, indeed, all overtures should. (Rousseau: "Ouverture.")

Unfortunately, the Paris opera orchestra did not keep step with such organizations as the Concerts spirituels with the result that many of the early abuses in execution still plagued that group. In studying opera orchestras in Europe, Rousseau tells us that the Dresden unit was probably the best in his time, and the Naples opera orchestra a close second. The Paris group, according to Rousseau, was hopelessly last.[9]

[8] Numbering thirty-eight musicians in 1725, this orchestra was composed of a personnel of fifty-eight in 1775. Mlle Bobilier, *Les Concerts en France sous l'ancien régime*, p. 312. The Revolution put an end to the activities of this festival orchestra. See Riemann, "Concert Spirituel," in *Dictionnaire*.

[9] La Borde, in his *Mémoire sur les proportions musicales*, 1781, notes a considerable expansion in the personnel of the Paris Opéra orchestra. Thus, in 1713 this organization

Here are some of the reasons for the local inferiority as set down by Rousseau in the article "Orchestre." (1) The ignorance of the French musicians. (2) The lack of ensemble. In the article "Ensemble" Rousseau asserts that French music precludes the possibility of any ensemble. Since the music says nothing, the musicians cannot feel the impulse to agree. (3). The interminable tuning-up.[10] (4) The Frenchman's hatred of routine.[11] (5) The deplorable habit of leaving instruments stranded overnight. (6) The poor location of the conductor. At this period the conductor stood, or more frequently sat, at one side during the rehearsals, and from his position at the harpsichord indicated the measure by waving his hand. But at the public performances of the Opéra the conductor stood in the pit with his back to the orchestra. Since he was entirely taken up with the singers, the musicians of the orchestra were directed by the first violin. Rousseau criticizes: "the poor placing of the conductor on the opera stage, where he can busy himself only with the actors on the stage and cannot properly see the orchestra behind him in the pit." (7) The distracting noise of his bâton. It will be remembered that at this time the conductor carried a cane of from three to four feet in length, with which he beat upon the stage to indicate the measure. Because of the racket caused by the conductor's pounding on the stage, Grimm called him "Holzhacker" (woodchopper). Thus, in 1755 the French opera orchestra left much to be desired. In this article Rousseau shows a keen understanding of its many shortcomings.

But perhaps the most advanced critic of instrumental music in France was Diderot,[12] who wrote the articles on instruments for the

---

numbered only forty-seven musicians and cost the king about 20,150 livres. In 1778 the orchestra had swollen to include sixty-four musicians, with an expense sheet of 69,482 livres.

[10] The outcry against this failing of the French orchestra was general: "Que dire," says Bollioud de Mermet in 1746, "de la longueur excessive du temps qu'ils employent à s'accorder entr'eux dans les concerts? de ces préludes sans fins, où les Symphonistes, chacun sur un mode différent, fatiguent l'auditoire par leurs essais?" *De la corruption du goût dans la musique française*, pp. 27–28.

[11] Even today, when French musicians do turn out for a rehearsal, considerable individuality and independence must be allowed. It is only with great difficulty that a conductor calls his orchestra to order in France. If he has something to say to the double-bass, it is usually more practical for him to traverse the various disputing choirs, and shout his message into that worthy's ear.

[12] For Diderot's illuminating criticism of the music of instruments, aside from the articles for the *Encyclopedia*, see his *Œuvres*, I, 358, apology for instrumental music; I,

Encyclopedia.[13] His organization of the material in these articles was as follows: (1) a short history of the instrument; (2) a brief account of the word; (3) a table setting forth the range of the instrument; (4) method of its manufacture; (5) the various methods of playing the instrument. The articles "Basson," "Musette," "Orgue," "Serpent," and "Viole" are models of descriptive writing, and it is no small tribute to Diderot that *La Grande Encyclopédie* follows his lead throughout. In the article "Instrumentation" of that work, we read: "In regard to each musical instrument we have given all the necessary details concerning its form, its history, its range, and its usage in musical works." This procedure was first established by Diderot in his *Encyclopedia.* In the article "Instruments" Diderot divides instruments into three main groups: (1) strings; (2) winds; (3) percussion. Under each heading he gives examples and the method of sound production. Each instrument, says Diderot, has its range and timbre, which a composer must know thoroughly before he can compose successfully. But it is not enough to be acquainted with the timbre of each instrument separately. The composer must experiment with various combinations of the several instrumental choirs in order to ascertain their effect in tonal expression.

We shall simply point out here that each instrument has its own range, tonal qualities and peculiarities that the composer must immediately master if he is to use the instrument effectively. Mastering the use of the various

---

335, as "le plus violent des beaux-arts," and praise of C. P. E. Bach; V, 409, against virtuosity; XII, 150, lauds good performance of Opéra orchestra; XII, 398, "les sons retournent du cœur au cœur"—Wagner later repeated this, *vide infra,* Chapter X; and XVIII, 438–439, XIX, 266–267, XX, 91–92, for praise of performance of Oginski (Harpe), Eckhardt and Bayou (Clavecin), and the note in praise of C. P. E. Bach, which Diderot addressed to that composer. See also his *Correspondance inédite,* I, 264, Schiester's concerts at Paris and Grandval, and his *Lettres à Sophie Volland,* Nov. 20, 1760. We recall that Diderot put up the German professor Bemetzrieder at his house, rewrote the latter's *Principes d'harmonie,* 1771, and gave him his first pupil, Diderot's own daughter, later Mme de Vandeul, who soon became a distinguished *claveciniste,* thanks to her father's patient and understanding supervision of her lessons. Diderot's letters are full of admiration for his daughter's prowess, and he reports faithfully every new composition she undertakes. *Œuvres,* XIX, 338–339, *Correspondance inédite, Lettres* XXI, XXII, XXIII, LXVII. Philidor spoke highly of her talent and mastery of harmony, and Burney praised her "knowledge of modulation." *The Present State of Music in France and Italy,* pp. 391–393, refer to Diderot.

[13] L. J. Goussier was responsible for the *planches* referring to musical instruments and their manufacture, as well as for a very important article on the organ, written for the *Encyclopedia* in conjunction with Thomas, *Discours préliminaire,* xliv.

instruments is no small achievement for the composer, because these are the voices with which he speaks to us. But it is not enough for the composer to grasp the individual possibilities of the instruments, he must also familiarize himself with their combined tonal production.

The article ends with the hope that further improvements may be made in the manufacture of musical instruments so that the composer can exploit the full tonal possibilities.

So intimately does Diderot discuss problems of instrumentation in this article, that we must conclude that a profound conviction of the future of instrumental music led the Encyclopedist to conduct long and arduous inquiries into orchestration. No doubt his many composer friends were of great help to him in this search, above all with regard to the technical aspects of the question. We know that whenever he had to document any article for the *Encyclopedia* he consulted his specialist friends. After wrangling over the subject with many authorities, Diderot managed to incorporate the best of their ideas in a superbly written article. In this way his articles were always more representative and commanded more respect than the opinion of any specialist in particular. Thus, Diderot must be granted the distinction of being the first non-musician to consider problems in instrumentation in terms of tonal color and the peculiar capacities of each instrument.

CHAPTER VI

THE DANCE

THE ART OF DANCE underwent numberless turbulent changes in the eighteenth century. The darling of the French court at the time of Marie de' Medici, the ballet showed a dramatic tendency with *Le Ballet comique de la royne* (1581). This tendency was continued in the *ballet de cour,* which became an immediate ancestor of French opera.[1] Brought to its apogee by Benserade, the *ballet de cour* did not finally begin to lose ground until the appearance of Molière's comedy ballets and Lulli's and Quinault's operas. Both of these genres showed the influence of the *ballet de cour,* which would seem to have had a renaissance in the work of La Motte-Houdard toward the end of the seventeenth century. Rameau created the opera ballet toward the middle of the eighteenth century, and as yet the art of dance showed no inclination toward an independent existence. The fixed dances of the old *ballet de cour* still held sway in the opera *divertissements,* and traditional costumes of a particularly unwieldy nature hampered the movements of the more progressive dancers. Mlle Sallé was the first to break the academic bonds, in *Pygmalion* (1734), wherein she shocked her audience by appearing in a light, loose costume. Cahusac then began his attacks on the antiquated nature of the dance routine (1754), immediately followed by Diderot's epoch-making *Entretiens sur le fils naturel,* especially the *troisième entretien* (1757), in which he set the stage for the modern ballet pantomime, furnishing an example of the new art utilized by Noverre in his revolutionary *ballet d'action.*

So close to the Frenchman's heart was the dance in any and all forms that no tortuous aesthetic of this art was necessary. In general,

---

[1] Láng, *Music in Western Civilization,* pp. 378ff. Cf. also Prunières, *Le Ballet de cour en France avant Benserade et Lulli,* and Silin, *Benserade and His Ballet de Cour.*

Encyclopedists agreed that the dance must imitate nature and that like music it must "paint." (Cahusac: "Figurant"; Rousseau: "Ballet"; Marmontel: "Pantomime"; Grimm: "Poème lyrique," *De la danse*.) But whether it was the old *ballet de cour* or the new ballet pantomime that the audience was viewing, whether the artists were depicting a dramatic action or just dancing, it is certain that the French gave the performance a cordial reception.

Marmontel likened the pleasure taken in enjoying the dance to that experienced in listening to a symphony. (Marmontel: "Pantomime.") But it remained for Montesquieu, that too-infrequent contributor to the *Encyclopedia,* to give the most eloquent appraisal of the dancing art.

The art of dancing pleases us because of its light and graceful movements and the beautiful variety of its poses. The dance pleases us also because of its fusion with music, the dancer being in many respects an accompanying instrument. Above all, dancing appeals to us because of a certain tendency of the mind to relate all movements to certain movements, all poses to certain poses. (Montesquieu: "Goût.")

Thus was the art of Terpsichore appreciated by the author of *L'Esprit des lois.*

By far the most important authority on the dance in the *Encyclopedia* was Louis Cahusac. It is difficult to ascertain exactly what his background was with regard to this art, but we do know that he wrote a good *Traité de la danse,* published in 1754. His articles for the *Encyclopedia* reveal that he was conversant with the works of the Jesuit Le Jay, with Bonnet's *Histoire de la danse sacrée et profane* (1723), and Père Ménestrier's monumental *Des ballets anciens et modernes selon les règles du théâtre* (1682), and that he was acquainted with the achievements of the outstanding artists of his time. On the whole, his articles are well documented and show a professional interest in the advance of the art. Moreover, he collaborated with Rameau in the creation of operas ballets, so that his interest in dancing must have been somewhat more than that of the intelligent amateur. In any case, most of the articles of the *Encyclopedia* referring to the dance were confided to him, and, short of calling in a specialist, which does not seem to have been the policy of the *Encyclopedia,* it cannot be said that the editors were mistaken in making this choice.

In the article "Ballet" Cahusac gives a brief history of the genre from the times of the ancients to date (1750). His sources for the dance in Greece and Rome are Plutarch, Sidonius Appollinaris, Athenaeus, Plato, and Lucian. He starts the modern ballet with the seventeenth-century *fêtes* of the Duchesse de Savoie, *Le Gris de lin,* and *La Verità nemica dell'apparenza sollevata dal tempo,* the last given at the birth of the Cardinal de Savoie (1634). Cahusac draws analyses of these *fêtes* from Père Ménestrier. He then speaks of the ballets given during the reign of Louis XIV up to 1671, mostly of Benserade's composition: *Le Ballet des prospérités,* given at Louis' majority, *Hercule amoureux,* performed at the time of the sun king's marriage, *Alcidiane* (1658), *Les Saisons* (1661), and *Amours déguisés* (1664). Here is Cahusac's judgment of Benserade: "This poet was particularly talented in the writing of the lesser aspects of works of this sort. We must admit that he did not show as much capacity in planning and developing a ballet." A not very flattering appraisal of the creator of the *ballet de cour.* Cahusac gives Quinault credit for the *Fêtes de Bacchus et de l'amour* (1671), which as we have seen above was composed almost entirely of excerpts from Molière's comedy ballets, and claims that *Le Triomphe de l'amour* (1681), by Lulli and Quinault, caused Benserade's *grands ballets* to disappear from the stage. In the meantime, the only haven of the dance was Molière's *intermèdes, Le Mariage forcé, Les Fâcheux, Psyché, Le Bourgeois gentilhomme,* and other plays. Quinault incorporated the dance into the opera as a minor element, and it was not until 1697, with La Motte's and Campra's *l'Europe galante,* that the ballet made its reappearance on the French stage as a major art form. This led directly to the opera ballet of Rameau's invention, principal among which was *Platée* (1749). For Cahusac, this *divertissement*-type opera was the highest expression of the ballet. In regard to the contemporary *ballet-en-action,* Cahusac maintains the cautious reserve of the historian.

In our own day authors have attempted to introduce the element of *merveilleux* into the ballet, and have created what they call the "action ballet," wherein the dance is the principal element of the presentation. This type of ballet we have found agreeable because of its novelty. It does possess, however, much more resourcefulness than the old ballet in keeping the spectator amused because it offers poetry, painting, and music more occasion to deploy their riches. In the lyrical theater this "action ballet" makes use of the machines, the principal attraction in that spectacle. But we must await public reaction to the revival of the *Fêtes de l'hymen de l'amour* [by Rameau, 1747] to decide which is the real genre for the ballet.

Part of this modesty was due, of course, to the fact that Cahusac collaborated with Rameau in this work.

Cahusac seems to have been the only Encyclopedist who insisted upon the inclusion of the dance in the opera, a fact which is surprising in view of the great popularity it enjoyed with the public and musicians alike. Indeed, he felt that the dance was the saving grace of the French opera, the only department in which the local composers could boast of superiority over the Italians. He defines the ballet as a figured dance in which the artists, accompanied by the music of instruments or of the human voice, represent by means of steps and gestures "a natural or fantastic dramatic situation." Cahusac goes so far as to suggest that in time the *ballet français* may displace the Italian opera, an assumption which the Italians never justified.

The main defect of the ballet, according to the other Encyclopedists —and Cahusac agreed in part—was that it presented a series of disconnected scenes which did not even have the interesting tonal relations of the dance suite. Consequently, Grimm suggests extracting the ballet from the opera altogether, on the grounds that dancing and singing are two distinct manners of imitating nature. Each has its proper method of imitation, and to confound the two is to destroy their several powers of artistic performance.

Is it not a violation of sound judgment and good taste to attempt the fusion of two distinct arts of imitating nature in the same performance? . . . Is it logical to confuse two different hypotheses in the same poem, the one asserting that the actors in the spectacle can converse only in song, the other maintaining that the dancers in the same piece can express themselves only by movements and gestures? (Grimm: "Poème Lyrique," *De la danse*.)

For this reason, adds Grimm, both the art of opera and the art of dance were mediocre in France. The *ballets* were brought in to cover the defects in the composition of French opera. But the dances themselves were mediocre, they had no connection with the main dramatic action, and served only to interrupt and belittle the opera. Thus, both arts remained at a standstill. So poor, indeed, was the dance in France, that Noverre had to go to Germany to create the modern ballet. Here is Grimm's analysis of the French ballets.

Each ballet is composed of two files of dancers lined up on each side of the stage. They soon mingle and form figures and groups having no particular significance. The best dancers, however, are reserved for solos, duos, and trios, and sometimes they dance in groups of four, five, and even six. For all these different types of *divertissements* the composer writes *chaconnes, loures,* sarabandes, minuets, *passepieds,* gavottes, *rigaudons,* and *contredanses.* If there is any occasion to represent a scene or a dramatic situation, it is certain to be performed by the duo or trio, after which the *corps de ballet* takes up again its insipid figure dancing. The only visible difference between one *fête* and another is that provided by the tailor who dresses the dancers today in white, tomorrow in green, and the next day in red, depending upon the policy and prescriptions of the house. Thus, the ballet in the French opera is merely a dancing academy, where mediocre dancers learn in public to form figures, break, and form them again, and where good dancers perfect themselves in more difficult studies using various noble, graceful, and learned poses.

Grimm's analysis, which is borne out by the facts, is at the same time as sound a condemnation of the rigid ballet as might have been penned by Noverre himself.

Just as Grimm had set forth the aesthetic theory of aria and recitative as conceived in the Italian opera, now again the Encyclopedist establishes the tenets of the *poème-ballet* based upon an examination of the works of Noverre. The modern ballet represents, according to Grimm, the combined efforts of a poet, a musician, and a ballet-master. The dance imitates nature by means of gesture and pantomime and must be accompanied by instrumental music, which serves the same office in this respect as in commenting song in the opera. Like the opera, the ballet must have a beginning, a middle, and an end. The action must evolve more rapidly than in the opera, and the scenes must be more varied. The poetic principles of opera apply exactly to the ballet. The same reserve must be observed in using dances as the composer exercises in employing the aria. As an opera cannot be song from start to finish, the ballet cannot be dance throughout. The creator of the *poème-ballet* must know how to lead up to the dance by distinguishing, as does the composer, the scenes of passion from those of tranquillity. The dance should be made to represent the high point or emotional crisis in the ballet, just as the aria indicates the climax or breaking out of passion in a scene of opera. As the aria is prepared and relieved by the recitative, the dance must also be led up to by the step, to which in turn it gives way. This step is in cadence, and has that relation to ordinary walking that the recitative has to everyday speech: it is artistic, not functional. As Grimm banished songs from the opera because they tended to be too loosely or not at all related to the musico-dramatic sequence which the aria was to further, and in a sense, the expression of its goal or highest significance, the dancing of minuets, gavottes, and *chaconnes* was likewise proscribed by him, on the grounds that they were not sufficiently adequate to interpret the key scenes of emotional crisis in the ballet. Rather, the dance should derive from the very fabric of the ballet. It should be pantomimic, gesticulative, well coördinated with the music in every detail and nuance. Each movement of the dancer should be replete with all the dramatic pathos of the scene in progress. Precisely as was the aria in the opera, the dance in the ballet was to be "the peroration of the scene being represented." The close coöperation of the arts of dance, music, and mime, then, was to result in the new ballet, the *ballet-pantomime*.

In examining the ballet, Marmontel, as usual, follows Grimm very closely and states that pantomimic dancing is far too powerful an art in itself to coöperate successfully with the opera, and that it should be developed separately. He does not see, however, why the old set-figure dances cannot be left in the opera as a tool of the *merveilleux*. (Marmontel: "Pantomime.") Rousseau expresses a similar sentiment in his article "Pantomime": "The idea of substituting dancing pantomime in the opera in the place of figured dances does not seem to me to be very advisable"; and the remainder of this sentence shows that Rousseau was categorically opposed to the modern ballet: "you do not dance to express your feelings and thoughts, but you dance merely to enjoy yourself."

Although he did not write many significant articles on the dance in the *Encyclopedia*, Diderot must be placed in the front rank of innovators of the revitalized ballet. Insofar as Noverre may be said to be a child of the *Encyclopedia*, it was Diderot's ideas concerning the ballet, as expressed in the *Entretiens sur le fils naturel*, that he was putting to work. Here is Diderot's appraisal of the dancing art.

The dance is still awaiting a man of genius. That art is everywhere poor because it has hardly been guessed by us that it can imitate nature. . . . The dance bears the same relation to pantomime . . . as natural declamation bears to song; dance is rhythmic pantomime. . . .
The dance is a poem. . . . As such it should have a particular presenta-

tion. The art of dancing is an imitation of nature by means of movements, and presupposes the collaboration of the poet, the painter, the composer, and the mimic. The dance has its own subjects which can be distributed into acts and scenes. Each scene may or may not be musically accompanied and the dance solo could be compared to the aria in the opera.[2]

The genius here appealed to by Diderot was to be none other than Jean George Noverre.

Sulzer, in the article "Ballet" of the Supplement, taken from his *Allgemeine Theorie der schoenen Künste*,[3] states that Noverre's type of ballet was the only one worthy of being classed as art. For purposes of thoroughness, and also to gauge the influence of the *Encyclopedia* upon Noverre's art, it is indispensable here to examine the French ballet master's ideas, together with their application, as set down by him in the work entitled *Lettres sur les arts imitateurs*.[4]

In the *Préface* to the 1807 edition of that book, Noverre, now an old man, looks back with pleasure upon the long road the ballet has traveled since he first took upon himself the task of remaking the art. The transformation of the old figure dances into *ballet-pantomime,* the banishment of masks and ridiculously cumbersome costumes, the new high standards required of the ballet master, these and a host of other innovations aided Noverre in bringing about as important a revolution in the dance as Gluck had effected in the opera.[5] Noverre asserts that he made the dance imitate nature, taught it to "paint," and to speak the "language of the passions." What is more, he showed how pantomime could attain heights of expression unknown to music. Encyclopedists had explained that song expressed a concentration of emotion that the spoken word was powerless to portray. Noverre asserted that when music itself must also be silent before a still higher degree of passion, there yet remained pantomime.[6] It was his mission to reveal to the world this powerful art.

[2] Diderot, *Œuvres*, VII, 157–158. Diderot knew Noverre. Cf. Diderot, *Œuvres*, V, 482.

[3] Sulzer and his collaborators expressed by and large in this work most of the Encyclopedists' aesthetic doctrines. *Vide infra,* Chapter X.

[4] This work includes in its entirety the earlier *Lettres sur la danse,* Stuttgart and Lyon, 1760. A good study of Noverre's contributions to the ballet is to be found in Levinson, *"Jean George Noverre und die Aesthetik des Balletts,"* in his *Meister des Balletts,* pp. 7–68.

[5] Sachs, *Eine Weltgeschichte des Tanzes,* pp. 297ff. sees a striking similarity between the principles expressed in the *Lettres* here examined and the Gluck manifesto in the preface to *Alceste*.

[6] See Abert, *J. G. Noverre und sein Einfluss auf die dramatische Ballettkomposition*.

All the foregoing apology, couched in the choicest language of the Encyclopedists' disciple, somewhat obscured the real accomplishments of this dancing master. Noverre found the ballet a hopeless victim of routine and tradition. An accomplished practitioner, he tried to remedy some of the many blights that beset the dance. The French Opéra spurned his offered reforms, so he took his ideas to Stuttgart. Then he tells us how he met Gluck in Vienna and how the first *ballet-pantomime* was born. Gluck was rehearsing for a performance of *Alceste* in that city. The singers were having difficulty in interpreting the highly-prized "chœurs en action." After two hours of relentless drilling, Noverre counseled Gluck to give them up; but the composer remained obdurate. Either the troupe learned to perform the choruses, or the performance did not go on. It was then that Noverre hit upon the idea of hiding the singers behind the scenes and having the dancers execute the action in pantomime. The result was an overwhelming success, and Noverre not only satisfied the outstanding composer of Europe, but, and this was infinitely more important, he found himself.

In a letter to Voltaire written September 1, 1763, Noverre sums up what he accomplished for the dance.

I felt that it was possible to give the ballet a plot. I abandoned the symmetrical figure dances and associated to the mechanical motion of arms and legs a dramatic significance derived from the varied expressiveness of the physiognomy. I threw out the masks and substituted a more real and exact costume. I revived the art of pantomime, once so celebrated in the reign of Augustus. Nature, which I took to be my guide and model, afforded me the means of making the dance talk, paint all the passions, and take its place in the ranks of the imitative arts.[7]

This art, to which he was to devote his entire life, Noverre came to learn only through long conversations with the principal actors of his day—among whom was Garrick [8]—by observing dancing technique in the crudest as well as in the most accomplished performers, through arduous study of the dance in the ancient world, and finally by acquainting himself with the allied arts of music, painting, poetry, stage decoration, and the like. In short, Noverre was the model disciple of the *Encyclopedia,* not only as regards specific reference to the dance, but also for his entire cultural background; what the French call "la formation de son esprit." In his *Belton et Elisa,* there is an interesting

[7] Noverre, *Lettres sur les arts imitateurs*, I, 2.   [8] *Ibid.*, p. 124.

reference that reveals Noverre's indebtedness to the *Encyclopedia*. The opening scene is: "A group of natives, Quakers, and English officers is disposed upon the stage. Some are gambling, others are drinking and conversing together, and the negroes and negresses are working." Then in a note Noverre adds: "The ballet-master could give this scene a lively and realistic air by consulting the *Encyclopedia* on the manner in which negroes work on sugar plantations." [9] Certainly, the *Encyclopedia* could not have been put to more edifying use.

Noverre divides the dance into two categories: (1) *danse mécanique*, and (2) *danse pantomime*. The first appeals to us because of its symmetry and grace, the quick change of tempi, and the regularity of execution. Noverre calls this part of the dance, *matérielle*. The second is the soul of the first, in that it gives expression and life to the movements. Each movement or gesture reveals the artists' interpretation of a scene, or shred of scene, of dramatic import.[10] For the creation of the second type of ballet Noverre turned to history, mythology, and poetry for subjects.[11] Not more than four principal dancers were to take part in the action. Above all, there must be no episodes, and the action must be well unified. Even the *coryphées,* or dance choruses, must constantly further the action of the ballet by means of pantomime. The ballet master, the painter decorator, the costumer, and the musician must all work in close collaboration. Many rehearsals are necessary to achieve perfection.[12]

The ballet master who is acquainted with many arts will compose the best dances for the *ballet-en-action*. The *maître* must be a bit of a painter, decorator, mechanic, geometer, and musician.[13] He must have a tincture of geometry in order to plan the various figures. A knowledge of mechanics will teach him to have the separate parts of the ballet cling together and depend upon each other, like the movements of an intricate machine. He must know painting for the arrangement of

[9] *Ibid.*, II, 477.   [10] *Ibid.*, I, 135; see Cahusac, "Ballet."
[11] Noverre, *op. cit.*, I, 156; see Cahusac, "Merveilleux," "Ballet."
[12] Noverre, *op. cit.*, I, 158–166; see Grimm, "Poème lyrique."
[13] In the preface Noverre claims that he studied ". . . la peinture, l'architecture, la perspective, et l'optique." He tells us later (*op. cit.*, I, 126–128) that he studied osteology, I, 128, along with painting and music. The entire Lettre XIII is a disquisition on anatomy, (*ibid.*, I, 169–188; see I, 190–199, for the requirements of the successful creator of ballet). For Noverre's relations to music, consult Niedeken, *Noverre, sein Leben und seine Beziehungen zur Musik*.

groups according to color, design, and draping. And a knowledge of music will give him a sense of phrasing and rhythm.

The dancers in the ballet must be well drilled. The principal should not take up all the creator's attention, at the risk of neglecting the secondaries. The ballet must be divided into scenes and acts that have a beginning, a middle, and an end.[14] Noverre proscribes singing from the ballet, because it slows up and cools the action on the stage. Moreover, a good dancer who fully possesses the art of pantomime does not need the aid of words.[15]

In the opera Noverre wanted the ballet to carry on the dramatic action in the scenes of the entr'actes. The only possible dance in the opera was that which would be allied to the main spectacle. For this reason the same close collaboration between composer, painter, poet, ballet master, and mechanic that prevailed in the composition of ballets should obtain. Though Noverre conceived the opera as primarily a spectacle which appealed to the eye and the ear rather than to reason and emotions, he saw clearly that a ballet which served only as ornament would detract from the interest of the spectacle.[16] Thus, a good portion of Gluck's reform opera, that is, ballets that aided the development of the main dramatic action, was owing to Noverre. Insofar as the successful opera was the result of the close collaboration of many artists, Noverre gives us to believe that he was responsible for the particular type of ballet to be found in Gluck's works. Instead of setting the ballet to a given dance tune, Noverre reversed the procedure and had music written to suit his steps.

Instead of arranging dance steps to fit the music, in the manner of those poets who write couplets to fit known tunes, I composed, if I may so express myself, the dialogue of my ballet and then had music written to suit each phrase and each idea.

It was in that manner that I dictated to Gluck the characteristic air of the *Ballet des sauvages* in *Iphigénie en Tauride*. The dance steps, the gestures, the poses, the facial expressions of the various personages that I outlined for him gave that celebrated composer the idea of the composition of that excellent musical work.[17]

[14] Noverre, *Lettres sur les arts imitateurs*, I, 244–245; see Grimm, "Poème lyrique, De la danse."

[15] Noverre, *op. cit.*, I, 268; see Grimm, *loc. cit.*

[16] Noverre, *op. cit.*, I, 274, 276; see Grimm, *loc. cit.*

[17] Noverre, *op. cit.*, Preface, I, xiv–xv.

In this way the *ballet-pantomime* arose. The opera, as well as the ballet proper, was indebted to Noverre's revolution of the dancing art.

But if Noverre borrowed liberally from the *Encyclopedia,* he also knew how to acknowledge his debt. With the exception of a slight pique toward the editors of the *Encyclopedia* for their refusal to call in a dancing master for the professional aspects of the ballet, Noverre had only the highest praise for Cahusac's articles on the dance: "M. Cahusac reveals the beauties of our art, proposes necessary embellishments, and seeks to point out to the dancers the sure road to success in their art." [18] This is followed by praise of Cahusac's *Traité de la danse.*[19] Then Noverre paid tribute to Cahusac the aesthetician.

He treated only the principles of dancing, but he was able to seize the spirit and character in the art. They are unlucky who can neither appreciate nor understand him. The genre Cahusac proposes is difficult, indeed, but does that make it any the less beautiful? It is the only genre that the dance can implement successfully.[20]

And, indeed, it is as aesthetician and theoretician of the dance that Cahusac is to be most highly prized.

Of still more importance is Noverre's avowal that he took the first scene of his *ballet-pantomime, Le Jaloux sans rival,* from Diderot's *scène de tric-trac* in *Le Père de famille.* Thus, Noverre took his ideas of pantomime not only from Diderot's *Plans* and discussions of the dance, but also from the Encyclopedist's plays and dramatic criticism. Noverre praises Diderot's ideas in the following excerpt.

M. Diderot, that philosopher friend of nature, that is, of true and simple beauty, seeks likewise to enrich the French stage with a genre that he found not so much in his imagination as in the faces of men. He would like to substitute pantomime for mannerisms in the ballet . . .[21]

Nothing, however, better reveals Noverre's allegiance to the *Encyclopedia,* together with his unbounded faith in the powers of leadership and reform of that organ, than the following admission: "If the advice of Diderot and Cahusac is not taken, if the road they indicate is not followed, can I hope to succeed? No, and doubtless it would be foolhardy of me to think so." [22] Noverre's willingness to defer to the

[18] *Ibid.,* II, 45.   [19] *Ibid.,* p. 46.   [20] *Ibid.,* p. 48.
[21] *Ibid.,* pp. 45–46; see also p. 36n, and p. 42.   [22] *Ibid.,* II, 50.

Encyclopedia, his expression of gratitude to Cahusac and Diderot, demonstrate once again that in the dance, as well as in the opera, the Encyclopedists were able to command the respect and attention of the men who really mattered.

PART II

POLEMICS
AND REFORMS

CHAPTER VII

THE BOUFFONS' QUARREL

THE ARTICLES ON MUSIC in the Encyclopedia may be considered as the storehouse from which Encyclopedists drew the raw material for their arguments in the Bouffons' Quarrel, the Rameau controversy, and the reform of the opera in general. Having studied the wide ramifications of the Encyclopedists' musical thought at rest, as exposed in the articles of the *Encyclopedia,* we are now prepared to study these men in action, championing the Italians in the Bouffons' Quarrel, guiding Rameau in his theories, and preparing the stage for the Gluck reform opera. Upon this public activity, upon their polemics and reform campaign, must rest the Encyclopedists' claim to significance in the field of musical criticism.

The first official act of the *Encyclopedia* as an organ of musical criticism was to launch an attack against French music which was to culminate in the Bouffons' Quarrel. The Bouffons were a wandering troupe of Italian comic-opera singers who had journeyed to Paris with a slim repertory of buffa operas by Pergolesi, Scarlatti, Vinci, Leo, and others. Before the Bouffons arrived, in 1752, Grimm had written his "Lettre sur Omphale," in the *Mercure,* anent the revival of this opera by Destouches.[1] Grimm's article is in the main a violent attack on French music. He scores the manner of singing in France[2] and criticizes in Destouches the French composers' tendency to write music which has no connection with the verse of the text.[3] Grimm believes, with Lulli and Perrault, that true musical expression is to be derived from verse declamation.[4] In general, he prefers the Italian recitative to the French, and he cites Rousseau's article "Récitatif" to support his

---

[1] February 2, 1752. See Richebourg, *Contribution à l'histoire de la querelle des Bouffons,* p. 21.
[2] Grimm, ed., *Correspondance littéraire,* XVI, 289.   [3] *Ibid.,* p. 293.   [4] *Ibid.,* p. 298.

claim.[5] In a long note Grimm upholds Italian supremacy in verse and music. The Italians have many *grands tableaux* in which are to be found numberless examples of "the furors of passion, of sorrow and tenderness." Above all, the Italians excel in portraying simple sentiments, whereas the French have gotten too far from simplicity.[6] Grimm calls Italian music European and French music national.[7] This letter aroused the ire of some patriotic writer, who answered in defense of French music.[8] Rousseau came to Grimm's rescue with his *Lettre à M. Grimm au sujet des remarques ajoutées à sa lettre sur Omphale.*[9] Thus, the conflict over the respective excellence of Italian and French music, already in progress when the Bouffons arrived, was developed into a controversy fomented by the Encyclopedists.

The first performance of the *opera buffa* troupe set all musical Paris at loggerheads, the Encyclopedists defending the Italians, or the *Coin de la reine*. The French camp, or the *Coin du roi,* was headed by Fréron, Cazotte, Castel, Jourdan, and a host of lesser lights. In the pamphlet *Ce qu'on a dit, ce qu'on a voulu dire,* attributed by Barbier to F. L. C. Marin,[10] D'Holbach is given credit for firing the first shot. This would be D'Holbach's *Lettre à une dame d'un certain âge sur l'état présent de l'opéra en Arcadie; aux dépens de l'académie royale de musique.*[11] This letter is a satire on French music, scoring principally the incapacity of the orchestra and singers of the Opéra. This is the only work that was published between August and December, 1752, so that a résumé of the first year of the war would show that the Encyclopedists had everything their own way.

Within the first two weeks of 1753 Grimm renewed his attack on French music and musicians.[12] In a dream the little prophet of

---

[5] *Ibid.*, p. 291. Rousseau's articles on music were ready by the summer of 1749; he gave them to Diderot in 1750; see his *Rousseau juge de Jean Jacques,* in his *Œuvres,* Hachette edition, VI, 218n. The volume containing the article "Récitatif" was not published, however, until 1765.

[6] Grimm, *Corres. Litt.*, pp. 303–305.   [7] *Ibid.*, p. 288.

[8] *Remarques au sujet de la lettre de M. Grimm sur Omphale,* March 17, 1752, according to Richebourg, *Contribution à l'histoire de la querelle des Bouffons,* p. 23.

[9] April, 1752; Richebourg, *op. cit.,* p. 25. Rousseau, "Ecrits sur la musique," in his *Œuvres complètes.*

[10] This work cannot possibly have appeared in 1752 as Barbier has it, for in it are mentioned Diderot's *Lettre au petit prophète* and other works definitely dated 1753.

[11] November, 1752; Richebourg, *op. cit.,* p. 45.

[12] Grimm, *Le Petit Prophète de Boehmischbroda,* January, 1753.

Boehmischbroda has been transported to the Opéra, where, after the performance, a voice informs him that it has caused the arts to pass from Italy to France. The voice disavows Lulli and his followers and says that Rameau has been appointed to remedy all, with the help of Mlle Fel and Jélyotte,[13] but that even this has been unavailing. Next, Manelli was appointed to introduce Pergolesi to the French, that they might model their operas upon his works. If this lesson is ignored, the voice threatens to make a desert of the *Académie de Musique*. This lesson became the gospel of the Encyclopedists throughout the quarrel.[14] It was answered in the *Réponse du coin du roi au coin de la reine,* January 25, 1753.[15] In this eight-page rebuttal, the first published by the opposition since the arrival of the Bouffons, Pidansat claims that Italian music is too light and coquettish, being in the manner of a *hors d'œuvre*. Whereas French music is solid and "depicts passions." He concludes by saying that Rameau is the greatest composer of the century.

The task of repulsing this attack fell upon Diderot. In the *Arrêt rendu à l'amphithéâtre de l'Opéra* Diderot scores Pidansat for drawing a parallel between Rinaldo da Capua's *La Donna superba* and Lulli's *Armide,* since the first is comedy and the second tragedy.[16] He further enjoins Pidansat to respect the composer of the *Venite exultemus,* now unfortunately fallen upon evil days with the opera *Titon et l'Aurore,*[17] and to consult Rameau's operas if he really desires to learn how to "depict passions." But Pidansat had by no means abandoned the field.

---

[13] Celebrated soprano and tenor of the Opéra. Cahusac had earlier appreciated the importance of their fine voices in the evolution of Rameau's operas. *Vide supra,* Chapter II, note 10.

[14] Scherer interprets the *Petit Prophète* in the following manner: a little Bohemian boy is sent to the Paris Opéra to see the state of decadence in which the French musical stage has fallen. He is told that the French used to be the chosen people musically, but have now fallen upon evil ways. The voice goes on to relate that a Messiah (Pergolesi) was sent to redeem them; however, if they did not repent, the opera house would be razed. Scherer, "Melchior Grimm." Cast in the form of the scriptures, Grimm's prophecy easily lent itself to such an interpretation.

[15] Barbier, Fétis, Chouquet, and Jansen attribute this work to the Abbé Voisenon, but the copy at the Bibliothèque Nationale, is signed Mérobert, whose full name was Mathieu François Mairobert de Pidansat, *Recueil de mémoires,* Vol. CCCXXXIV, No. 23.

[16] Rinaldo da Capua, active as composer of operas from 1737–1771, had two of his works presented by the Bouffons in Paris: *La Donna superba* and *La Zingara.*

[17] This opera by Mondonville, book by the Abbé de la Marre, was given its première January 9, 1753, to combat the Bouffons.

After the *Déclaration du public au sujet des contestations qui se sont élevées sur la musique,* and Jourdan's *Le Correcteur des Bouffons à l'écolier de Prague,*[18] Pidansat brought out his *Les Prophéties du grand prophète Monet,* a witty parody of Grimm's *Petit Prophète.*

Cazotte now made his appearance on the side of the French with *La Guerre de l'Opéra, lettre écrite à une dame de province par quelqu'un qui n'est ni d'un coin ni de l'autre.* This is a brief, dispassionate account of the quarrel, which contains some interesting criticism of *Titon et l'Aurore* from the point of view of music. Among other things, Cazotte points out that the music and text of the French opera are inseparable and that French music expresses well the typical *galanterie* of the text. However, Cazotte failed to see that it was exactly this *style galant* that defeated Rameau and the French serious opera. The young Suard closed the January onslaught upon the Encyclopedists with his *Lettre écrite de l'autre monde par l'abbé D. F. [Des Fontaines] à M. F. . . . [Fréron].*

In February, 1753, the Bouffons' Quarrel reached its peak. The most telling blows of the war were delivered by each side in the course of this month. Caux de Cappeval loosed four poems in succession against the Queen's Corner: "L'Anti-scurra; ou, Préservatif contre les Bouffons italiens," February 6; "La Réforme de l'Opéra," February 9; "Epître aux Bouffonistes," February 12; and "Réflexions lyriques," February 16. In the "Epître" he asks:

> Are these savants fit arbiters of artistic pleasure,
> And must we defer to them concerning artistic tastes? [19]

He goes on to say that the entire responsibility for the Quarrel is to be laid at the door of the Encyclopedists.

> The Bouffons' reign was heralded by the *Philosophes;*
> They prepared the throne for such conquerors as these.
> Your influence, O wise men, guaranteed their success.[20]

This charge has become the classic reproof of Encyclopedist activity. For two centuries critics of eighteenth-century music in France have cast it into the teeth of the *philosophes.*

---

[18] January 9; Richebourg, *Contribution à l'histoire de la querelle des Bouffons,* p. 51.

[19] Unless otherwise stated all references are to the *Recueil de mémoires,* Bibliothèque Nationale Vol. CCCXXXIV, which contains twenty-six pamphlets relating to the Bouffons' Quarrel, paginated 1–602. P. 484.

[20] *Ibid.,* p. 487.

Diderot entered the lists again on February 21 with his pamphlet *Au petit prophète de Boehmischbroda et au grand prophète Monet.* This work represents the high point in musical criticism for either camp. Let us put joking aside, says Diderot, and examine without prejudice the two schools of music in order to ascertain the merits and demerits of each.[21] Since comparison is the order of the day, Diderot continues, let us compare similar scenes musically. Take, for instance, the last three scenes of Act II of *Armide,* Lulli's masterpiece, beginning with the famous air "Plus j'observe ces lieux et plus je les admire" and concluding with the monologue "Enfin il est en ma puissance." Compare these scenes to Terradellas' opera *Nitocris,*[22] wherein the same number of scenes is employed to represent a highly similar dramatic situation. Both operas are tragic, and in each case the heroine is on the brink of destroying her enemy when an internal conflict forces her to drop the weapon. It is evident that the composers will be responsible for the differences in these two operas. The question is, how aptly does the music in either case interpret the dramatic situation?

Don't tell me that the music of *Armide* is the best that can be composed to a French text. Instead of defending our melody by such a reservation, you are belittling our language. Let us consider here nothing but the music. It is not a question of comparing Quinault to Metastasio. . . . We must compare the music of Lulli to that of Terradellas; the music of Lulli, the great Lulli, and this an excerpt that even his great rival, the jealous Rameau, found sublime.[23]

Diderot was the only critic who saw that both camps were fumbling in the dark. In these paragraphs he offers the only basis for comparison from which profitable conclusions may be drawn. He says, in effect, that as long as the Quarrel concerns musical superiority, it is time to cease the flow of insult and vilification in favor of a serious, fruitful, musical controversy. One week later, the author of *L'Apologie du sublime bon mot* greeted Diderot's plea for saner criticism by saying that nothing is ever settled by reason, so let us continue the battle of mutual abuse.

At least one member of the opposition, however, turned out an attack

[21] Diderot, *Œuvres,* XII, 153.

[22] Domenico Terradellas, or Terradeglias, 1711–1751, opera-composer of the Neopolitan school.

[23] Diderot, XII, 153–155.

against the Encyclopedists which bears quoting. This was Claude de Ruhlière's *Jugment de l'orchestre de l'Opéra*. He condemns the experimental spirit in music, the desire to express everything, and the tendency toward realism in artistic imitation. The trouble with these geometers, he says, in reference to the Encyclopedists, is that just because they have experimented with theories of sound, they think themselves capable of criticizing music. "They are as close to music as the person who knows that green is composed of blue and yellow is to the art of painting." [24] They teach that music must express everything; for this reason no doubt they approve of the trivial and low scenes of the Italian *opera buffa*.[25]

These *philosophes* who have studied the nature of sounds are not content with setting forth the scientific aspects of tonal production, but would like to introduce scientific systems into the art of composition itself. According to them, "a composer who sets himself the task of interpreting everything musically will on many occasions offer compositions whose significance will escape the vulgar ear. All that we can conclude from this fact, however, is that after having established an art of learning music we should discover a method of listening to it. (Note: *Discours préliminaire de l'Encyclopédie*.)" One can easily see that they have examined music quite apart from the genius required to compose it and without any regard for the pleasure the art affords. The error they have fallen into proves once again that you cannot consider an art purely from the theoretical point of view. Music has a mechanical aspect which makes it possible for us to learn the art. If one who has studied music obtains more enjoyment from listening to a composition than one who has not, it is merely due to the fact that through the aid of the mechanical apparatus of music he can appreciate the beauties of the art and can enter into the composer's spirit more effectively. That is the proper way to listen to music.[26]

This pamphlet, quoting chapter and verse, must have thrown some confusion into the Encyclopedist camp. However, as we shall soon see, the Encyclopedists in no way deserved this indictment. As a matter of fact, one of the prime achievements of the *Encyclopedia* was to sever once and for all science and music.

On March 1 Rousseau entered the field as a composer with the opera *Le Devin du village*. In this work he conceived the idea of presenting the French with an Italian-type *opera buffa*. We have seen that the only

[24] *Recueil*, p. 349.   [25] *Ibid.*, p. 353.   [26] *Ibid.*, pp. 354–355.

attempt to engage the Bouffons on musical grounds in the preceding months of the Quarrel was the production of Mondonville's *Titon et l'Aurore*. The *Coin du Roi* seized upon this performance to confound the opposition, because it was taken to represent French musical tradition. Rousseau's "opera" was meant as an object lesson, as if to say that this was the sort of opera that could be produced in France if Italian precepts were followed. But Rousseau, who wrote pamphlets and letters in defense of the Italians, composed opera like a Frenchman. French recitative, French songs, the important Lullian traditions are all represented in this little opera. *Le Devin* was a real success; it was the only opera composed by a Frenchman that stood the test of comparison with the works in the Bouffons' repertory. Diderot was quick to grasp the import of Rousseau's opera. In *Les Trois chapitres,* written soon after the première of *Le Devin,*[27] Diderot points out to Grimm that Rousseau has answered his *Petit Prophète.*[28]

After the February flurry interest in the Quarrel died down considerably. Throughout the spring and summer the only pamphlet of interest was Jourdan's *Seconde Lettre du correcteur des Bouffons,*[29] in which he renews the indictment against the Encyclopedists as geometers.

The first sortie of the Quarrel had been led by Grimm, ably supported by Diderot. In the fall of 1753 the war entered on a new phase. In the middle of November Rousseau brought out his epoch-making *Lettre sur la musique française,* which, he tells us, prevented a political revolution in France.[30] This attack upon French music called forth no less than twenty-five works by way of reprisal. But it is significant that no other Encyclopedist came to Rousseau's rescue, nor did he deem it necessary to write again in defense of his position. This devastating letter won the war for the Encyclopedists.

Rousseau starts his *Lettre* by saying that he did not publish it earlier in the Quarrel because everyone was so heated and unreasonable. Now that the animosity has cooled somewhat, the point to decide is, "Do we French have music?"[31] It is evident that the author did not believe

[27] March 6; Richebourg, *Contribution à l'histoire de la querelle des Bouffons,* p. 61.
[28] Diderot, XII, 157–170.   [29] May 4; Richebourg, *op. cit.,* p. 62.
[30] Rousseau, *Confessions,* Livre VIII, 1753; *Œuvres,* V, 586.
[31] Rousseau, *Œuvres,* IV, 411.

in the existence of French music. Vocal music is impossible because the French language does not lend itself to musical adaptation.[32] The lack of open vowel sounds forces the composer to give music the upper hand, and since the language is dull, the music will appear bombastic.[33] The high frequency of consonants excludes the use of many words from the opera poem. This lack of variety in diction gives rise to a similar lack in the music, which is thereby rendered monotonous. The slow movement of the music is also due to the language; should the composer attempt rapidity, his music would resemble the motion of a hard angular object bumping along the pavement.[34] Because the language is so uninteresting musically, French composers naturally turned to harmony and created "une musique savante" to cover the defects of melody. This inordinate insistence on harmony overwhelms the verse, so that musicians and singers at the Opéra are constantly getting in each other's way.[35] The French are incapable of having instrumental music as a result of their deficient vocal music; the latter has always preceded the former in the order of creation and consequently instrumental music took its character, measure, and form, from the vocal.[36] For Rousseau melody is the mainstay of music, and in this department the French are signally poor.[37] Finally, French recitative is not properly based on declamation.[38] Conclusion: the French do not and can not have music.

I think I have shown that French music has neither measure nor melody because the language is not susceptible to musical adaptation. I have shown that French song is nothing more than a continual howling unbearable to the unprejudiced ear. Our harmony is crude, lacking in expression, and smacks of the conservatory. French airs are not airs at all, and our recitative is not recitative. From which I conclude that the French do not and cannot have music, and that if they ever do have music, it will be a pity.[39]

This paragraph was obviously not intended to please the supporters of the *Coin du Roi*. Rousseau seems to have waited for heads to cool merely to precipitate a bomb that was destined to raise the heat of strife to a feverish pitch.

---

[32] *Ibid.*, p. 410.
[33] *Ibid.*, p. 413. We recall again the theory that good music was to be derived from verse declamation.
[34] *Ibid.*   [35] *Ibid.*, p. 414.   [36] *Ibid.*
[37] *Ibid.*, p. 432.   [38] *Ibid.*, p. 433.   [39] *Ibid.*, p. 440.

Of the letters that immediately followed in response to Rousseau's attack, that is, those written by Fréron, Cazotte, and Yzo, by far the most important was Cazotte's *Observations sur la lettre de J. J. Rousseau au sujet de la musique française.* Why should there be any question of a comparison between French and Italian music at all? asks Cazotte. Although French opera, like the Italian, may be said to have originated from the Greek tragedy, it has a particular appeal for the French in that the recitative is drawn from the declamation of classical French tragedy. For this reason the opera poet may be credited with most of the beauties of the local opera. The Italians have their form of opera, we have ours.[40] This attitude of "let us be satisfied with what we have and never mind the Italians" was carried on by Morand in his *Justification de la musique française contre la querelle qui lui a été faite par un allemand et un allobroge, . . .* (1754). Morand has French music say that the beauty of the local opera results from the perfect union of words and music. Properly rendered by French artists, it can be adequately appreciated only by French audiences.[41] This, of course, was the "reservation" that Diderot alluded to in his *Au petit prophète,* whereby French music appears magnificent when looked at in this provincial manner. It is noteworthy that the main objection to Rousseau's *Lettre,* and almost all of his critics made this point, is that just because Italian music is better does not mean that French music does not exist. Bâton even goes so far as to agree with Rousseau, and then exposes "a plan for a type of music proper to our language."[42]

But Rousseau left himself open to another charge. The *philosophe* signified his willingness to agree with French operatic traditions when he asserted that good music was to be derived from verse declamation. Accordingly, the partisans of French opera rediscovered the reasons for Lulli's excellence, that is, recitative based on classical declamation, and threw this at Rousseau in a vain last attempt to narrow the field of combat to local and patriotic grounds. In so doing, however, they abandoned a campaign for newer and better operas to satisfy newer and better minds. The Bouffons' Quarrel was over, and Rousseau felt that he had had the last word: "The King's Corner wanted to joke,

---

[40] Cazotte, *La Guerre de l'opéra,* in *Recueil,* pp. 102–104.
[41] *Recueil,* p. 168.
[42] Bâton, *Examen de la lettre de M. Rousseau sur la musique française.*

and was laughed at by *Le Petit Prophète;* when later it tried to reason, it was overpowered by the *Lettre sur la musique française.*" [43]

As a postlude to the Bouffons' Quarrel there appeared in Switzerland two books that were more comprehensive than the pamphlets and the letters of Paris. Although both works are dated 1754, their great remove from the center of struggle is evident in their cool analyses and deliberate reasoning. They are C. H. Blainville's *L'Esprit de l'art musical,* Geneva, and Rochemont's *Réflexions d'un patriote sur l'opéra français et sur l'opéra italien,* Lausanne. The first of these was written by a professional musician, theoretician, and composer, who says in answer to Rousseau that a nation whose legitimate theater is known the world over as the school of beautiful declamation cannot fail to possess a language fit for 'musical adaptation.[44] He admits that the Italian opera contains nuances and pleasing dexterities which the French at present lack, but can certainly acquire.[45] He gives the palm to the Italian orchestral accompaniment in the opera as being more pantomimic,[46] whereas the French lacked brilliance and vigor.[47] In a word, the Italian composers were masters of expression in music. Lulli was such an outstanding exception to the ordinary run of French composers because he knew how to express musically various passions, such as rage, despair, and love, and mythological characters, such as furies, heroes, and divinities.[48] Lulli sought to make his protagonists speak rather than sing, thus showing that the genius of French music resided in theatrical declamation.[49] And the secret of musical expression in the French opera, adds Blainville, is still to be found at the *Comédie Française.*[50] The upshot of this comparison between French and Italian music is that each nation has an operatic rhetoric largely determined by language.[51] Blainville ascribes the lack of variety in French music to a similar lack in the language.[52] He realizes, however, that the great disadvantage of the French is that they are too much inclined to follow rules and to argue and rationalize about music, whereas the Italians just compose. This remarkable diagnosis was valid throughout the history of opera.

Rochemont is much more severe toward the Italians. Granted the

[43] Rousseau, *Œuvres,* V, 585.   [44] Blainville, *L'Esprit de l'art musical,* p. 2.
[45] *Ibid.,* p. 19.   [46] *Ibid.,* p. 24.   [47] *Ibid.,* pp. 30–31.   [48] *Ibid.,* p. 33.
[49] *Ibid.,* p. 34.   [50] *Ibid.,* p. 53.   [51] *Ibid.,* pp. 43–44.   [52] *Ibid.,* pp. 38–39.

excellence of Italian music, Rochemont points out that one must not
be blind to the dramatic imperfections of the Italian opera. If their
music is sublime, their recitative, which contains most of the drama,
is usually given very little attention, and the dramatically insignificant
ariette is repeated.[53] He scores the Italian opera as containing two
glaring defects: overemphasis and digression. Italian composers are
guilty of the first when they tend to overdo the expression of an emotion, and of the second when they permit themselves to be side-tracked
by a charming dissonance or a happy modulation. The *da capo* aria is
in itself a digression from the dramatic action.[54] The important element in the Italian opera is patently the music; proof, everyone agrees
that Vinci's opera *Arteserse,* based on Metastasio's play, is a masterpiece, yet the capricious Italian audience, avidly seeking varieties of
musical expression, would prefer to hear Metastasio's text set to music
by a mediocre composer rather than hear Vinci's masterpiece twice.[55]
The French, on the other hand, have preferred to emphasize the dramatic aspects of opera; music is ushered in merely to give greater relevancy to the *poème*.[56] Rochemont concludes that Italian opera is "a
poor spectacle, often accompanied by very beautiful music; while
French opera is a magnificent spectacle, whose music seems mediocre,
but really is not." [57] This dictum, as fair an appraisal as was given
by either side during the course of the Quarrel, still loses sight of
the fact that the chief element in the opera must be music and that
consequently the Italians were on the right track.

In summing up the points at issue in the Bouffons' Quarrel it may
be said that the supporters of the local opera were purely on the de-
fensive, while the Encyclopedists were primarily interested in the advancement of French opera. It is evident that all the important features of French operatic traditions were subscribed to by the Encyclopedists: Grimm, Diderot, and Rousseau, in turn, stated that song
and recitative were to be based on verse declamation and that music was
to imitate nature and be a painter of sentiments. Moreover, Rousseau
composed a French "opera" that remained faithful to local traditions
of declamation. The *Devin du village* is a play with incidental music
exactly corresponding to St. Evremond's desires for the French musical

[53] Rochemont, *Réflexions d'un patriote sur l'opéra français* . . . , p. 14.
[54] *Ibid.,* pp. 16–17. [55] *Ibid.,* pp. 21–22. [56] *Ibid.,* pp. 24–25. [57] *Ibid.,* p. 42.

stage. Where the *Coin du Roi* went astray was in the insistence on the *status quo* of French opera, as if to say that opera in France was fatally what it was, and therefore as good as it could be.

Many years after the war was over the final decision on the Quarrel was given by D'Alembert, one of the coolest heads of the eighteenth century. In his essay *De la liberté de la musique,* which appeared for the first time in the 1759 edition of his works, he says of Rousseau's *Lettre* that it was "much attacked but little refuted." [58] As for the *Coin du Roi,* some of its partisans tried to defend French music by reason, but the great majority resorted to insult and vituperation.[59] All this Quarrel was useless, says D'Alembert, since the Bouffons did not create a revolution in French opera.[60] The French continued to prefer the local productions when the remaining European nations had overwhelmingly decided in favor of the Italians.[61] Thus the Quarrel went for nought, and the *Encyclopedia,* by espousing the cause of the Italians, lost considerable popularity in France.

The *Encyclopedia,* whose authors had the misfortune to agree with Rousseau and the boldness to say so, was not spared in these circumstances. The musical war was the first spark in a great blaze which has since succeeded in warming a great many enemies of that work. The contributors to the *Encyclopedia* are regarded in France as a society formed for the purpose of destroying at one blow religion, authority, morals, and music.[62]

But the hard and simple fact remains, says D'Alembert, that of the flock of pamphlets that appeared anent the Bouffons' quarrel only two are still remembered: Grimm's *Petit Prophète* and Rousseau's *Lettre sur la musique;* "we have even forgotten the titles of the other works." [63]

---

[58] Alembert, *Œuvres,* III, 515.   [59] *Ibid.,* p. 518.   [60] *Ibid.,* p. 521.
[61] *Ibid.,* p. 522.   [62] *Ibid.,* pp. 517–518.   [63] *Ibid.,* p. 518.

CHAPTER VIII

THE RAMEAU CONTROVERSY

WE HAVE ALREADY SEEN that toward the middle of the eighteenth century Rameau was the outstanding composer in France. Before turning his hand to operatic composition, Rameau had written several works on harmony that were to revolutionize musical theory. When he had been established in Paris for only five years, he had already built up an enviable reputation as a theorist.[1] By 1740 he had become more widely known through his operas. At first stubbornly opposed by the followers of Lulli, he finally came to be recognized as the rightful heir to Lulli's by now long-vacant throne. Thus, by the time he met the Encyclopedists, Rameau's work as a theorist and composer was finished; he was an old man who was jealously guarding a reasonably safe reputation.

In 1748 Diderot speaks at some length of Rameau's *Génération harmonique,* which he calls "un système admirable." [2] In 1752 D'Alembert brought out a practical edition of Rameau's theory entitled, *Eléments de musique théorique et pratique suivant les principes de M. Rameau.* Rameau was delighted to have these very capable men popularize his works, for besides being friendly with them, he had the highest confidence in the powers of understanding and exposition of both Diderot and D'Alembert.

[1] The following extract from the *Journal de Trévoux* attests this: "Il est peu d'ouvrages dont le mérite soit aussi décidé d'avance que le sont désormais tous ceux de M. Rameau." An 1728, p. 472.

[2] Diderot, *Mémoires sur différents sujets de mathématiques, Œuvres,* IX, 115. In reviewing this work of Diderot's for the *Correspondance Littéraire,* the Abbé Raynal says: "Il [Diderot] vient de publier quelques mémoires sur cela [les mathématiques] dont quelques' uns roulent sur la musique et sont extrêmement curieux. Cet écrivain puise en bonne source: il est intime ami avec M. Rameau, dont il doit dans peu de temps publier les découvertes. Ce sublime et profond musicien a donné autrefois quelques ouvrages où il n'a pas jeté assez de clarté et d'élégance. M. Diderot remaniera ses idées, et il est très capable de les mettre dans un beau jour." *Correspondance Littéraire,* I, 202.

Then came the *Encyclopedia,* and the trouble started. Rameau was asked by his friends to do the articles on music. The composer refused. It was all very well for Diderot and D'Alembert to popularize his works in monographs, but when it came to being a mere collaborator, Rameau hedged. Diderot, at least, was aware of the composer's crotchet. In the *Mémoires,* just cited, Diderot suggests that someone draw out Rameau's theory to make it more accessible: "not so much for the greater glory of its inventor, as for the advancement of the science of sounds." [3] Not thinking less highly of Rameau's achievements because of his refusal to join the *Encyclopedia,* Diderot appointed Rousseau to do the articles on music and, of course, to set forth Rameau's discoveries. Rousseau set to work with a will, and on the whole acquitted himself rather creditably. Taken altogether Rousseau's articles are a tribute to Rameau, as are, indeed, those written by D'Alembert. Yet the composer brought out his *Erreurs sur la musique dans l'Encyclopédie* (1755), in which he does nothing but sulk at the mistreatment he felt he had received at the hands of the Encyclopedists and is almost sorry that they made so few mistakes.

Another reason for Rameau's animosity to the Encyclopedists grew out of the Bouffons' Quarrel. Rousseau's and Diderot's attacks upon French music were taken by Rameau as a personal insult. He did not notice that Diderot, in the *Arrêt rendu* etc., praises his music repeatedly, that Grimm lauds his operas throughout the *Lettre sur Omphale,* and that D'Alembert speaks of Rameau's operatic revolution in the highest terms in *La Liberté de la musique.*

There is no occasion to belittle Rameau's magnificent theory. His discovery of chordal relations, their progressions and inversions, forms the basis of our theory of harmony. A disciple of Descartes, Rameau thought it necessary to couch his ideas in the typical pseudo-scientific language of the day and to give a geometrical justification for his musically sound acoustical theories. The Encyclopedists were quick to perceive this mistake and tried to keep Rameau from going astray. Diderot and D'Alembert, both good geometers, sought to retrieve Rameau's theories from a meaningless synthesis created *in abstracto,* wherein music was the all-in-all, the universal principle of all things.

In his theoretical works Rameau insisted that his discovery or princi-

[3] Diderot, IX, 115.

ple was the first principle that philosophers had been seeking for generations. According to his theory, the ear was to be the only perceptor of reality, and all other arts and sciences were to benefit by his discovery.

When one considers the infinite relationships the fine arts have to one another . . . is it not logical to guess that they are governed by one and the same principle? And is it not demonstrable that this principle is to be found in Harmony, which itself derives from it? [4]

It is to music that nature seems to have assigned the physical principle of those purely mathematical principles about which all the sciences revolve. I mean the harmonic, arithmetic, and geometrical proportions from which related proportions derive and which manifest themselves the moment a resounding body is made to vibrate.[5]

Music is a science which must have certain rules, these rules must derive from an evident principle, and this principle cannot be known to us without the aid of mathematics.[6]

In music is to be found most clearly perceptible the underlying principle of the fine arts.[7]

It was this principle that should have been the main preoccupation of the Encyclopedists, not the analyses of his harmonic theory.[8] When the Encyclopedists wisely refused to be impressed, Rameau lashed out at them in his controversial writings.[9]

In the article "Fondamentale" D'Alembert set out to criticize Rameau's theory. After stating succinctly the facts anent the *basse fondamentale,* D'Alembert suggests that the word "scientific" be thrown out of these considerations altogether, especially since Rameau himself in his compositions was never limited by scientific preoccupations. The geometer has the amusing task of pointing out to the composer that the ear is the final judge of music, not geometry. D'Alembert ridicules the idea that good melody grows out of good harmony. Indeed, harmony may enhance melody, but "it does not follow that all the beauty of this melody exists in the harmony." Moreover, Rameau himself has listed twenty different fundamental tones for *do-sol.* How can melody be said to be suggested by its fundamental tone, asks D'Alembert, if a melodic line may have several basses equally good?

---

[4] Rameau, *Nouvelles Réflexions sur le principe sonore,* p. 63.
[5] Rameau, *Démonstration du principe de l'harmonie,* Preface, pp. vi–vii.
[6] Rameau, *Traité de l'harmonie,* Preface, p. iii. [7] Rameau, *Nouvelles Réflexions,* p. 50.
[8] Rameau, *Erreurs sur la musique dans l'Encyclopédie,* p. 12. [9] *Ibid.,* pp. 113–114

Nothing is as useless to the theory of music as geometrical considerations, says D'Alembert. The geometer showed in his *Eléments* that a good theory of harmony could be deduced from Rameau's principles without having recourse in any way to geometry. Rousseau has shown in the article "Consonance," continues D'Alembert, that the study of the geometrical relations and proportions of sound in no way defines the pleasure we derive from music. Thus, the scientific aspects of music are so slight as to be quite negligible: "The exposition of facts and not verbiage is the great rule of physics as well as of history. I think that in my capacity as a geometer I will be pardoned if I protest against this ridiculous abuse of geometry in music." (D'Alembert: "Fondamentale.")

In the article "Gamme" D'Alembert states that, after all, Rameau's theory must remain arbitrary and that it can never be scientifically demonstrable. The *Académie des Sciences* had approved of Rameau's thesis as a working theory of harmony and not at all as a scientific demonstration.[10] Rameau's book did not carry the title *Démonstration du principe* when it was first presented to the Academy; consequently, this body had no inkling of Rameau's scientific pretensions. D'Alembert tells us that his own *Eléments* were intended as a tribute to Rameau for having developed the best theory of harmony to date. The geometer approved of it as musical theory, not as scientific experimentation: "Moreover, we reserve the right to examine and adopt any good ideas that may come from other sources." Which would seem to indicate that D'Alembert was not altogether oblivious to Rameau's difficult nature.

Rameau answered these attacks in *Lettre à M. D'Alembert sur ses opinions en musique insérées dans les articles Fondamentale et Gamme de l'Encyclopédie.*[11] Rameau accused D'Alembert of turning traitor to himself and to the Academy in these *Encyclopedia* articles, but added nothing in support of his scientific claims for music. The composer next tried to engage D'Alembert on geometric grounds, although he had admitted in the *Erreurs:* "I have learned whatever geometry I know from music." [12] This new effort at vindication was a *Controverse* on the origins of the sciences (1760). In his *Lettre à M. Rameau,* pub-

---

[10] D'Alembert, Mairan, and Nicole were chosen by the *Académie des Sciences* to report on Rameau's theory.

[11] Published in his *Code de musique pratique.*   [12] Rameau, *op. cit.,* p. 235.

lished in the *Mercure,* March, 1762, D'Alembert reiterated that neither he nor the Academy had subscribed *in toto* to the composer's theory, nor were they prepared to adopt the singular opinion of music as science. Indeed, how could D'Alembert, a geometer, seriously countenance such statements as: "I have discovered the true principles of geometry by studying music"? [13]

Thus, Rameau's warm friendship for D'Alembert the *philosophe* turned into an undying hatred of D'Alembert the Encyclopedist. On the publication of D'Alembert's first edition of the *Eléments de musique suivant les principes de M. Rameau* (1752), the composer made a public avowal of his indebtedness to the *philosophes* in general, and in particular to D'Alembert.

Among those savants, whom I am proud to call my judges and my masters, there is one who is particularly outstanding thanks to the simplicity of his life, his high-minded principles, and the extent of his learning. It is from him, sir, that I receive the most glorious acknowledgment to which an author can aspire . . .[14]

Rameau goes on to say that D'Alembert did not look for faults in his theory of harmony, but concentrated his efforts upon an analysis and an exposition of the salient features, the whole set forth in the inimitably clear and concise manner of the geometer, giving an essentially complicated theory a simplicity which the author had guessed, but could never express. Ten years later this glowing eulogy is exactly contradicted in the *Lettre à M. d'Alembert* (1762), in which the author of the *Encyclopedia* articles is accused of treachery and of having sapped the very foundations of Rameau's harmonic theory. But D'Alembert tells us that he has had enough of this fruitless controversy. The articles in the *Encyclopedia* express his views sufficiently: "I think that therein I have acquired the right to keep silent for the future." [15]

While Rameau was obstinately and bitterly chastising the Encyclopedist for his alleged treachery, D'Alembert continued to point out Rameau's achievements. In sketching the history of French music, D'Alembert states that Rameau's operatic revolution was tremendous. The composer was all the more deserving of credit in that he showed no inclination to outstrip his audience, although it was patent that he

[13] Rameau, *Réponse à la lettre de M. d'Alembert.*
[14] Rameau, *Lettre à l'auteur du Mercure,* mai, 1752.
[15] Alembert, *Eléments de musique,* 1762 edition, p. 231.

could have done so. Rameau brought the French opera a considerable distance forward, but he gave the French not the best music he could have written, but the best they were capable of attending to.[16] And let us remember that this essay of D'Alembert's is in general an attack on French music.

Still another reason for the rift between Rameau and D'Alembert grew out of the composer's animosity to Rousseau. Rameau interpreted D'Alembert's "treachery" as a generous desire to shield Rousseau.[17] In any case, the *Erreurs* were meant chiefly as an attack on Rousseau. Rameau cites here the episode of the ballet Rousseau asked him to judge. This was the first performance of *Les Muses galantes* at La Popelinière's in 1745. The composer tells us he was impressed by the mixture of good and bad in this little work, but soon concluded that Rousseau had written the French sections of the music, which were very bad, and that he must have been aided by a professional musician in selecting the Italian airs.[18] These observations gave rise to the lifelong enmity between these two men.[19] Rousseau never forgot Rameau's harsh judgment of his music, nevertheless, when he came to write the articles on music for the *Encyclopedia*, he followed Rameau's lead throughout. Indeed, Rousseau's antagonism coincided precisely with D'Alembert's objections to Rameau's theory that melody is to be derived from harmony, and that music is a science. (Rousseau: "Harmonie.") Rameau's theory is faithfully rendered throughout the Supplement to the *Encyclopedia*, which contains articles taken from Rousseau's *Dictionnaire de musique*. Tiersot tells us that in Rousseau's *Leçons de musique*, which are to be found in manuscript among the *philosophe's* papers at the *Bibliothèque de Neuchâtel*, Rousseau shows the same blind respect for Rameau's authority. Out of the apparent confusion of these papers, Tiersot carried away the conviction that Rousseau waged a lifelong struggle to master every ramification of Rameau's theory.

If, on occasion, the ideas jotted down at random in the *Leçons* seem to us somewhat confused, we gradually learn that these ideas emerge more clearly, are amalgamated and classified in a very logical manner, and the great discoveries of the author of the *Traité de l'harmonie* are ultimately

---

[16] Alembert, *La Liberté de la musique*, in his *Œuvres*, III, 517.
[17] Rameau, *Réponse à la lettre de M. d'Alembert*.
[18] Rameau, *Erreurs*, pp. 42 and 44.   [19] Rousseau, *Muses galantes; Avertissement*.

exposed with much more lucidity than the original author possessed. Rousseau may have been Rameau's enemy, but his intervention in the latter's field was no small factor in explaining and propagating Rameau's works.[20]

Rousseau thus ranks with D'Alembert as a popularizer of Rameau's theories, and Rousseau's studies, as explained by Tiersot, indicate the high esteem in which the Encyclopedist held Rameau's accomplishments in the field of musical theory.

However, as might be expected, Rousseau answered Rameau's attack at great length. In his *Examen de deux principes avancés par M. Rameau dans sa brochure intitulée Erreurs sur la musique dans l'Encyclopédie,* written in 1755 and not published until after Rameau's death in 1764, Rousseau states that no one is more dissatisfied with the articles on music in the *Encyclopedia* than himself, but that Rameau, who attacks them, has little reason to complain, since his theory is to be found extolled at every turn. Rousseau explains that he really had very little time in which to do these articles; [21] nevertheless, in all fairness to himself as well as to Rameau, he had sincerely done his best to do justice to the composer's ideas.[22] But Rameau published the *Erreurs* out of spite. When passion no longer blinds him, Rousseau adds, the composer will judge better than anyone else the usefulness of the *Encyclopedia* articles.[23] Getting away from personalities, Rousseau reminds Rameau that melody is not drawn from harmony, but is only enhanced by it.[24] As for the assertion that in music is to be found the universal principle of all arts and sciences, Rousseau admits that he can find no answer to this "marvelous conclusion." [25]

In his *Lettre à M. Grimm,* written just before the arrival of the Bouffons in 1752, Rousseau extols the discovery of the *basse fondamentale* as epoch-making in the history of musical theory.[26] As com-

[20] Tiersot, "Les Leçons de musique de J. J. Rousseau."

[21] Rousseau, *Examen de deux principes,* IV, 446. See also the preface to his *Dictionnaire de musique,* in which Rousseau explains that he was given a task to do in three months that would normally have taken three years to achieve. *Œuvres,* IV, 565.

[22] Rousseau, *Examen de deux principes,* IV, 446. Even the *Journal de Trévoux,* a distinctly anti-Encyclopedist publication, recognized the value of Rousseau's music articles: "L'auteur de ce bon article ["Accompagnement"] et de plusieurs autres tels que "Accord," "Accorder," "Air," etc., est M. Rousseau de Genève, déjà si connu par les ouvrages éloquents qu'il a publié contre les sciences et les arts. Il est honorable à l'*Encyclopédie* d'avoir sçu s'attacher cet homme de lettres et ce bon écrivain." Janvier, 1752, p. 160. The editors go on to show how well Rousseau served Rameau.

[23] Rousseau, *Examen de deux principes,* IV, 446.   [24] *Ibid.,* IV, 447.

[25] *Ibid.,* IV, 453.   [26] *Ibid.,* IV, 487.

poser, Rameau rejuvenated the opera which had fallen into insignificance and staleness with the successors of Lulli, and opened up new vistas of composition. Rameau was a master of harmony and melody. In comparing him with Lulli, Rousseau tends to give the palm to Rameau "from the point of view of expression," though Lulli was the more sensitive artist. Lulli's recitative is more natural, but Rameau's more varied.[27]

The official judgment of Rameau insofar as the *Encyclopedia* was concerned appeared in D'Alembert's *Discours préliminaire*. In summing up briefly the history of art, D'Alembert asserted that in France, perhaps, the art of music has made the greatest advance in the last fifteen years (1735–1750), thanks to the compositions and theories of Rameau.

Thanks to the works of a virile, bold, and fecund genius, foreigners, who heretofore could not bear our symphonies, are beginning to enjoy them, and the French seem to be convinced at last that Lulli left much to be done in this field. M. Rameau, in carrying his performance to such a high degree of perfection, has become at once the model and the object of envy of a great many artists, who criticize him but try to imitate his works. But what renders Rameau particularly distinguished are his works on musical theory . . . I seize this occasion to honor this artist philosopher.

Thus did D'Alembert pay tribute to one of the greatest musical geniuses in French history.

When Rameau brought out his *Erreurs,* Diderot, in his capacity as editor-in-chief, took up the pen in defense of the *Encyclopedia*. In the *Avertissement des éditeurs,* in the sixth volume (1756), Diderot says that it was the intention of the editors to ignore all attacks. An anonymous writer has seen fit to take exception to Rousseau's articles on music,[28] ascribing to the ignorance of the editors the host of alleged errors permitted to appear in the *Encyclopedia* on that subject.

Its author should not regard this statement as a tacit or an indirect avowal of the justice of his remarks. M. Rousseau, who joins to a knowledge and taste for music the talent of being able to express himself with clarity, a talent with which all musicians are not gifted, is too well equipped to defend himself for us to think of taking up his cause here. . . . As for us,

27 *Ibid.,* IV, 488.
28 Not until his *Lettre à M. d'Alembert,* 1762, did Rameau admit authorship of the *Erreurs.*

without bothering to take part in a dispute which would deter us from our purpose, we cannot believe that the celebrated artist to whom this book is attributed can be really its author. Everything tends to disprove this: the scant success that the book enjoyed among the general reading public, the unreasonable accusations made in such poor taste against two men of letters who have always rendered the composer a distinguished justice could never have come from the pen of Rameau since he did not disdain consulting them on occasion regarding his own works, the harsh manner in which the author handles M. Rousseau who has always praised the composer in question and was never lacking in respect toward him even in the few instances he felt he could differ with Rameau, and finally, the more than singular notions harbored by the author of this book, which do not speak in his favor, namely, that geometry is founded on music, that all sciences must be compared to harmony . . . if these are the truths that we are accused of ignoring, neglecting, and dissimulating, then we shall have the misfortune of meriting this accusation for a long time to come.

This beautiful Olympian rebuttal was typical of the *Encyclopedia's* policy of hammering away at Rameau to make him drop his scientific pretensions. A less mathematically minded group than the Encyclopedists might very well have been taken in by Rameau's metaphysical nonsense. Yet the Encyclopedists did not scoff and triumph when they pointed out to Rameau the danger of submerging his theory of harmony in a so-called scientific system. Though perhaps they did not understand all its ramifications and worldwide significance in the art and practice of music, they clearly saw the usefulness of his discovery, drew it out of its would-be physicogeometrical shell, and set it forth as the best working theory of harmony to date.

In an article on the new edition of D'Alembert's *Eléments de musique* (1762) Grimm defends D'Alembert against Rameau's accusation of treachery by observing that the theoretician had changed his position so frequently in the space of a dozen years that it was perfectly possible for a critic to have accepted Rameau's first efforts without necessarily subscribing to all of his subsequent works. In any case, Grimm pursues, everyone knows that both D'Alembert and Diderot were the first redactors of Rameau's theories, a collaboration which was invaluable to Rameau's reputation. "It seems to me that M. Rameau should be very grateful to M. Diderot and M. D'Alembert." [29] In an article on the *Erreurs* Grimm again takes up the relations of Rameau and the

[29] Grimm, ed. *Correspondance Littéraire,* janvier, 1762, V, 20.

Encyclopedia. He admits that perhaps the articles on music are not as good as they could be, yet such as they are, it is certain that neither Rameau nor anyone else could have done any better.[30] Even before the *Encyclopedia* began to appear, Grimm wrote that it was thanks to the *philosophes* that France had improved its musical taste and that "Rameau owes to their praises of him the justice and honor that the entire nation now grants him." [31] And as if in proof, Grimm adds a paragraph of appreciation of Rameau's operas, in which he praises *Pygmalion, Zoroastre,* and *Platée.*[32]

As a theorist, Rameau made two far-reaching discoveries: [33] first, that the physical and artistic material of music is one; thus, acoustics is the basis of musical aesthetics. Against this phase of Rameau's theory we have seen that the Encyclopedists protested most vigorously, on the grounds that science could not seriously be taken as a guide for artistic creation; otherwise stated, a knowledge of acoustics is not indispensable to musical composition. This position is admirably stated by Professor Láng: "The laws of acoustics are different from the laws of the stylistic musical effects and consequences produced by acoustics, it being an aesthetic impossibility for the acoustic values to reach musical values." [34] The second, and greatest, contribution made by Rameau to the field of musical theory was the discovery of fundamental tone and the concomitant classification of fundamental chords. Viewed from this angle, the chords of the tonic, dominant, and subdominant form a hierarchy of *accords fondamentaux,* of which individual chords are a functional manifestation.

By establishing the doctrine of "fundamental chords" he gave the first impetus toward the modern doctrine of functional harmony, not fully realized until the late nineteenth century. This epoch-making doctrine established the fact that all possible harmonies can be reduced to a limited number of fundamental forms (*accords fondamentaux*) called "tonic," "dominant," and "subdominant," the individual chords being functional representatives of the primary or fundamental forms. This theory ended the former equality of all chords and created a unity of harmonic conception which was both simple and profound. Until his time musicians did not, properly

---

[30] *Ibid.,* novembre, 1755, III, 129.
[31] Grimm, *Lettre sur Omphale,* in *ibid.,* XVI, 301.   [32] *Ibid.,* XVI, 307.
[33] These analyses of Rameau's theory are drawn from Professor Láng's "Rameau," in his *Music in Western Civilization.*
[34] Láng, *Music in Western Civilization,* p. 546.

speaking, think in chords—they measured intervals—and to most of them Rameau's conception was sheerly unintelligible.[35]

It is not likely that the Encyclopedists could have followed Rameau more than half way into this part of his theory; but then, besides the musicians, the outstanding theorists of Europe misunderstood or belittled Rameau's contribution.

If the Encyclopedists had been less perspicacious and more musically than scientifically minded, they might have written concerning Rameau's theory as did Mattheson in his *Grosse General-Bass Schule* (1731), in which he treats Rameau's works as entirely irrelevant and insignificant,[36] and concerning his operas as did Collé in the *Journal historique,* in which this author confuses moral and artistic issues and charges Rameau with having reduced the opera to a symphonic mess and with the destruction of operatic poetry in France.[37] Moreover, the great J. S. Bach knew Rameau both as composer and theorist, but did not appreciate him, and Marpurg and Kirnberger misunderstood his theories. The last two, theoreticians of note, used Rameau's discoveries, (Marpurg: *Handbuch bei dem Generalbasse,* 1756; Kirnberger: *Das Kunst des reinen Satzes,* 1774-1779) but gave the great Frenchman no credit.[38] Even Hugo Riemann, the modern German theoretician, points out that Rameau misunderstood Descartes [39] and Zarlino's theory of the dual nature of harmony,[40] a mistake which Rameau later admitted and corrected. Riemann dilates upon the fact that the most epoch-making acoustical material offered Rameau by the physicists Mairan and De Gamaches, that a resounding body communicates its vibrations not only to the particles of air capable of receiving and transmitting these vibrations but also to the fibers which cover the tympanum of the ear, thus rendering this organ an instrument corresponding exactly to the original resounding body in the matter of receiving and transmitting vibrations, was completely lost upon the composer. Rameau stated these data only once, thus proving, says Riemann, that

---

[35] *Ibid.,* p. 546.

[36] See Arnold, *The Art of Accompaniment from a Thorough Bass as Practised in the Seventeenth and Eighteenth Centuries,* p. 273.

[37] Collé, *Journal,* II, 212, 375.

[38] See Hirschberg, *Die Encyklopädisten,* p. 9; and especially Riemann, "Musikalische Logik," in *Geschichte der Musiktheorie,* Kapitel 16.

[39] Riemann, *Geschichte de Musik-Theorie,* p. 476.   [40] *Ibid.,* pp. 474–475.

he did not grasp the significance of these statements or the truly scientific basis of his field. Riemann speaks of Rameau as a great composer, but esteems him only mediocre as a mathematician, physicist, and logician.[41] In the light of the foregoing remarks, we may state that on the whole Rameau did not fare so badly at the hands of his contemporaries the Encyclopedists.

In reviewing the Encyclopedists' relations with Rameau it is to be noted that as a group they did yeomen's service in spreading the master's theory. D'Alembert's *Eléments* was put into German by Marpurg as early as 1757, and such important theoreticians as Eximeno and Arteaga studied Rameau's theories in D'Alembert's little masterpiece. To this very day music scholars have realized that the clearest approach to Rameau's theories is to be found in D'Alembert's *Eléments*. It is now safe to say that Rousseau's articles on music in the *Encyclopedia* offered a faithful if somewhat jumbled and at times inept picture of Rameau's discoveries. It is also certain that Rousseau believed sincerely in Rameau's importance in the history of music and did his best to aid the popularization of the theory of harmony. The wholesome and understanding criticism these men offered Rameau was of great benefit to the history of musical theory. In general, the objections recorded by these men are still valid and attest to the high integrity and sincerity of purpose of a body grossly maltreated by a man confessedly their superior in musical knowledge and composition. As a composer, too, Rameau owed much to the Encyclopedists, since they took every opportunity to point out excellence in the work of the master. To the *Encyclopedia* belongs the credit of being able to overlook the ungenerous and hostile remarks of a man patently its debtor, in favor of the propagation and dissemination of a theory of far-reaching significance in the history of musical art.

[41] *Ibid.*, p. 476.

CHAPTER IX

GLUCK'S REFORM-OPERA

THE REFORM OF THE OPERA in the eighteenth century was a movement set on foot and inspired by Frenchmen. The reform of the Italian opera-libretto toward the middle of the century by Zeno and Metastasio was based upon the classical tragedies of Corneille and Racine. The innovations that characterized the revitalized music-dramas of Jommelli and Traetta were due to the direct inspiration of the *tragédie lyrique.* And the literati, from Martelli and Marcello, Quadrio and Ortes, to Algarotti and Calsabigi, Gluck's librettist, all paid allegiance to one or more of the French critics of opera.

Professor Láng has shown that Gluck's revolution was an assimilation of the various aspects of reform movements already under way in Italy and France.[1] Gluck's repeated reversions to the old *opera seria* when reform librettists (Du Roullet, Calsabigi) were not available, he takes as proof that Gluck was wholly dependent upon his literary associates for his reform ideas.[2] Professor Láng maintains that Gluck's essential departure was the decision to turn from the *opera seria* to the *tragédie lyrique.*[3] The consummation of the reform would thus take place in Paris, when Gluck would reset *Armide,* using Quinault's text and some of Lulli's music.[4]

We have already seen that after Lulli's death French opera remained unchanged until the coming of Rameau and that the latter's fine musico-dramatic talents were hampered by the prevailing mode of *divertissements.* However, French writers did not fail to voice their discontent with the stagnant *tragédie lyrique,* and the arrival of the Bouffons touched off the powder-keg of Encyclopedist animosity. Diderot pointed to the works in the Bouffons' repertory as an object

---

[1] Láng, *op. cit.,* p. 558.   [2] *Ibid.,* p. 560.   [3] *Ibid.,* p. 566.   [4] *Ibid.,* p. 563.

lesson, and French composers immediately responded. The new *opéra-comique,* as composed by Philidor, Duni, Grétry, and Monsigny, took possession of Paris and soon spread to foreign lands. German and Italian presentations of French *opéra-comique* awakened in those countries an interest in the *tragédie lyrique.*[5] The literature that surrounded the French versions of the lyrical stage, from St. Evremond to Diderot, were known on the continent from Parma to Berlin. Diderot's ideas of reform were known to Algarotti and Jommelli, to Marpurg and Hiller. It is very likely, then, as Dr. Láng suggests, that Calsabigi guided Gluck's reform-opera with principles culled from Algarotti, who in his turn derived them from the French.[6]

As Grimm had launched the Bouffons' Quarrel and D'Alembert publicized Rameau's theories, Diderot prepared the French for Gluck. Although Diderot mentions the name of Gluck only once, his ideas of operatic reform bear that relation to Gluck's reform-opera as the saying is to the doing. The Bouffons taught Diderot that French classical declamation was not the only declamation that suited the French tongue.

These wretched little Bouffons appeared in Paris in 1751 [1752] and permitted us to hear some excellent music. Our own poor, monotonous, and uninspired brand of music was freed from its shackles as a result. The prejudice we had held that Lulli's and Rameau's melodies were the only ones suited to our prosody and language fell away, and we now have comic operas that are greeted with applause in all the opera houses of Europe.[7]

In remaining true to the French tradition that music is enhanced declamation, Diderot sought to enlarge the sphere of declamation to include the expression of elemental passions. Get into the spirit of the character you are portraying, he tells Grétry. How will a man in a violent passion express himself? Learn this "tone of passionate outcry," and you will have your air: "If the singer would only limit himself to an imitation in cadence of the inarticulate accents of passion in an aria . . . the reform would be greatly advanced."[8] This *cri,* or *accent,* which is to be found often in Diderot's reform campaign, is certainly far removed from the cold control of classical stage declama-

---

[5] Jansen, *J. J. Rousseau als Musiker,* p. 350.
[6] Láng, *Music in Western Civilization,* p. 561.
[7] Diderot, *Miscellanea Dramatiques* in his *Œuvres,* VIII, 458.
[8] Diderot, *Dorval et Moi,* in his *Œuvres,* VII, 157.

tion. In *Le Neveu de Rameau* this "natural declamation," as opposed to classical declamation, receives its fullest expression.[9] In this satire Diderot records three abuses of French opera which may be traced to classical declamation: first, a stereotyped vocabulary revolving about such words as *vols, lance, gloires, triomphe,* and *victoires;* secondly, standardized musical mannerisms which grow out of the above terms; thirdly, fixed situations and opera plots largely drawn from mythology, wherein the afore-mentioned mannerisms and limited vocabulary could flourish.[10] As correctives to these abuses Diderot offers an exemplary "natural" declamation based on the actual accents inspired by fear, love, hate, and the like,[11] and tells the French to study the scores of Italian operas to learn how vigorous music may be drawn from this type of declamation.[12]

This new "natural declamation" Diderot found in the typical *recitativo* and *aria* of the Italian operas, of which certain selections had been intercalated into the *intermèdes* of the Bouffons' repertory, while others had been presented in concert form.[13] In the article "Intermède" of the *Encyclopedia,* Diderot speaks of the Italian composers as being "profound composers, great imitators of nature, and great *déclamateurs.*" In *Le Neveu de Rameau,* he has Rameau's nephew say that the French composers do not yet know what type of poem is proper for musical adaptation. For this reason the opera has yet to be born in France: "but as a result of constantly listening to Pergolesi, the Saxon,[14] Terradeglias, Traetta, and the rest, by dint of reading Metastasio, they will finally see the light." [15] The only hope for the French opera, then, was to follow the lead of the Italians, who knew how to give music the upper hand without destroying the beauty of the poem.

Diderot's visions of the ideal opera were based on the power of music to imitate "natural declamation," and he insisted on the value of a good libretto; he saw no reason why excellent music could not be

---

[9] Diderot was inspired by Mlle Dumesnil's "natural" stage declamation—see his *Entretiens sur le Fils Naturel*—as was Marmontel by Mlle Clairon's *déclamation simple;* cf. his *Mémoires,* II, 39–44.

[10] Diderot, *Le Neveu de Rameau,* V, 461–462.

[11] See his detailed commentary on the excerpt from Racine's *Iphigénie,* Acte V, scène 4, in which Diderot shows exactly how the composer is to proceed; VII, 162–165.

[12] Diderot asserts that Philidor's *Ernelinde,* book by Poinsinet—corrected later by Sedaine —resulted from just such a study; VIII, 458–459.

[13] Diderot, *Miscellanea Dramatiques,* VIII, 458–459.

[14] Johann Adolf Hasse (1699–1783).   [15] Diderot, *Le Neveu de Rameau,* V, 464.

written to excellent poetry. In his *Lettre au sujet des observations du Chevalier de Chastellux sur le Traité du mélodrame* [16] Diderot states that the poet must submit powerful scenes for musical adaptation,[17] and later in the same work, "a great poet who is a great composer as well, will do much better than he who is neither the one nor the other." [18]

In pointing out that the tragedy, and specifically Racine's *Iphigénie,* may serve as a fit subject for musical treatment, Diderot insists that music must take the upper hand in the opera. "In the opera the poem is written for the composer . . . for this reason the poem will not be as perfect as poetry that is not intended for musical adaptation." [19] This statement would seem to presage Mozart rather than Gluck, but we shall see that Gluck, too, gave music full sway in the opera. The restraint that obstructed the composer's art for more than a century in France was to be transferred to that of the poet. Diderot was among the first Frenchmen to admit that the lyrico-dramatic form known as opera was primarily not literature, but music. This admission implied a recognition of the fact that the type of opera given currency by Lulli and Rameau was not the best sort of composition.

A great composer, then, aided by a revitalized ballet and a strong dose of pantomime, was to lay the basis for the new opera. In his supposed dialogue with Dorval, Diderot suggests that neither the composers, nor the poets, nor the dancers have any idea of what really constitutes the opera. A new genius must arise to create a new lyricism.

When the opera is badly done it is the poorest of all the arts; however, if it is well done it is the best. But how could it be done well unless the composers turn to an imitation of nature? What is the value . . . of setting to music that kind of poem which cannot even be recited? Is there not one opera writer who can make lyrical poetry descend from the enchanted regions to the solid earth we live on? [20]

A wise man was formerly a philosopher, a poet, and a musician. These

---

[16] Laurent Garcin, *Traité du mélodrame; ou, Réflexions sur la musique dramatique.*

[17] Diderot, *Lettre au Sujet des Observations du Chevalier de Chastelleux sur le Traité du Mélodrame,* VIII, 507.

[18] Diderot, *Ibid.,* 510. We have already seen in what high esteem the Encyclopedists held Metastasio, poet and composer, as a factor in the reform movement. Later, Jansen was to say of Rousseau that the *philosophe* had made disciples all over the world for the composer-poet type. Jansen, *Jean Jacques Rousseau als Musiker,* p. 174.

[19] Diderot, *De la poésie dramatique,* in his *Œuvres,* VII, 375.

[20] An allusion to the mythological sources of French opera plots.

talents degenerated when they were separated from one another. The field of philosophy has shrunk, poetry lacks ideas, and song needs energy and force . . . A great composer and a great opera poet would soon repair all this damage.

   . . . Let him appear, then, this man of genius who will place the true tragedy and the true comedy on the operatic stage. Let him cry out . . . *Adducite mihi psaltem;* "Bring me a composer," and he will create the true opera.[21]

The composer here appealed to was to be found presently in the person of Christoph Willibald Chevalier Gluck.

   Gluck's biographers have given the composer credit for having nursed ideas of reform from the very earliest Italian operas.[22] Other writers have seen the definite influence of Algarotti [23] and of Diderot and the Encyclopedists.[24] In any case, it was Du Roullet, Encyclopedist emissary to the court of Vienna, who engaged Gluck to write a French opera and wrote to Dauvergne, director of the *Académie Royale de Musique,* beseeching that worthy to make a bid for Gluck's operas.

   In a letter written to the *Mercure* Gluck took especial pains to point out that he subscribed *in toto* to French tenets. Among the points made were first, that the poet must inspire the composer, secondly, that music must imitate nature, and thirdly, that the music in the opera must be enhanced declamation, several are stated in a manner that is strongly reminiscent of Diderotian musing on this subject.

No matter how gifted an opera composer may be, he will produce only mediocre works if he is not inspired by the poet. . . . All arts must imitate nature. That is the goal I try to achieve with my music, which, insofar as possible, I try to keep always simple and natural, merely attempting to stress or lend greater expression to the poetic declamation.[25]

In adhering to Encyclopedist doctrines in this letter, Gluck took occasion also to speak of Rousseau in the most glowing terms as composer and critic.

   Although Gluck had been writing Italian operas for thirty years, he knew that Paris was the proper scene for the unfolding of his reform-

---

[21] Diderot, *Dorval et Moi,* VII, 156–157.

[22] Notably Newman, *Gluck and the Opera,* and Tiersot, *Gluck.*

[23] Charles Malherbe, "Un précurseur de Gluck, le comte Algarotti."

[24] Rolland, *Musiciens d'autrefois,* pp. 207–225.

[25] Gluck, *Lettre au Mercure sur la musique,* février, 1773. Compare Diderot, VIII, 507, and VII, 164.

operas, which fit exactly into the Lulli-Quinault tradition. For this reason he felt certain of conquering the old guard defenders of Lulli and Rameau.[26] Actually, as well as theoretically, Gluck identified his music with the theories of Diderot and the Encyclopedists. He gave music full sway over words—though, a true Machiavellian, he says in his preface to *Alceste* (1776), "I sought to reduce music to its true function, which is to enhance poetry"—as even a superficial study of his scores will show. He collaborated with excellent librettists; first Calsabigi, and later Du Roullet. Lastly, he insisted on mime and dance as an essential part of the opera, even going so far as to make the dance a link in the dramatic action.[27]

Gluck's theories of operatic composition, as gleaned from his letters and prefaces, also show a strong Encyclopedist bias. Thus, in the dedication to *Alceste* (1769), Gluck takes the opportunity to point out again how much he owes to Calsabigi for having entered into his spirit of composition. Calsabigi had done away with the superfluous and the sententious and had emphasized "a sincere diction, strong passions, interesting situations, and an ever varied spectacle." In the dedication to *Paride ed Elena* (1770) the composer tells us that he always thought that in the opera, song was nothing more than a substitute for declamation; for this reason he thought to preserve the rude Spartan character of Helen in the music he had composed for her part; "and I felt that in order to preserve this character in the music I might be pardoned an occasional concession to the trivial." This fitted the tradition set up by D'Alembert in the *Discours préliminaire* of the *Encyclopedia*, wherein music is seen to be an art which can paint situations and delimit character.[28] Finally, the following selection from Gluck's "Lettre à La Harpe," published in the *Journal de Paris*, October 12, 1777, might have been written by Diderot himself.

[26] Dr. Burney reports that: "If it is possible for the partisans of old French music to hear any other than that of Lulli and Rameau with pleasure, it must be M. Gluck's *Iphigénie*, in which he has so far accommodated himself to the national taste, style and language, as frequently to imitate and adopt them." *The Present State of Music in Germany, the Netherlands, and United Provinces*, p. 255.

[27] For Noverre's influence on Gluck, together with his relations and indebtedness to the *Encyclopedia, vide supra*, Chapter VI.

[28] It will be recalled that during the Bouffons' Quarrel the Encyclopedists were accused of fostering a realistic theory of imitation, and that Ruhlière quoted the *Discours préliminaire* as approving just such a condescendence to the trivial.

I was simple enough to believe that music, like other arts, interpreted life and could represent the divers passions of the soul. I thought that music should not please less when it is presenting the vagaries of the madman or the outcry of anguish than when it treats of the sighs of a lover. . . . I was persuaded that song saturated with the feelings it had to express had to be modified in the same degree as those feelings and express all the nuances thereof. I was convinced that the voices, the instruments, all sounds, and even silences, should be used to attain the same end, which is the expression of feelings. And, finally, I felt that the union between words and music should be so perfect that the words seem to be made for the music, and the music for the words.

We recognize in this passage elements of Rousseau's theory of operatic dramaturgy, that even silence could be expressed musically, but by far the greatest debt is to Diderot. Compare, for example, the analysis he offered of the scene from Racine's *Iphigénie*.

Clytemnestra's anguish should prompt her to utter cries which the composer should bring to our ears in all their nuances . . . his music should be filled with Clytemnestra's sorrow and despair. . . . What character this music can have! It depicts for us entreaty . . . sorrow . . . fright . . . horror . . . fury. . . .
The air begins with *Barbares arretez*. Let the composer declaim this *barbares* and this *arretez* in as many ways as possible. He will prove to be surprisingly sterile if these words do not provide a never ending source of melody. . .[29]

It is in confrontations such as these that we can realize the full force of Rolland's statement to the effect that Gluck's operatic revolution was prepared, announced, and expected by the Encyclopedists.[30]

In accepting Diderot's challenge and Du Roullet's libretto, Gluck made an observation that coincided with another of Diderot's dicta, that what the French lacked most was a good operatic poet.

. . . The French genre was the true one for musical dramaturgy. The fact that this form has not yet reached its perfection is not the fault of the truly estimable French composers, but of the opera poets, who, underestimating the power of musical expression, preferred wit to sentiment in their works.[31]

He assiduously pointed out that Du Roullet had succeeded in retaining the spirit of Racine's *Iphigénie* in his libretto.[32] Thus, possessing all

29 Diderot, *Dorval et Moi*, VII, 162ff.   30 Rolland, *Musiciens d'autrefois*, p. 225.
31 Gluck, *Lettre à M. Dauvergne*.   32 *Ibid.*

the prerequisites that Diderot demanded in the ideal poet-composer, using as a libretto the very play that the philosopher had indicated, subscribing to French tenets of operatic dramaturgy, and praising Rousseau, Gluck could not fail to be welcomed by Diderot and the Encyclopedists. He came to Paris in 1774 with this same *Iphigénie,* his first great lyrico-dramatic success in the new reform movement.

Within the space of five years Gluck composed his five great operas: *Iphigénie en Aulide* (1774), *Orphée* (1774), *Alceste* (1776), *Armide* (1777), and *Iphigénie en Tauride* (1779). The Parisian audience went literally mad over this new opera. The very capable, but unwilling, Italian composer Piccini was brought in as a competitor, and another quarrel started, more foolish and less respectable than the *Querelle des Bouffons.* Although Piccini's *forte* was *opera buffa,* he scored a real success with *Roland* (1778). Moreover, the later works of the Italian master show that he had the deepest respect and appreciation for Gluck's genius.

Diderot did not take any part in the Gluck-Piccini war, and this does him honor. His letters to his friends, usually so full of contemporary events, are singularly silent with respect to Gluck. Characteristically, then, his work in connection with the reform opera having been terminated, Diderot turned his attention to other matters; his ideas had passed into history.

Diderot's relations to the reform opera are typically those of a *chef de file.* In general, the articles that bear on the reform opera by Rousseau, Grimm, D'Alembert, and Cahusac are refinements of Diderot's ideas. But, as was usual in any discussion of musical moment raised by the Encyclopedists, Rousseau was an ardent champion of their position. Thus, in the Bouffons' Quarrel, in the Rameau controversy, Rousseau may be considered as the *Encyclopedia's* strong second line of defense. As he had ably supported Diderot's ideas, Rousseau became a devoted admirer of Gluck's reform-opera. Accordingly, on April 17, 1774, he wrote Gluck the following note: "I have just come home delighted with your opera, *Iphigénie.* You have realized what I held to be impossible up to this very day. Please accept my sincere congratulations and respects." [33] Later, Gluck gave Rousseau a copy of his opera *Alceste* for comment, but withdrew the score without asking for Rousseau's re-

---

[33] Rousseau, *Correspondance générale; à Gluck,* XX, 291.

marks, which Rousseau tells us were in a very confused state and only just begun.[34] However, in his *Fragments d'observations sur l'Alceste italien de M. le Chevalier Gluck,* written toward the end of his life, Rousseau again pays tribute to Gluck: "what will always remain real and true in these observations is the testimony they bear in regard to my deference for M. Gluck's desires, and my esteem for his works." [35] In a note Rousseau acquaints us with the fact that the composer had profited by his remarks in composing the French version of *Alceste.*[36]

Gluck was not behindhand in his praise of Rousseau. In the *Lettre au Mercure,* Gluck states that he should have liked to collaborate with Rousseau, since he was convinced that the Encyclopedist had musical talent and could have accomplished what he, Gluck, did for the opera, had he devoted his life to music. In the *Dédicace d'Orphée* (1774), the composer pays a priceless compliment to Rousseau's modest lyrical genius: "I have seen with satisfaction that the natural tone is the universal language . . . M. Rousseau used it successfully in the simple genre. His *Devin du village* is a model which no one has yet imitated." Taken as an adventure in musical criticism, the foregoing statement as it stands offers a sample of what Diderot and his associates looked for in the opera.

The only Encyclopedist who took an active part in the Gluck-Piccini Quarrel was Marmontel. Marmontel has been taken as the principal champion of Piccini, and, indeed, it is difficult to imagine how it could have been otherwise, since he prepared the libretti for Piccini's French operas. In any case, his part in the Quarrel was not at all representative of the *Encyclopedia's* position. He was called in to prepare the articles for the Supplement, long after the main body of the *Encyclopedia* had been completed. For many years Marmontel had been dreaming of writing French libretti for Italian music, an escape from classical French operatic traditions that was entirely his own and not in the least countenanced by the *Encyclopedia.* So that when Carraccioli asked him to prepare a book for Piccini, Marmontel felt that his moment had come. "I had taken upon myself the task of grafting Italian music onto our lyrical stage." [37] After having met Piccini, he was completely won over to the Italian's cause. "It was then I realized that I had met the

---

[34] Rousseau, *Lettre à M. Burney.*   [35] Rousseau, *Œuvres,* IV, 464.
[36] *Ibid.*, note.   [37] Marmontel, *Mémoires,* III, 161.

man I was seeking. He was master of his art, and music did as he directed. Thus was composed the music for *Roland,* which in spite of the cabal enjoyed the greatest success." [38] While the statements referring to Piccini in this passage are perfectly allowable, we must discount Marmontel's share in the fine success of the opera *Roland.*

Thus, Marmontel's attitude in the Quarrel was motivated by personal interest, since he became the official librettist of Gluck's opponent. It was in this spirit that he published his controversial poem *Polymnie* in defense of Piccini's operas. "I was not the only one insulted by my adversaries; I had to avenge an artist inhumanly attacked in his sincerest interests." [39] But Marmontel was not oblivious to the merits of Gluck's works. In an article concerning Marmontel in the *Correspondance littéraire* for May, 1777, the author cites the following passage from the Encyclopedist's *Essai sur les révolutions de la musique* (1777).

Gluck made musical declamation move more swiftly, forcefully, and energetically. By exaggerating its expression he at least may be said to have avoided the pitfall of boredom. He used harmony with excellent effect, forced our singers to observe the same measure as the orchestra, fused the chorus into the dramatic action, and linked the dances to a suitable scene. His art is a composite work, in which German taste prevails, but in which is implied the manner of conciliating the outstanding characteristics of the French and Italian opera. [40]

Moreover, Marmontel admitted later that Gluck outdid Piccini in the *Iphigenia* duel. [41]

Paving the way for the Gluck reform-opera must remain the highest achievement of the *Encyclopedia* in the field of musical criticism, for Gluck summed up the whole of French operatic tradition with which these Encyclopedists identified themselves. Gluck demonstrated the practical application of those reforms that Diderot and his associates thought the French opera was susceptible of. It may be that Diderot tended more toward the type of music drama created by Traetta and Jommelli, or even towards Mozart's operas. But in the final analysis, if he wished to remain true to French traditions he had to point inevitably toward Gluck's reform, with its "more economical," though "pregnant,

38 *Ibid.,* p. 168.   39 *Ibid.,* p. 213.   40 Grimm, ed., *Correspondance littéraire,* XI, 465.
41 Marmontel, *Mémoires,* III, 225–226.

use of music." [42] In his *Lettre sur les drames-opéra* (1776) Du Roullet sets forth the *Encyclopedia's* plan for reform and comments on the manner in which Gluck realized every one of its items, thus bringing together in a contemporary document perhaps the cause and effect of the so-called Gluck reform.

[42] Láng, *Music in Western Civilization*, p. 697.

PART III

THE INFLUENCE OF THE
ENCYCLOPEDIA ON THE
CRITICISM OF MUSIC

CHAPTER X

THE INFLUENCE OF THE
ENCYCLOPEDIA ABROAD

AT THIS TIME Paris was a clearinghouse for all ideas concerning art and literature, with the *Encyclopedia* as the principal organ of propaganda. Grimm's *Correspondance littéraire* went to most foreign courts and was very influential in spreading Encyclopedist ideas. At times the Encyclopedists were able to evaluate and give currency to some foreign theory, but more often the idea originated in Paris, probably at one of the numerous *salons,* was overheard by a German or Italian ambassador, written down at the latter's request by a foreign man of letters, and returned to the capital as something entirely new. The writings of Algarotti and Calsabigi and the Bailli du Roullet's rewriting of Gluck's prefaces and letters—not to mention the works of the Abbé Galiani—are very instructive in this respect. Ideas were so rife and cheap in the Encyclopedist stronghold, however, that no French author thought of invoking copyright laws. So long as the idea gained circulation, its author was amply repaid.

The Italian who most evidently reflected Encyclopedist influence abroad was the Count Francesco Algarotti (1712–1764). For many years attached to the court of Frederick the Great (1740–1753), Algarotti learned early to write libretti for that sovereign in the French tongue and to pride himself on his many French correspondents. He carried on a steady correspondence with Voltaire, deeply admired Fontenelle, whose disciple he considered himself, and quoted frequently from Molière, Racine, Corneille, and Quinault. Above all, he admired the French tragedy, whose spirit he sought to include in his opera poems. After nine years service in Berlin, Algarotti retired from public life because of ill health, and later he returned to Italy, where he continued to read French literature and wrote two very important works: (1) *Saggio sopra l'opera in musica,* and (2) the libretto *Iphigénie en Aulide.* In the latter, Algarotti shows that he was the first to take up Diderot's challenge to construct a libretto on the model of Racine's play. Throughout the *Saggio* Algarotti insists that he is primarily interested in the reform of Italian opera, yet he wrote his *Iphigénie* in French, on the grounds that French was the universal language. However, when one is as familiar with operatic prosody and the violent wars that were being waged over the preëminence of this or that language from the point of view of music as was Algarotti, the reason given by him seems weak, indeed. Moreover, French writers were convinced to a man that the Italian language more easily lent itself to musical adaptation than the French. Rather does this act reveal a deep interest in French culture, together with a desire to establish the reformed French opera based on Encyclopedist tenets. It is more than likely that Du Roullet, in presenting Gluck with his version of *Iphigénie,* was not entirely ignorant of Algarotti's libretto, published in the *Mercure* as early as 1755. Indeed, Grimm tells us that "the Chevalier Gluck set Algarotti's *Iphigénie* to music and had it performed in Vienna. It was a great success." [1]

Algarotti was a keen literary critic, who differed from his compatriots concerning the interpretation of music. His attitude toward the opera, for instance, was entirely French. He went so far as to point out the mistakes in diction in the performance of the local operas, and suggested to the Italians that they follow the French in studying stage declamation.[2] He further counsels local composers to study the French dance, which he asserts leads the world.[3] But the touchstone of the *Encyclopedia's* influence upon Algarotti's works is patently to be found in the *Saggio.* This work, which appeared for the first time in 1762, contains all the reforms demanded by the Encyclopedists. The collaboration of all the arts,[4] the welding of the ballet into the dramatic action,[5] the primacy of poetry over music,[6] the orchestra as a means of heightening the expression of the recitative,[7] the appeal to reason

---

[1] Grimm, ed., *Correspondance littéraire,* avril, 1773, X, 230. See also Malherbe, Un Précurseur de Gluck, le comte Algarotti," *Revue Musicale,* 1902. Rolland, *Musiciens d'autrefois,* p. 225.

[2] Algarotti, *Saggio,* in *Opere,* III, 285–288.   [3] *Ibid.,* pp. 298–299.

[4] *Ibid.,* p. 253.   [5] *Ibid.,* p. 263.   [6] *Ibid.,* p. 269.   [7] *Ibid.,* p. 273.

and verisimilitude,[8] and even satisfies the oft-repeated Encyclopedist phrase that music attains its fullest expression only when allied to words;[9] all these precepts are restated by the Italian *philosophe*. He quotes, either in the original or in literal translation of the "Discours préliminaire" in the *Encyclopedia*,[10] Grimm's retort that it is no more unnatural to die singing than reciting poetry[11] and Diderot's statement that in ancient times a sage was at the same time poet, philosopher, and musician.[12] The *Saggio* is a wholesale tribute to the authors of the *Encyclopedia*, including a mention of D'Alembert's *Liberté de la musique*,[13] D'Alembert's and Rousseau's objection to counterpoint in the opera,[14] Rousseau's theory of the role of the overture as an introduction to the opera,[15] and Grimm's assertion that the dance must, like the drama, have a beginning, a middle, and an end.[16] *The Saggio* even repeats Fontenelle's *boutade,* which Algarotti terms *graziosissimo*.[17] Thus Algarotti represents one of the finest conquests of the Encyclopedists' foreign influence.[18]

Stefano Arteaga, the Spanish Jesuit who found refuge in Italy when his order was driven out of Spain (1767), underwent the influence of Italian writers on musical subjects and wrote what is, perhaps, the finest compendium of the virtues and abuses of eighteenth-century Italian opera. His chief thesis, *Le Rivoluzioni del teatro musicale italiano* (1783), contains every one of the Encyclopedists' reforms for the opera, along with frequent quotations from the *Encyclopedia* proper. In the preface to the second edition (1785), for example, Arteaga gives the Italian version of the Abbé Arnaud's argument, to

[8] *Ibid.*, p. 275.   [9] *Ibid.*, p. 269.   [10] *Ibid.*, p. 279.

[11] *Ibid.*, p. 269; see Grimm, "Poème lyrique."

[12] Algarotti, *Saggio,* III, 269; see Diderot, VII, 156–157.

[13] Algarotti, *Saggio,* III, 293, note.

[14] *Ibid.*, III, 283. See articles "Contre-Point" by these authors. Gluck also shared this objection. Newman, *Gluck and the Opera*, p. 216.

[15] Algarotti, *Saggio,* III, 270–271. See Rousseau, "Ouverture."

[16] Algarotti, *Saggio,* III, 297–298. See Grimm, "Poème lyrique."

[17] Algarotti, *Saggio,* III, 279. Also repeated in Italy by Beccaria. See Jansen, *Jean Jacques Rousseau als Musiker*, p. 351.

[18] Algarotti's influence on Frederick the Great may be gathered from the note the king-philosopher attached to his plan of the opera *Coriolanus:* "Io mi sono assoggettato alle voci de' musici, al capriccio degli apparecchiatori delle scene, ed alle regole della musica . . . vi prego di fare che quest'opera si assomigli un poco alla Tragedia Francese." Michelessi, *Memorie intorno alla vita ed agli scritti del Conte Francesco Algarotti*, prefixed to Volume I of *Le Opere*, p. xciii. Yet, Italian composers ignored Algarotti's theories.

the effect that the author is trying to provide a rhetoric of the art of opera, in contrast to the many scientific treatises already available.[19] Like the Encyclopedists, Arteaga felt that the opera was a conglomerate art, in which music was to be the handmaid of poetry.[20] He agrees with D'Alembert that music must paint,[21] and that the successful composition must put us in the same frame of mind and call up the same emotions as the sight of the object itself.[22] He calls upon the authority of Grimm to show that the libretto must express succinctly what the tragic poet expands upon and presents in a rather prolix manner.[23] In this connection Arteaga betters Grimm's definition of song, when he says that the singer elevates the listener to an illusory world.[24] He agrees with Grimm that the aria must be the high point of a given scene, the safety valve to an emotional crisis.[25] He bears with Grimm and Marmontel in admitting that mythology is the best source of opera plots and that the French got their love of the *merveilleux* from it, but does not agree that French opera should be preferred to the Italian for this reason.[26] Rather, says Arteaga, the aims of opera and drama should be similar; to wit, Aristotle's theory of purging the emotions through scenes of pity and terror. We recall that D'Alembert called the opera a spectacle of senses and that Marmontel considered this spectacle a dramatization of the epic. Arteaga insists that for pur-

---

[19] Arteaga, *Le rivoluzioni del teatro musicale italiano*, I, 1. Compare Abbé Arnaud, *Lettre sur la musique à M. le Comte de Caylus*, pp. 1–2. This work essentially sums up Encyclopedist doctrines, although Arnaud was not officially connected with the *Encyclopedia*. See also his *Soirée perdue à l'Opéra* and his articles and reviews in the *Variétés Littéraires* for his Encyclopedist leanings.

[20] Arteaga, *Le rivoluzioni del teatro musicale italiano*, pp. 1–2. This made him as unacceptable to the Italians as Algarotti.

[21] *Ibid.*, p. 15. See Alembert, *Discours préliminaire*.

[22] Arteaga, *op. cit.*, pp. 9–10. See above, Chapter V, for an analysis of D'Alembert's position.

[23] Cf. Grimm, "Poème lyrique":

> "Rendimi il figlio mio:
> Ahi! mi si spezza il cor:
> Non son più madre, o Dio!
> Non ho più figlio".
>   Metastasio.

"Ma questi quattro versetti soli accompagnati dalla mossa e vivacità, che ricevano da una bella musica, faranno, come riflette saggiamente Grimm nel suo Discorso sul Poema Lirica, un effetto vieppiù sorprendente sugli animi degli uditori, che non la tragica, e artifiziosa scena della *Merope* di Voltaire." Arteaga, *De rivoluzioni del teatro musicale italiano*, I, 17–18. See above, Chapter III, for Grimm's statement.

[24] Arteaga, *op. cit.*, p. 20.   [25] *Ibid.*, p. 28.   [26] *Ibid.*, p. 45.

poses of verisimilitude the technique of dramatic writing must be observed by the librettist. Thus, he is convinced that Quinault would have written better opera texts had he paid more attention to dramatic verisimilitude than to the *merveilleux*. It is curious to see this Italian opposing Encyclopedists with their own arguments. However, he consults "le bon sens," and in general heads for the same musico-dramatic compromise as was maintained in the *Encyclopedia*.[27]

So closely does Arteaga follow dramatic trends in the opera that he devotes one hundred pages to an analysis of Metastasio's plays, which he feels represent the high-point in operatic composition.[28] This tendency to evaluate the opera mainly on the basis of the excellence—or lack of it—in the libretto, is entirely French, bringing to mind the works of the earliest critics of opera in France. Arteaga states, for instance, that the Italian opera began to decline after the death of Metastasio; as if to say that once the technique of creating libretti became lost or vitiated, successful opera could no longer be composed. Or again, that the combination of poetry and music as an art form declined because of the weakness of the poetry; as if music were only an accessory in the opera. The overemphasis of the role of the poem in the opera reveals to how great an extent Arteaga was following French theorists. Among other things, the opera declined in Italy because of the over-importance given to the orchestra. This preoccupation with the instrumental score led to a neglect of the libretto and, consequently, of the drama. Because instrumental music failed to imitate nature successfully, the singers became all-important, and the bane of virtuosity was upon the Italians. The inappropriateness of music to words in the Italian opera and the ignorance of dramatic declamation on the part of the singers were other French reasons Arteaga found for the dissolution of the local opera.[29] Finally, Arteaga blames modern composers for being ignorant of the works of such theorists and aestheticians as Rameau, Blainville, D'Alembert, and Grimm.[30]

There follows a curious paragraph, of maximum importance to us, in which Arteaga traces the changes—for the worse, of course—in the Italian opera to the *philosophes,* those heralds of French taste.

The plots taken from history and the prevailing general trend of Italian opera no longer make good theater. To which may be added the fact that

[27] *Ibid.,* pp. 53–55.   [28] *Ibid.,* II, 84–200.   [29] *Ibid.,* pp. 272–275.   [30] *Ibid.,* pp. 318.

the victorious influence of the French and the brilliant sophisms of the *philosophes* caused the Italians to begin to renounce the beauties of the local opera in favor of foreign whims, modeling this unique Italian product to suit the taste of the inhabitants of the Seine.[31]

Never doubting that he was also a product of Encyclopedist thought, Arteaga laments the French influence on the local opera, criticizing in detail the libretti Calsabigi prepared for Gluck. He takes Calsabigi as an egregious example of French imitation and says of Gluck's music that although such compositions may have been pleasing to the ancients, they were too monotonous for the Italians.[32] This turnabout is especially surprising when we consider that Arteaga desired to have the dance form a part of the dramatic action of the opera, that he praises the works and articles of Cahusac, and that he has the profoundest esteem for Quinault's use of the dance,[33] as well as for Noverre's *poème-ballet*.[34] Moreover, he quotes Rousseau's *Lettre à M. Burney*,[35] makes frequent reference to the latter's *Dictionnaire de musique*,[36] cites Diderot's *Observations sur le chronomètre*,[37] and ends his work by translating the Abbé Arnaud's plan for the reform of the opera, as expressed in the latter's *Lettre sur la musique à M. le Comte de Caylus*.

Arteaga represents in one person the various French reactions towards operatic dramaturgy from St. Evremond to Diderot. It is evident that he is dissatisfied with both the French and the Italian forms of opera (which he came to know through first-hand acquaintance), but it is not immediately apparent why he should have charged the Encyclopedists—his masters—with the decline of the lyrical stage. At the time of Arteaga's writing, 1783, the Gluck revolution had been consummated and there were already in France post-Encyclopedist critics of the stamp of La Harpe who began to object to *Alceste* as the *ne plus ultra* of operatic composition. Arteaga's remove from the scene of Gluck's triumph did not permit the critic an eyewitness's reaction to the new French opera. This may be understood as proof that he came by his knowledge of French opera primarily through literary sources. Such an admission must imply the wide inroads made in foreign lands by the Encyclopedist invasion. The literary activity of the French in regard to the opera preceded as a harbinger the reform gestures of

[31] *Ibid.*, III, 111.   [32] *Ibid.*, pp. 119–125.   [33] *Ibid.*, pp. 180–200.
[34] *Ibid.*, pp. 203–204.   [35] *Ibid.*, pp. 119.   [36] *Ibid.*, especially I, 295ff.   [37] *Ibid.*, III, 89.

Gluck, Jommelli, and Traetta in Germany and Italy. Arteaga is, then, the first of a long line of critics to inveigh against the nefarious influence of the *Encyclopedia* on the opera in Europe. By a strange quirk of fate this unhappy Spanish Jesuit, who took refuge in Italy for many years, came to die in 1799, in Paris, the city to which he owed his greatest spiritual debt.

Another Spanish Jesuit who found a retreat in Italy was D. Antonio Eximeno (1729–1808). In his *Dell'origine e delle regole della musica, colla storia del suo progresso, decadenza e rinnovazione* (1774) the author is mainly interested in separating music from mathematics, following D'Alembert's lead.[38] Eximeno came by his knowledge of Rameau's theories exclusively through D'Alembert's *Eléments de musique,* which he feels gave currency to Rameau's ideas by dissipating the general confusion that reigned therein.

This part of Rameau's theory of music is given more of a semblance of truth in D'Alembert's little treatise entitled *Elémens de la musique,* in which this great philosopher and mathematician by eliminating from Rameau's theory the false suppositions and the glaring contradictions of the author reduces it to a series of clear and concise propositions which make Rameau's theory of music worthy of being compared with Newton's theory of physics.[39]

It is in testimonials such as the above that the fine work done by the Encyclopedists in propagating Rameau's theories can be gauged. Like Algarotti and Arteaga, Eximeno is a convinced disciple of the Encyclopedists. He concurs with them in holding that music must enhance the text in the opera.[40]

Among other writers who reflected the opinions of the *Encyclopedia* in Italy was Antonio Benedetto Bassi, who insisted in his *Lettre adressée à la société olympique de Paris* (1787) that the composer should be inspired by the librettist and that the music should identify itself with the text.[41] This work, written in French—one might almost say Diderot's French—shows a keen acquaintance with the fortunes of the Italian opera in Paris. Bassi tells us that about 1780–1787 the French were disgusted with the Italian *opera buffa.* Italian music was being written to poorly conceived French libretti. Since in the opera

[38] Eximeno, *Dell'origine e delle regole della musica,* Preface, p. 7.
[39] *Ibid.,* p. 6.   [40] *Ibid.,* p. 4.
[41] Bassi, *Lettre adressée à la Société olympique de Paris,* pp. 15–16.

music is inseparable from the text, Bassi intelligently advises the French to have Italian opera alongside the national opera. Giovanni Antonio Bianchi (1686–1758) advocated Encyclopedist operatic reforms in his *De I vizi e de I defetti del moderno teatro* (1753).[42] Raniero di Calsabigi (1719–1795), Gluck's librettist, to whom the composer attributed the major part of his reform opera, defended Gluck's operas and his own libretti in the controversial *Risposta che ritrovò nella gran città di Napoli alla critica ragionatissima delle poesie drammatiche del Cavaliere di Calsabigi* (1790). In August, 1784, he wrote *Lettre à l'auteur du Mercure,* in which he vehemently claimed his share in the reform of the opera.

Still other aestheticians and theoreticians of note who came to maturity before the *Encyclopedia* got under way, and therefore could not be said to reflect directly Encyclopedist thought, repeated French ideas which were later espoused by the *philosophes.* Such was the eminent author of the *Della storia e della ragione d'ogni poesia* (1739–1752), Francesco Saverio Quadrio (1695–1756). This distinguished author extended the arc of St. Evremond's influence by repeating verbatim the French critic's theory of correct operatic situations and diction.[43]

In Germany, the foremost interpreter of the *Encyclopedia's* musical criticism was the Swiss-German, Johann Georg Sulzer (1720–1779). His *Allgemeine Theorie der schoenen Künste* (1771–1775) followed the lead of the *Encyclopedia* even in the matter of form, his theory being presented in a dictionary of aesthetics. For the musical section Sulzer was able to secure the services of Johann Philip Kirnberger (1721–1783) and later of his pupil J. A. P. Schulze (1747–1800). These men, both musicians and theoreticians of note, quoted frequently from the *Encyclopedia* and the Encyclopedists and from Rousseau's *Dictionnaire de musique.*[44] Of greater significance was the attitude of the editor-in-chief, Sulzer himself, who in *Lettre à un de ses amis où il expose le plan de son Dictionnaire sur les sciences et les arts,* published by Arnaud in the *Variétés littéraires* (1768), plainly shows himself to

[42] Bianchi, *De i vizj e de i defetti del moderno teatro,* especially pp. 123–125.
[43] Quadrio, *Della storia e della ragione d'ogni poesia,* Lib. 3, Distinzione IV, Capo II, p. 443.
[44] Sulzer, *Allgemeine Theorie der Schoenen Künste,* see especially the articles "Musik" and "Oper."

be a disciple of the *Encyclopedia*.[45] The editors of the Supplement to the *Encyclopedia* included fifteen articles on music taken from Sulzer's dictionary. At least five of these, "Aria," "Art," "Ballet," "Mesure," and "Rhythme," develop earlier Encyclopedist doctrines. In this way the *Encyclopedia* reaped the fruits of its foreign influence. Sulzer joins Chastellux in rebelling against the theory of art as an imitation of nature and outlines a theory of the useful and the beautiful. Man, says Sulzer, naturally tends towards an embellishment of the objects in his environment. This ornamentation increases the beauty of those objects and thus renders them more dear to us. The need for artistic creation is accompanied in man by a need to be exalted by representations in color, sound, form, or writing.[46] The theory of art should result from the solution of a half psychological and a half political problem. How can art, by appealing to the finer sentiments in man, lead him to discharge his debt to society? The composer, for example, can stir the sentiments by sound. Since he speaks directly to the emotions, his message is relayed more immediately than that of other creative efforts. Thus, Sulzer concludes, music is the most powerful of the arts.[47]

The authors of the Supplement incorporated articles taken from Sulzer, because they felt that he was heading in the same general direction in his aesthetic doctrines as the descendants of the Encyclopedists at home. Other German writers on musical subjects did not show such obvious affiliations with the *Encyclopedia,* but the writings of Encyclopedists on music appeared in one or more of the musical periodicals of Germany soon after their publication in France. Riedel's *Ueber die Musik des Ritters von Gluck* (1775) contains the monographs on Gluck by Arnaud, Moline, and other Frenchmen. Marpurg (1718– 1795), generally conceded to be one of the outstanding German theoreticians of the eighteenth century, gives a translation of D'Alembert's *Eléments de musique* in his *Historisch-kritische Beyträge zur Aufnahme der Musik* (1754–1760), and comments upon practically all French writings of musical interest. He published the detailed analysis

---

[45] Arnaud, *Variétés Littéraires,* III, 17–132. The letter here referred to may have been directly inspired by Diderot's article, "Encyclopédie." See especially the two paragraphs which are aimed to introduce the reader to the manner of using his *Dictionnaire;* III, 130.

[46] Sulzer, "Art"; cf. Chastellux, "Idéal."

[47] See Marmontel "Art," and Diderot, Chapter V, note 12, of this work.

of Rousseau's *Lettre sur la musique française* as it appeared in the *Journal des Savants* (1754). Forkel (1749–1818), the German historian of music, also includes in his *Musikalisch-kritische Bibliothek* (1778–1779) French articles on Gluck, and analyzes Bemetzrieder's theory of music in a study of twenty-six pages; we now know that Diderot rewrote and published this work. He also quotes frequently from Rousseau's *Dictionnaire,* in his *Allgemeine Litteratur der Musik* (1792). The critic Hertel brought out a *Sammlung musikalischen Schriften Grosstentheils aus den Werken der Italiänen und Franzosen übersetzt* (1757–1758). These publications could not fail to disseminate Encyclopedist ideas throughout Germany.

Lessing, a devoted disciple of Diderot's in his *Laokoön*,[48] translated the Encyclopedist's plays and dramaturgical essays into German as early as 1760.[49] Johann August Eberhard took up Diderot's ideas of the opera as a conglomerate art—a worthy predecessor of Wagner's *Gesamtkunstwerk*—in his *Allgemeine Theorie des Denkens und Empfindens* (1776).[50] Wagner gave the German equivalent of Diderot's phrase: "[Die Musik] kommt vom Herzen und geht zum Herzen." [51] Moreover, we know that it was Goethe who first published, in German, Diderot's *Le Neveu de Rameau* (1805), with its vivid discussions of music illustrated by pantomime.

As for Rousseau, Jansen has shown the vast repercussions that his theories and compositions had upon German art and thought. We learn that *Pygmalion* appeared in Vienna seven years before the French première in 1775. This performance was based on Ramler's translation (1768).[52] Goethe praised *Pygmalion* highly in his *Bemerkungen zu Diderot's Versuch über die Malerei*.[53] Mylius and Schink translated *Le Devin du village* in 1781.[54] Rousseau's theoretical writings on music were spread throughout Germany by Ramler in his *Vertheidigung der Oper,* by Wieland in his *Geschichte der Abderiten,* and by Herder and Marpurg.[55] Goethe found Rousseau a constant source of edification: compare, for instance, "Die Tonkunst ist nichts ohne die

---

[48] See Werner Leo, *Diderot als Kunstphilosoph,* p. 34.
[49] Consult Schink's edition of Lessing's *Sämmtliche Schriften,* 1825, I, 56.
[50] Hirschberg, *Die Encyklopädisten und die französische Oper,* p. 103n.
[51] Quoted in Jansen, *Jean Jacques Rousseau als Musiker,* p. 405.
[52] *Ibid.,* pp. 315–316.   [53] *Ibid.,* pp. 316–317.   [54] *Ibid.,* p. 183.   [55] *Ibid.,* p. 402.

menschliche Stimme" [56] with Rousseau's predilection for the human voice. The German poet's preoccupation with the *mélodrame* and the musical comedy in his youth, together with his love of Rousseau's songs, must also be mentioned in this place. Jansen draws thirteen points of comparison between Rousseau and Wagner, at least eight of which are very significant: (1) The human voice is supreme in music. (2) Poetry and music are inseparable (this idea could be more fairly ascribed to Diderot). (3) A national opera is inseparable from the local language. (4) Music is at its best when allied to words. (5) Instrumental music heightens and develops the power of words. (6) Eliminate counterpoint in the opera. (7) Instrumental music is too general. (8) Words render musical meaning specific.[57] It is clear that Wagner's ideal of a conglomerate art, at least as expressed in his writings *Oper und Drama* and *Das Kunstwerk der Zukunft,* is in the same direction as that of the Encyclopedists.

Rousseau's criticism of French music aroused such interest in Germany that "hardly a pamphlet appeared against Rousseau [during the Bouffons' Quarrel] which did not immediately find its way into Germany." [58] Rousseau's *Lettre sur la musique française,* as well as Grimm's *Petit prophète,* were in great demand, and as late as 1800 Rousseau's *Observations sur Alceste* was "in everybody's thoughts." [59] Weisse's and Hiller's preoccupation with the *opéra-comique,* a form abetted and protected by Diderot and the Encyclopedists, owes more than a nod to Rousseau's *Devin,* which furthered the development of the local *Singspiel.* Nor must we forget that it was Rousseau's *Pygmalion* that suggested Benda's *Ariadne* (1775), the earliest German predecessor of Wagner's music-drama.[60] Finally, Mozart's opera *Bastien et Bastienne* was inspired by Rousseau's *Le Devin du village.*

In England the chief propagandist for the Encyclopedists was the eminent Dr. Charles Burney (1726-1814), who undertook a voyage to France and Italy in connection with his *History of Music* (1776-1789). While in France (1770), Burney made the acquaintance of the Encyclopedists, with whose works he was already familiar. In 1760 he

[56] *Ibid.,* p. 403.   [57] *Ibid.,* p. 405.   [58] *Ibid.,* p. 216.
[59] Karl Spazier, *Grétry's Versuch über die Musik,* quoted in Jansen, *Jean Jacques Rousseau als Musiker,* p. 400.
[60] Láng, *Music in Western Civilization,* pp. 581-584.

had given at the Drury Lane an English adaptation of Rousseau's *Devin* under the title *The Cunning Man*. The account of his travels in *The Present State of Music in France and Italy* (1771) contains a glowing paragraph relative to Diderot's mastery of matters musical.

With M. Diderot I had the happiness of conversing several times, and I was pleased to find, that among all the sciences which his extensive genius and learning had investigated, there is no one that he interests himself more about than music. . . . He entered so zealously into my views concerning the history of his favorite art, that he presented me with a number of his own Mss. sufficient for a volume in-folio on the subject. These from such a writer I regard as invaluable.[61]

Burney does not tell us what use he made of this treasure, nor do we know which works of Diderot's bearing on the art of music were in it. At any rate, so abundantly did the English doctor's own writings express the Encyclopedist viewpoint, that his criticism was immediately put into French by Drack (1772).

Another representative of Encyclopedist opinion in England was Charles Avison (1710–1770), a pupil of Geminiani. His *Essay on Musical Expression* (1752) reveals gleanings from D'Alembert's *Discours préliminaire* as well as from Rousseau's articles on music in the first two volumes of the *Encyclopedia*. The following excerpt is a typical foreign version of a cardinal Encyclopedist precept; music as an agent of natural imitation must give rise in the listener to passions similar to those expressed in sounds.

The force of sound in alarming the passions is prodigious. Thus the noise of thunder, the shouts of war, the uproar of an enraged ocean, strikes us with terror: so again there are certain sounds natural to joy, others to grief or despondency, others to love; and by hearing these, we naturally sympathize with those who either enjoy or suffer. Thus music either by imitating these various sounds in due subordination to the laws of air and harmony, or by any other method of association bringing the objects of our passions before us . . . does naturally raise a variety of passions in the human breast, similar to the sounds which are expressed.[62]

The composer who would aim at true musical expression, "is to blend such a happy mixture of air and harmony, as will affect us most strongly with the passions or affections which the poet intends to

[61] Burney, *The Present State of Music in France and Italy*, pp. 391–393.
[62] Avison, *An Essay on Musical Expression*, pp. 3–4.

raise." [63] And "the composer is culpable, who for the sake of some low and trifling imitation, deserts the beauties of expression." [64] Avison agrees with the Encyclopedists in concluding that "the finest instrumental music may be considered as an imitation of the vocal." [65] In a note the author counsels the student of music "to take a particular survey of Rameau's *Principles of Composition,* now translated into English." [66] The translation referred to is that made by French in 1752.

The impact of Encyclopedist activity was tremendous in foreign countries. The influence of their opinions made itself strongly felt on the musical thought of Italy and Germany, where the various reform movements bore the mark of Encyclopedist propaganda. As early as the last quarter of the eighteenth century the French took the lead in the literary form that came to be known as musical criticism.

[63] *Ibid.,* p. 69. See Alembert, "Contre-sens," and Marmontel, "Chant."

[64] Avison, *An Essay on Musical Expression,* p. 108. Compare Cahusac, Rousseau, articles "Expression."

[65] *Ibid.,* p. 117. See Cahusac, "Chant"; Grimm, "Motif."   [66] *Ibid.,* pp. 80–81.

CHAPTER XI

THE INFLUENCE OF THE
ENCYCLOPEDIA IN FRANCE

OF THE FRENCH CRITICS who were contemporaries of the *Encyclopedia,* many, as we have seen, opposed Encyclopedist thought. Yet the great majority of writers whose names carried weight subscribed to the musical doctrines of the *Encyclopedia.* Such were Condillac (1715–1780), who stated in the *Traité des sensations* (1754) that "the pleasures of the ear consist principally in melody"; [1] Jean Adam Serre, who called D'Alembert one of the outstanding musical theoreticians of the age in his *Observations sur les principes de l'harmonie, occasionnées par quelques écrits modernes sur ce sujet, et particulièrement par l'article Fondamentale de M. d'Alembert* (1763); Du Roullet, who acted as go-between for the Encyclopedists in their relations with Gluck; and the poet Saint-Lambert (1716–1803). The last-named was a true Encyclopedist of the younger generation, counting the *philosophes* among his closest friends and showing strong intellectual kinship to that group.

In 1768 Saint-Lambert published, in the *Variétés littéraires* a *Lettre à M. le B . . . d'H . . . sur l'opéra,* in which the poet develops a curious thesis. Neither the Italians nor the French have hit upon the correct form for the opera, says Saint-Lambert, the one having no cohesion between the various parts, the other, although better unified, having little variety. In preferring the Italian opera, Saint-Lambert is accepting the lesser of two evils. But as he is more interested in the improvement at home, he draws up a list of grievances concerning the French opera. First of all, from the point of view of accent the French language is far inferior to the Italian. French regard for politeness knocked strong accents—which Saint-Lambert takes to be indispensable to the por-

[1] Condillac, *Traité des sensations,* p. 128.

trayal of "the natural outcry of passion"—out of the language.[2] In this
way the French poets not only would not but also could not represent
violent passions. Thus, Quinault and his successors had to limit themselves to *maximes galantes*. As for the composers, they failed miserably
when they attempted to write music for this lackluster poetry. It should
have been their business to point out that this sort of poetry could never
lend itself to musical interpretation. Thus, the mediocrity of the local
opera was due to the shortsightedness of both librettists and composers.[3] Weak poetry and expressionless music led to the idea of the
merveilleux, wherein the voluptuous, the gracious, the sugary-sweet,
and *le tendre* became the only fit subjects of opera. Composers soon
learned that the ballet was a far better vehicle for these sentiments
than the opera, and so the ballet came to take the place of the lyrical
tragedy in France. This type of criticism, while essentially deriving
from the Encyclopedists, is refreshing in its interpretation; it is the first
to take into consideration the many factors that led to various transformations in the French opera. Synthesis was not one of the virtues
of the *Encyclopedia.*

The generation that immediately followed the *Encyclopedia* was
overwhelmingly dedicated to the musical precepts of that organ. None,
perhaps, so completely bore the stamp of the Encyclopedists as the Abbé
Arnaud (1721–1784). Like Rousseau, he was self-taught in the art of
music, as, indeed, were all the other Encyclopedist critics of music.
He made wide appeal for the reform of the opera according to their
dictates and heralded Gluck as the composer the world was waiting
for.[4] Cofounder of the *Variétés littéraires,* with Suard, Arnaud carried on in that periodical, as well as in his correspondence, a steady
campaign in favor of the Gluck reform opera. His great activity as a
partisan of Gluck in the so-called Gluck-Piccini quarrel may to some
extent account for the Encyclopedists' silence on that head, so well
did the Abbé Arnaud defend the reform opera.[5] In any case, Grétry,

[2] Arnaud, *Variétés Littéraires,* 1804 edition, III, 309.   [3] *Ibid.,* pp. 311–312.
[4] See Briqueville, *L'Abbé Arnaud et la réforme de l'opéra.*
[5] Besides the works mentioned above, chap. x, note 19, consult Arnaud's *Lettres* to
Mme d'Augny, Mme la Comtesse de B., Condorcet, le Père Martini, and to La Harpe,
as well as the comments he published along with his résumé in French of Marcello's *Il
teatro alla moda* and his translation of Sulzer's *Lettre,* all in Arnaud, *Œuvres complètes,*
1808. Leblond's *Mémoires pour servir à l'histoire de la révolution opérée dans la musique
par M. le Chevalier Gluck,* 1781, may also be consulted with profit in respect to Arnaud's
musical criticism.

in his *Mémoires,* mentions Diderot and Arnaud in the same breath as enthusiasts and inspirers of musical composition.

> It was not always advisable to heed the Abbé Arnaud or M. Diderot when they gave free rein to their imagination, but the first spark of these two burning minds was divinely inspired.
>
> . . . a Diderot, an Abbé Arnaud, who used to throw guests into an up-roar with their ideas, communicated to each and all by the power of their eloquence a burning desire to write, paint, or compose.[6]

This juxtaposition is indicative of Arnaud's Encyclopedist bias, and of Diderot's all-pervading influence.

The Abbé distinguished himself as a music critic by insisting that the composer study language prosody. Arnaud felt that much of the confusion over French and Italian music, as well as the poor grade of the local opera, was due to a neglect of this department of composition. Just as each language has its own prosody, says Arnaud, each must have its own melody, since melody must follow prosody.[7] Hence the impossibility of adapting French words to Italian music. Language prosody determines melody, which Arnaud defines as a series of pro-portionate sounds that are interdependent.[8] He is careful to distinguish between French and Italian opera, pointing out that the Italian is melodrama or musical fantasy, while the French is drama heightened by music.[9] In underlining the dramatic content of the opera Arnaud identifies himself with the old current of French musical criticism. He ridicules the old French opera "in which the instruments accompany the voice like a valet his master." [10] Yet this man, who represented the *Encyclopedia,* asserted that Gluck realized all his demands. Arnaud summed up the two main currents of musical criticism in France and showed that what the Encyclopedists and their opponents really de-sired was identical: a good play set to French music.[11]

In his *Lettre sur Iphigénie en Tauride,* June 15, 1779, Arnaud shows that he really appreciates the import of Gluck's "revolution," since he points out especially the beauties of orchestration in that work. Arnaud's *Lettre au Père Martini* sums up what Gluck did for the opera: he de-

---

[6] Grétry, *Mémoires,* I, 225–226; II, 134.   [7] Arnaud, *Œuvres,* I, 10–11.
[8] *Ibid.,* I, 21.   [9] Arnaud, *Essai sur le mélodrame,* in his *Var. litt.,* III, 23–30.
[10] Arnaud, *La Soirée perdue à l'Opéra,* in his *Œuvres,* II, 390.
[11] Arnaud, *Lettre à Mme D'Augny,* in his *Œuvres,* II, 263–264.

veloped both music and text; [12] he found the perfect form of French musical prosody by using only as many notes as there were syllables in a verse; [13] he created the dramatic chorus; [14] he was the first to use the overture as a musical indication of what was to follow in the opera; [15] and finally, Gluck was the first and only composer to present a well-coördinated spectacle in which all the parts complemented each other.[16] Disregarding for the moment the fine works of Jommelli and Traetta in connection with the music drama, we may state that every one of the reforms claimed by Arnaud for Gluck had been accomplished before the German master's advent on the scene. The careful weighing of note distribution was a procedure familiar to Lulli; he rarely gave less than a quarter note to a syllable. This aspect of musical prosody based on a close study of classical stage declamation was a cardinal point in Lulli's conception of the *tragédie lyrique*. Many years later, Nietzsche was again to overlook Lulli in imputing to Gluck the first attempt since the Greeks to base musical prosody upon principles of accentuation.[17] Gluck got the idea of the active chorus from Rameau, and the mid-seventeenth-century opera symphony "gave a condensed picture of the drama they prefaced." [18] Insofar as the *grands ensembles* in music are concerned, it was Traetta who introduced the ensemble technique of the *opera buffa* into the *opera seria*.[19] Moreover, Lulli, and again later Rameau, presented in the *tragédie lyrique* an extremely well-coördinated music drama that was never again matched in the history of the French lyrical stage. Thus, Gluck's achievement, as far as the French were concerned at least, reduced itself to a freshening of the musical aspects of the *tragédie lyrique* without in any way damaging its dramatic integrity. And this was exactly the slogan of the Encyclopedists in their reform drive.

The violinist and aesthetician, C. R. Brijon, evidently opposed to Encyclopedist doctrines, nevertheless shared their sentiments regarding instrumental music. He begins his *Réflexions sur la musique, et la vraie manière de l'exécuter sur le violon* (1763) with a brief apology for the music of instruments, stating that the power of music to imitate

---

[12] Arnaud, *Œuvres*, II, 405–406.   [13] *Ibid.*, p. 408.
[14] *Ibid.*, p. 411.   [15] *Ibid.*, p. 413.   [16] *Ibid.*
[17] Nietzsche, *Einleitung zu den Vorlesungen über Oedipus rex*, quoted in Professor Moody Campbell's article, "Wagner—Nietzsche, to January, 1872."
[18] Láng, *Music in Western Civilization*, p. 366.   [19] *Ibid.*, p. 559.

is unlimited, even when not allied to words.[20] This he aptly proves by the effect of Mondonville's motets upon women, who, of course, did not know Latin, and the unprecedented success of the Bouffons.[21] He conceives the sonata as a discourse, or *ode en musique,* the concerto as a dialogue or discussion, and the *symphonie* as a large canvas upon which may be depicted battle scenes, tempests, earthquakes, and similar striking natural phenomena.[22] These ideas were current among eighteenth-century aestheticians, and although the Encyclopedists may have shared them with their contemporaries, they did not invent them. However, Brijon walks into the Encyclopedist stronghold when he states that the composer of instrumental music must have a definite subject in mind and must exactly label his creations.[23] This idea was widely discussed in the *Encyclopedia,* beginning with D'Alembert's *Discours préliminaire* and continuing through the articles, "Expression," by Cahusac, and "Instrumentale." [24]

It must not be supposed, however, that the disciples of the *Encyclopedia* were all willing slavishly to follow its precepts. Ange Goudar (1720–1791), who admired the Encyclopedists and subscribed to most of their musical criticism, reveals a striking personality and a genius for sarcasm in his *Remarques sur la musique et la danse* (1773). Goudar flays the "improvements" wrought by the Italians upon the opera, wherein "perhaps the least blunder is to have Alexanders, Caesars, and Pompeys settle the destiny of the world with women's voices." [25] He scores the tendency to go back to the Greeks and Romans for models and advises composers to depend upon themselves.[26] Goudar holds that the best vocal music is that which approaches closest to the spoken language. For three thousand years, he says, man sang pretty much as he spoke, then music took the upper hand and vocal music was ruined forever.[27] Goudar argues that Handel changed the course of the English opera by introducing Italian *ariettes* and that Rameau forced too many notes into the *tragédie lyrique.*[28] Music must be simple, easy, and natural, a sort of embellished declamation, not a mess of notes, trills, and so forth; and here Goudar accepts the Encyclopedists' precepts, carried on still later in France by Lacassagne and

[20] Brijon, *Réflexions sur la musique,* pp. 1–2.   [21] *Ibid.,* p. 2.   [22] *Ibid.,* p. 3.
[23] *Ibid.,* p. 12.   [24] *Vide supra,* chap. v.   [25] Goudar, *op. cit.,* Introduction, p. 2.
[26] *Ibid.,* pp. 21–22.   [27] *Ibid.,* p. 27.   [28] *Ibid.,* p. 29.

Blanchet.[29] The appeal of Gregorian chant—"the only monument that remains of that type of melody which affects the soul without sickening it"—has never flagged, whereas the complicated modern opera passes through as many modes as there are composers.[30]

In another section Goudar ridicules dancing pantomime, and calls Noverre's revolution a fantastic and impracticable dream, for, to execute dancing pantomime a soul is indispensable, and "dancers only have feet." [31] The following paragraph is representative of the caliber of withering sarcasm that Goudar leveled against all classical imitation, and especially at Noverre's revival of the late classical dance.

A celebrated dancing master is going to give his version of the *Annals* of Tacitus in a heroic ballet, in which the entire Roman Empire will dance. On the stage will be represented the founding of Rome, the conquest of Africa, the affair of Cannes, and the destruction of Carthage performed by tumblers. Hannibal and Scipio will dance a *pas de deux*. The performance will end with the death of Julius Caesar, who will be killed in cadence by Brutus, who will also expire on the stage to the sound of violins. To round off the finale Cicero will address the Senate with his accustomed eloquence by executing double *entrechats*.[32]

Goudar claimed that Rome introduced dancing pantomime in its decadence. To try to restore these rules of vice would be to "seek to become great by imitating the Romans in their pettiness." [33] What is more, and here again he speaks like an Encyclopedist, of what use are the conquests we have made in the fields of knowledge and art if we are to constantly preserve the prejudices of the ancients as models? [34] This reactionary music critic, who held faith with Gregorian chant and Lulli, this purist in art who opposed the ancients on moral grounds, was, together with his wife Sara, to whom some of his works are by some attributed, among the century's most unbridled adventurers.[35]

M. P. Gui de Chabanon (1730–1792), composer, theoretician, and man of letters, betrayed in his criticism of music the most violent animosity to the *Encyclopedia*. In his *Eloge de Rameau* (1764), and again in his *Observations sur la musique* (1779), he agrees that the aim of all music

[29] *Ibid.*, p. 45.   [30] *Ibid.*, p. 46.   [31] *Ibid.*, p. 54.
[32] *Ibid.*, p. 60.   [33] *Ibid.*, p. 67.   [34] *Ibid.*
[35] See Michaud, "Goudar," in *Biographie universelle;* and Casanova, *Mémoires*, VI, 367, 485, VII, 7, and especially VI, 462ff., and VIII, 107–108, 139–140,

must be melody.[36] But the appeal of this melody must be immediate, and there must be no question of imitation in the D'Alembertian sense, for music cannot paint.[37] By the same token, it is not necessary to have words accompany each musical composition, since the appeal of the sounds produced by the instruments is sufficient.[38] Moreover, melody is quite distinct from declamation—and Chabanon injects this disturbing thought—otherwise we could not have expressive music written to Latin, since we are ignorant of correct Latin prosody.[39] He agrees that music expresses passions, but he advises the musician to forget the "natural outcry" when composing song, for, "how can you make a song out of a cry?" [40] At a rehearsal of *Orphée* Gluck had asked the singer to render the natural accents of sorrow, "l'accent naturel de la douleur." [41] The singer did so well that Gluck was forced to soften the effect of that passage: "The composer had stepped outside the bounds of his art to get closer to nature, but his artistic instinct pushed him back within the pale. As a result the imitation lost in truthfulness, but it gained in musical quality and was better liked." [42] The practical application of this Encyclopedist theory by Gluck revealed to the composer its inherent weakness: music is not an imitation of nature. The composer puts down the sounds he has in his head, and these sounds, as Chabanon states it, are not the representation of an object, but are the object itself.[43] This thought—later repeated by Schopenhauer, "Music does not represent the image of an idea as the other arts, but the idea itself"—is further expanded by Chabanon. The interjection "ah!" for instance, is one of those sounds that takes its meaning from the inflection of the voice; in this manner it may express sorrow, joy, wonder, or other emotions. It is the function of music to melodically accentuate words, so that even those words which normally are bereft of all expression may be given an added vigor by means of music. And here Chabanon agrees with Goudar, Blanchet, and Lacassagne in subscribing to the Lulli-Perrault tradition that music embellishes words. This was also an Encyclopedist theory.[44]

Chabanon admits that since music has become the subject of everyday conversation, newer, finer, and profounder observations have ap-

---

[36] Chabanon, *Eloge*, p. 26; *Observations*, p. 15.
[37] Chabanon, *Eloge*, pp. 25–26; *Observations*, pp. 31, 43.
[38] Chabanon, *Observations*, p. 47.   [39] *Ibid.*, p. 59.   [40] *Ibid.*, p. 64.
[41] *Ibid.*, p. 66.   [42] *Ibid.*   [43] *Ibid.*, pp. 145–146.   [44] *Ibid.*, p. 151.

peared in Paris on that art than Italy produced in its two centuries of
musical history.[45] He agrees with Cahusac that half the beauties of
the art of music depend on adequate performance,[46] he bears with the
Encyclopedia and Gluck in stating that the most beautiful melody is
also the simplest, the freshest, and the most natural,[47] and shares
D'Alembert's belief that a large place must be made for habit in the
criticism of music.[48] Like so many other French critics, Chabanon was
forced to follow the lead of the *Encyclopedia* in spite of himself.

Perhaps the most distinguished author of the century to fall in with
Encyclopedist doctrines of musical criticism was Beaumarchais. In
Tarare, he tried to bring the libretto up to the level of Salieri's music.
As he himself says in his dedication to that composer: "My greatest
claim to merit in this work is to have divined the opera *Tarare* in *Les
Danaïdes* and *Les Horaces.*" But more important than the opera itself
were the few pages of introduction which accompanied the 1787 edition, entitled "To the subscribers of the opera who would like to enjoy
the opera." In this exordium Beaumarchais states that he does not want
to reform the opera, but to renew interest in the spectacle. An interest
which in Paris has flagged because the divers elements that compose
the opera have pulled in different directions and the correct hierarchy
of those elements has not been observed. According to Beaumarchais,
the order of preference should be: first, the poem; secondly, the music,
"which is only a new expression added to the charm of the verse"; and
thirdly, the dance. He then asks himself the question, how did these
ranks become confused so that music became more important than the
poem, and the dance even more interesting than the other two factors?
In Beaumarchais' explanation, the spectator, having tired of trying to
understand the words, turned to the music, which amused him for a
time, but soon gave way to the "evident" pleasures of the dance. What
is the trouble with the contemporary opera? It "stinks of music," as
Gluck had said. Music had ruined the French opera in particular by
engulfing the libretto, both in sound and in content: the words were
inaudible, and their meaning was betrayed. The playwright turned to
the creation of opera because he met the composer Salieri, who fell in
with his views immediately. He was a born poet, says Beaumarchais,

[45] *Ibid.,* Preface, p. vii.   [46] *Ibid.,* pp. 147–151; *see* Cahusac "Exécution."
[47] Chabanon, *Observations,* p. 178.   [48] *Ibid.,* p. 185; *see* Alembert, "Echo."

and since the playwright was something of a musician, they seemed to be destined to write the perfect opera. But this was not enough. If the poet and the composer were in agreement, it was still necessary to win over the singers and the musicians. To the first Beaumarchais said, "pronounce clearly"; to the second, "calm yourselves." Thus, in strict accordance with Encyclopedist demands, each factor of the opera was to coöperate in presenting a finished performance.[49]

[49] Other disciples of the *Encyclopedia* in France and their significant writings were: Jean Blanchet (1724–1778), who consulted Cahusac and Diderot concerning his *Principes philosophiques du chant*, 1756. J. G. Noverre (1729–1810), whose comments regarding the opera in his *Lettres sur les arts imitateurs*, 1807, show him to be a disciple of Cahusac. N. Bricaire de la Dixmérie (c. 1731–1791), shows Diderot announcing Gluck in his *Lettres sur l'état présent de nos spectacles*, 1765. Julie de Lespinasse (1732–1776), the Encyclopedists' admirer. Cf. her *Lettres*, 1773–1776. J. B. Suard (1734–1817), who made propaganda for Gluck in the *Journal de Paris* and in the *Mercure*. Laurent Garcin (c. 1734–1788), *Traité du mélodrame*, 1772, quotes the *Discours préliminaire* of the *Encyclopedia* to support his contention that music must paint, p. 303. J. B. de la Borde (1734–1794), *Essai sur la musique ancienne et moderne*, 1780, cites Diderot's article "Instruments." Pascal Boyer (b. 1743), *Lettre à M. Diderot sur le projet de l'unité de clef dans la musique*, 1767.

CHAPTER XII

POST-ENCYCLOPEDIST CRITICISM
OF MUSIC IN FRANCE

THE MEN WHO MADE the Revolution in France were even more pro-Encyclopedist than their predecessors. Pierre Nougaret (1742–1823) invokes the authority of Rousseau and Diderot for the *raison d'être* of the *opéra-bouffon* in his *De l'art du théâtre en général* (1769).[1] He deplores the fact that neither the *Encyclopedia* nor its Supplement contains an article on the *opéra-bouffon* and suggests that his book will supply this lack.[2] He defines this form of the opera as a spectacle in which everyday realities, and even low scenes of comedy, are to be portrayed. There will be plenty of good music, but the spectator will be more interested in novelty than in the sublime and the beautiful.[3] Dramatic rules are to be observed, however, as closely in this spectacle as in the opera.

The popularity of the *opéra-bouffon* was overshadowing the development of the *tragédie lyrique* in France. Nougaret suggests that in order to save the opera, the *opéra-bouffon* should be joined to it, much as Corneille's tragedies were followed by a light comedy at the *Théâtre Français*. Thus *Castor et Pollux* (Rameau) would be followed by *On ne s'avise jamais de tout* (Sedaine-Monsigny) at the Opéra. He is convinced that this is the only way to save the *grand opéra* in all its refulgence.[4] As we may imagine, Nougaret prefers the *opéra-bouffon* to the *opéra-sérieux*.[5] He holds the *Devin du village* to be a model of *opéra-bouffon*, and Rousseau as the only poet composer that France can boast of.[6]

---

[1] Nougaret, *De l'art du théâtre en général*, I, 85–86.   [2] *Ibid.*, I, 127.
[3] *Ibid.*, pp. 128–129.   [4] *Ibid.*, II, 244–245.
[5] *Ibid.*, pp. 286–289.   [6] *Ibid.*, I, 205, and II, 294.

The revolutionist-to-be as music critic reveals strong Encyclopedist attachments. In *Le Lecteur y mettra le titre* (1777) Mirabeau concurs with the *Encyclopedia* in stating that music must be imitative, that the composer must have a definite object in mind, and that music gets its fullest expression only when it is allied to words.[7] To illustrate his theory concerning the technique of instrumental composition, he gives the scheme for a tone-poem to be called *Télémaque,* in which the *dramatis personae* are Mentor (violoncello) and Telemachus (violin): "By means of sweet and voluptuous sounds the flute will express Calypso's love; her jealousy will be announced by rapid variations." Encyclopedist propaganda had interested everyone in musical criticism; the results were not always happy.

Perhaps the first critic in France successfully to divorce music from words was the distinguished *savant* Lacépède (1756–1825). Yet, in *La Poétique de la musique* (1785) this critic confirms Encyclopedist belief as to the manner in which music may imitate nature: first, by reproducing natural sounds; secondly, by representing Diderot's "cri de l'homme passionné"; and thirdly, by D'Alembert's theory of interpretation, by musically retracing the inspiration that objects may offer.[8] The *Poétique* was to be a definitive rhetoric of the art of musical composition, but the better part of these two volumes is nothing more than a series of hints, most of which are to be found more adequately stated in the articles of the *Encyclopedia*. He asserts, for instance, that the overture must announce the tragedy,[9] musical imitation must always be vague in comparison to the other arts,[10] and so forth. On his own initiative he considers the symphony to be three acts of drama, and he counsels the composer of string quartets to study opera duos and trios. There is one passage in this work that reveals a deep love for the art of music. In it Lacépède tells us that when listening to music, often an extraneous interest will intrude, or the listener may be profoundly moved by some event entirely foreign to the music being played. In any case, each time the listener is exposed to that particular composition, that interest or event will be present to his mind.[11] Lacépède deserves considerable credit for publishing a work in which music is considered

---

[7] Mirabeau, *Le Lecture y mettra le titre,* pp. 65–70.
[8] Lacépède, *La Poetiaue de la musique,* I, 83–84.
[9] *Ibid.,* II. 2.   [10] *Ibid.,* pp. 330.   [11] *Ibid.,* I, 88.

aside from its relations to words. The author succeeds in divorcing instrumental music from words, but not from song.

Framery (1745–1810), the *littérateur-musicien,* who edited for a time the *Journal de Musique,* founded by Mathon de la Cour, in 1764,[12] and attacked Gluck in the *Mercure,*[13] was chosen as coeditor of the section pertaining to music in the *Encyclopédie méthodique.*[14] In the *Discours préliminaire* to this work Framery tells us that he has taken the *Dictionnaire de musique* by Rousseau as a model and that he has liberally drawn from the original *Encyclopedia* as well as from the Supplement all those articles that still commanded attention.[15] This work was not a success. Fétis asserts with justice that the contradictions and confusion that reign in this section of the *Encyclopédie méthodique* render it useless as a reference work.[16] Yet, the idea of renewing the articles on music in the *Encyclopedia* was a good one; Framery proved elsewhere that he was capable of sound musical criticism, and he kept in touch with the new trends. In his "Quelques réflexions sur la musique moderne," an article published in the *Journal de Musique* for May, 1770, when he was a youth of twenty-five, Framery foresaw that the future of music belonged to the Germans. He pointed to Germans such as Gluck, Hasse, Stamitz, and Bach, probably C. P. E. Bach, as masters of the art. He made so bold as to state that Philidor took his rise neither from the French nor from the Italians, but from the Germans who came to study in Italy. Like them, Philidor carried away from that country what the Italians neglected most, the full harmony of church music. Furthermore, he rightly pointed out in this article that the quarrel between French and Italian music really began in the early part of the century, with Raguenet.

It was high time that Encyclopedists' successors performed the necessary lopping off of antiquated material for there were those in France who discarded not only the articles and comments on music in the *Encyclopedia,* but everything else that that work represented. A more implacable enemy of the *Encyclopedia* than the postrevolutionary critic La Harpe (1739–1803) would be hard to find. In his *Cours de lit-*

12 See Carlez, *Framery, littérateur-musicien.*
13 Framery, *Lettre à l'auteur du Mercure,* septembre, 1776.   14 Volume I, 1791.
15 Framery, *Encyclopédie méthodique, discours préliminaire,* pp. vii and xi.
16 Fétis, "Framery," in *Biographie universelle des musiciens.*

térature [17] he places Diderot among the sophists [18] and flays the most highly prized article penned by that *philosophe* for the *Encyclopedia*— "Encyclopédie." [19] As a critic of opera, La Harpe reverts to the standards of Boileau and the late seventeenth-century commentators, considering the opera from the point of view of literature only [20] and labeling that spectacle a voluptuous orgy.[21] With Cahusac he holds that Quinault wrote the ideal type of *tragédie lyrique* and that mythology is the best source for the opera poem. He agrees with Marmontel in advising that the Italian form be given to Quinault's libretti. La Harpe insists that the *tragédie en musique* is an impossible genre.[22] If music is given the upper hand, he says in another connection,[23] then the drama must suffer; if, however, the music is sacrificed to the play, then the play had best be given alone, since tragedy set to music can never be as effective a dramatic performance as straight drama. It was this type of reasoning, literary on the whole, that led La Harpe to condemn Gluck's operatic compositions, which he attacked in the *Journal de Politique et de Littérature* (1777). He admits that Gluck dramatized music, and he composed a *tragédie chantée* as against the old Quinault type of *tragédie déclamée*.[24] But then he makes the unenviable blunder of comparing Du Roullet's libretto based on Racine's *Iphigénie en Aulide* with the original classic, with the intention of pointing out the many weaknesses of the opera.[25] Paradoxically enough, this critic was willing to admit that music was the more important element of the opera.[26] He argues, therefore, that the Italians should serve as models. For La Harpe, Gluck's dramatico-operatic revolution had failed, just as half a century earlier the Encyclopedists considered Rameau's revolution (which gave music the upper hand in the opera) an evil.

As seen through the writings of the critics of music in France, the

---

[17] First edition 1799, *Philosophie*, 1805; 1825 edition used for this work.
[18] La Harpe, *Les Sophistes*, Chapter III, "Diderot," in *Cours de littérature*, Volume XVI.
[19] La Harpe, Vol. XV, *De l'Encyclopédie et de d'Alembert*.
[20] La Harpe, Vol. VI, *De l'opéra dans le siècle de Louis XIV*, Chapter 8.
[21] La Harpe, *Cours de littérature*, XII, chap. 6, Sec. IV, *De l'opéra italien comparé au nôtre*.
[22] *Ibid.*
[23] *Ibid.*, Appendix: "*Observations sur un ouvrage de M. Grétry intitulé Mémoires; ou Essais sur la musique.*"
[24] La Harpe, *De l'opéra*, Vol. XII, chap. 6.
[25] *Ibid.*, Section IV.   [26] La Harpe, *Cours de littérature*, Vol. VI, chap. 8.

opera would seem to have run the following course in that country from 1670 to 1770. Lulli's contemporaries, Boileau, Fénelon, St. Evremond, La Bruyère, and others, considered the composer the creator of the opera. This meant that they took music to be the important feature and praised Lulli at the expense of Quinault. Yet when they came to criticize the opera, it was only Quinault's *poème* that they wrote about. They analyzed the opera as tragedy, censuring the poet's poor verses—from the literary standpoint—and deploring the emphasis on love. When Voltaire rehabilitated Quinault as opera poet, the French reversed the judgment of Boileau, accepted Quinault as a fine poet—again from the literary view—and proceeded to forget Lulli's music in their accounts of the opera. Thus, when Rameau came on the scene, Quinault was considered the creator of opera; all its virtues were attributed to him, and its failings were ascribed to Lulli's inadequate music. This was essentially the position of the Encyclopedists, who lamented the fact that the drama had become so important in the opera. Rameau's efforts they merely tolerated, judging that he had far overshot the mark and had overwhelmed the drama with his music. Therefore they turned to the Italians for musical guidance, in the hope that some composer would appear on the scene who could successfully unite music and text. Gluck realized all their ideals, and he came to France to show how, as he stated, he had "put music in its proper place," that is, as a handmaid of poetry, although in reality music was on a footing more than equal to the drama in his operas. The Encyclopedists were apparently satisfied, but La Harpe, along with Marmontel, Framery, and others, even Grétry, were afraid that Gluck had given too much importance to the drama. Yet they still criticized the opera on dramatic grounds. So with the exception of the Encyclopedists, French critics of opera from the beginning up to the end of the eighteenth century were extremely literary in their aspirations for the opera. Even the Encyclopedists insisted that the successful opera must be based on good drama. Gluck came to Paris to show that they were right, but the upshot of his "revolution" served only to convince once and for all the post-Encyclopedist critics, especially La Harpe, of exactly the contrary: that, after all, music is the most important element of opera. The greatness of the Encyclopedists' victorious revolution lay in making that fact finally acceptable to the French—a fact that one hundred years of polemical writing had failed to establish.[27]

[27] Other writers on music at this time in France were: Olivier de Corancez (d. 1810), a Gluck partisan and a great admirer of the *Encyclopedia* in his *Lettre sur Gluck* (1788) and again in *Jean Jacques Rousseau* (1798). Grétry (1741–1813) considered himself, though on a humbler plane than Gluck, the disciple of the Encyclopedists and did not disdain to take suggestions on musical composition from Diderot. See his *Mémoires* and the *Réflexions d'un solitaire*. For his position as regards Gluck see his *De la vérité* (1801), II, 18ff. Momigny (1762–1838), the famous theoretician and editor of Volume II of the musical section of the *Encyclopédie méthodique* (1818). His criticism of music in that work already reveals a departure from the cautious reserve of the eighteenth century, and plunges into the hopeless gibberish of the nineteenth-century impressionists. In analyzing, for instance, the first movement of Haydn's D major Symphony, he says: "Elle a pour motif *ré, ré, ré, la,* et pour réponse, *ré, ut♯, ut♯, ut♯,* et ce motif semble dire: Devant les dieux prosternons-nous," II, 408.

CHAPTER XIII

CONCLUSION

FEW WORKS HAVE BEEN as roundly abused as the music articles in the *Encyclopedia*. Voltaire misquoted Cahusac's article "Expression," in his *Questions sur l'Encyclopédie* (1770).[1] Lefebure considered D'Alembert a traitor to Rameau's theories and took him to task for his errors in harmony in the *Encyclopedia* articles, as well as in the *Eléments*.[2] Berlioz delivered a scathing condemnation of the *philosophes'* musical criticism, thereby setting the entire nineteenth century at loggerheads with the Encyclopedist program.[3] René de Récy tried to view the Encyclopedists' position with regard to Rameau in a dispassionate manner, but his effort bore no fruit.[4] The close of the nineteenth century saw the critic Adolphe Jullien apparently triumphing over the editor Tourneux, in their differences regarding Diderot's musical criticism.[5]

[1] Voltaire quoted Cahusac as saying: "En général la musique vocale de Lulli n'est autre, on le répète, que le pur récitatif, et n'a par elle-même aucune expression du sentiment que les paroles de Quinault ont peint." Voltaire, *Questions sur l'Encyclopédie*, II, 247. The Encyclopedist had said: "En général la musique vocale de Lulli, autre, on le répète, que le pur récitatif, n'a par elle-même aucune expression etc." A typical example of Voltaire's journalistic negligence, all the more striking when we remember that it was he who contradicted Boileau's judgment of Quinault, and that only four pages earlier in the same work he renewed his attack on Boileau, saying: "C'était au contraire Quinault qui réchauffait Lulli." Voltaire, *Questions sur l'Encyclopédie*, II, 243.

[2] Lefebure, *Bévues, erreurs . . .* , p. 35.

[3] "O Philosophes, prodigieux bouffons! Oh! les bons hommes, les dignes hommes que les hommes d'esprit de ce siècle philosophique, écrivant sur l'art musical sans en avoir le moindre sentiment, sans en posséder les notions premières, sans savoir en quoi il consiste!" Berlioz, *Les Grotesques de la musique*, 1859, p. 247.

[4] The author showed how Rameau refused to write the articles on music for the *Encyclopedia*, and then antagonized the Encyclopedists by publishing his *Erreurs*. Récy added that Rameau's greatest mistake was his attempt to prove his harmonic theory mathematically: "*Le Traité de l'harmonie* avait émancipé la musique; le *Nouveau Système théorique* la fit retomber sous la tutelle des physiciens et des algébristes." Récy, "Rameau et les Encyclopédistes."

[5] The editor, with Assézat, of Diderot's works, sharply reprimanded the critic for

With the turn of the present century more and more critics took an interest in the Encyclopedists' musical criticism, and some began to consider the *Encyclopedia* seriously. J. G. Prod'homme cited Cahusac's article "Chanteur" in the preface to his study of the celebrated eighteenth-century singer Jélyotte.[6] Eugen Hirschberg wrote a doctoral dissertation on *Die Encyklopädisten und die französische Oper im 18. Jahrhundert* (1903). Romain Rolland devoted an entire chapter of his *Musiciens d'autrefois* (1908) to the Encyclopedists' writings on music, in which for the first time an authoritative music critic took up the defence of the *Encyclopedia*.[7] But on the whole, music critics remained obdurate. F. Hellouin, in his *Essai de critique de la critique musicale* (1906), admitted the vast influence of the *Encyclopedia* upon the music of the eighteenth century, but like Berlioz, he taxed the *philosophes* with ignorance and ineptitude, and like Hirschberg, he considered their effect to be nefarious in French musical history. The eminent harpsichordist Mme Wanda Landowska agreed with Hellouin in her book entitled *Les Allemands et la musique française au dix-huitième siècle* (1911).[8] Mme Landowska found, for example, that German music was practically unknown in France at this time, thanks to the tyrannous *Encyclopedia,* whose contributors would have found it "trop savante." She scored Encyclopedists for preferring the Italians to the French, quoting Rousseau as the oracle or high priest of this villainy. The Encyclopedists exaggerated everything, threw more smoke than light on French music, and ridiculed a form of the art that had inspired the great Bach himself.[9]

---

basing all his remarks concerning Diderot and music upon the *Neveu de Rameau* in *La Musique et les philosophes au dix-huitième siècle.* Diderot, *Bijoux indiscrets,* IV, 174*n.* Whereupon Jullien republished his essay as Part III of his book entitled *La Ville et la cour au dix-huitième siècle,* and added an Appendix on *Diderot musicien,* 1881, in which he confirms his opinion of eight years standing, that *Le Neveu de Rameau* was Diderot's best work on music: "cette admirable satire de mœurs, dans laquelle il faudra toujours aller chercher son dernier mot sur la musique." Jullien, *Diderot musicien,* p. 200.

[6] Prod'homme, "Pierre de Jélyotte."

[7] Earlier still Rolland had defended the Encyclopedists in his article on "Gluck."

[8] See also her *Musique ancienne, le mépris pour les anciens . . .* in which she quotes the *Encyclopedia* often.

[9] Landowska, *Les Allemands et la musique francaise,* pp. 14–16. German music was known in France at this time. Telemann made an eight-month stay in 1737, during which, says Riemann, he was "entouré comme un homme célèbre." He was known in France long before his arrival, as there were numerous editions of his instrumental music printed in Paris. The reforms of the Mannheim school were immediately accepted in France.

In our own day the *Encyclopédie du conservatoire* gives high praise to D'Alembert's *Eléments*. The scholar, Lucien Chevaillier, presents Rameau's theory as seen by D'Alembert in the *Eléments*.[10] The collective work *La Musique française du moyen âge à la Révolution* (1934), edited by MM. Gastoué, Leroquais, Pirro, Expert, and Prunières, gives full credit to the vulgarizing and clarifying influence of D'Alembert's *Eléments*.[11] M. Trahard speaks with praise of Diderot's *Leçons de clavecin,* in his *Les Maîtres de la sensibilité française* (1933),[12] but says little of his musical criticism. He considers Rousseau a link between Rameau and Gluck, but incorrectly asserts that Rousseau maltreated Rameau in the articles "Accord," "Accompagnement," and "Chiffrer." [13] Thus, the tendency to brush aside as negligible Encyclopedist criticism of music has not altogether disappeared.

The charge most frequently made against these men was that they did not know music. André Billy, Diderot's biographer, is of the opinion that the editor-in-chief's musical instruction was limited to dilatory conversations with Blainville, Philidor, and Rameau.[14] According to Diderot's own testimony, he first began the systematic study of music on January 18, 1751.[15] At this time Diderot was thirty-eight and had already published the *Principes généraux d'acoustique* (1748), so that we must understand him to mean that he began at that date to study music as an art, being already conversant with its scientific aspect. One of his earliest published works, the *Cinq mémoires sur différents sujets de mathématiques* (1748), contains three monographs on music con-

The *Concerts spirituels* performed a Stamitz symphony, April 12, 1751, and the German master had a successful season in Paris, 1754–1755. Many disciples of the Mannheim group took up permanent abode in Paris. Of these Anton Filtz, Schobert, and Eckardt received high praise at the hands of Encyclopedists. Consult Grimm, ed., *Correspondance littéraire,* VII, 422; and Diderot, XII, 180, 289, 302, 321, 328; XIX, 266. See also Riemann's *Dictionnaire* under these composers' names.

[10] *Encyclopédie du Conservatoire,* I, 546–548, Part II, *Esthétique.*

[11] Seventeenth and eighteenth centuries by Prunières.

[12] "Elles sont la plus familière et la meilleure initiation à l'harmonie classique que nous possédons." Trahard, *Les Maîtres de la sensibilité* . . . , II, 248.

[13] *Ibid.,* III, 175–193. In the article "Accompagnement" Rousseau praises Rameau's new method of accompaniment, the *basse fondamentale,* and the composer's method of scoring. In "Accord" he follows Rameau's lead. In "Chiffrer" Rousseau sets forth Rameau's method of scoring accompanying chords, and states that of all systems Rameau's is the best; that it was abandoned not because of lack of merit, but "Elle était nouvelle, elle était proposée par un homme supérieur en génie à tous ses rivaux: voilà sa condamnation."

[14] Billy, *Diderot,* p. 184.   [15] Diderot, I, 373.

sidered scientifically. We know that Diderot gained his earliest renown as a mathematician. It is therefore an exceedingly interesting commentary on his musical leanings that even as a mathematician his preponderant interest in that science was of a musical nature.[16] Thus, equipped with a solid knowledge of the theories and experiments of his day on musical subjects,[17] Diderot set out to learn at a relatively late date the art and practice of music. He tells us that he had a good ear [18] and a good voice.[19] With these excellent prerequisites, he went to learn composition from Rameau, Philidor, and Blainville.[20] We recall that the Abbé Raynal considered Diderot capable of clarifying Rameau's theories [21] and that Collé, who hated Diderot, admitted that the Encyclopedist had rewritten Poinsinet's book to Philidor's opera *Ernelinde*.[22] It is not likely that either of these composers would have allowed Diderot to tamper with their works if he had been ignorant of music. Moreover, we have the testimony of composers such as Duni, Grétry, and Philidor and of theoreticians and critics such as Burney, La Borde, Bemetzrieder, Boyer, and Cahusac to the effect that Diderot was accepted as an authority on matters musical.[23]

Rousseau has been the most violently attacked of all the contributors of articles on music to the *Encyclopedia,* mainly, perhaps, because he

[16] See above, chap. viii, for the Abbé Raynal's criticism of this work.

[17] See Appendix B for complete list of writings on music and acoustics consulted by the Encyclopedists.

[18] Diderot, II, 333.   [19] *Ibid.,* XIX, 428.   [20] *Ibid.,* XII, 525.

[21] Grimm, ed., *Correspondance littéraire,* I, 202.

[22] Collé, *Journal et mémoires, 1748–1772,* III, 172–173.

[23] The composer Duni (1709–1775) wrote French operas at the court of Parma, came to Paris in 1757 and helped establish the *opéra-comique,* largely through Diderot's influence. Anton Bemetzrieder (1743–1817), an obscure professor and theoretician, came to Paris in 1770, where he enjoyed a moderate vogue, thanks to Diderot's rehandling of his theories. See Grétry's *Mémoires* concerning this composer's change of an entire aria from *Zémir et Azor* under Diderot's direction, I, 225–226, and for his high opinion of Diderot, II, 134, III, 377–378. Also his "Réflexions d'un solitaire," where he recalls that he extracted a *roulade* to suit Diderot. *Mercure de France,* nov.–déc., 1913, pp. 280–285.

Cahusac expressed his esteem for Diderot's musical authority in his *Traité de la danse,* foreword, p. xi. La Borde looks upon Diderot as a writer on music of considerable importance in his *Essai sur la musique ancienne et moderne,* III, 615–617. In these three pages La Borde upholds Diderot's theory of musical appreciation as being derived from the "perceptions des rapports," examines the *philosophe's Principes d'acoustique* and praises him for his attacks on the metronome of the period.

The self-styled "ci-devant maître de chapelle," Boyer, openly sought the Encyclopedist's support in his quarrel with Lacassagne over the single-clef idea. Boyer, *Lettre à M. Diderot sur le projet de l'unité de clef dans la musique.*

was the chief authority on music in that work, extravagantly denied the
possibility of creating French opera, and maintained that he himself
was a composer. But it is not always safe to take Rousseau as the oracle
of Encyclopedist precepts.[24] Often, indeed, his ideas run directly counter
to majority Encyclopedist opinion. Diderot regarded music as Rousseau's major interest and therefore confided the section on music to
his care. Rousseau used this confidence to develop many ideas peculiar
to himself. In any case, writers from Rameau down to Adam[25] and
Trahard[26] did not fail to point out the obvious faults in Rousseau's
articles and to hold these up as a reflection on the *Encyclopedia*—where
in many cases the errors already stood corrected in other articles of the
Encyclopedia by D'Alembert, Grimm, and others—and as a proof of
his musical ignorance.[27] If Rousseau was as ignorant of music as his
articles show, they argue, then he could not have composed *Le Devin
du village, Pygmalion,* and the group of songs known as *Les Consolations des misères de ma vie.*

There is no need to trace the various attributions of the *Devin du
village.* It is sufficient to say that more books and pamphlets have appeared concerning the authorship of this little forty-minute operetta
than of any other composition of major importance. Here are the facts
according to Rousseau. The desire to give the French an Italian-type
opera-buffa gave him the idea for the *Devin,* in 1752. Within three
weeks the work was ready for presentation. This first draft Rousseau
claims to be entirely his own.[28] For a later performance Rousseau admits that three small parts belonged to Collé, Cahusac, and D'Holbach,
respectively.[29] Since all three are in the *divertissement,* the essential
portions of the opera remained unchanged. Then the news got about
that Rousseau had plagiarized other works in creating his opera. No
composer's name was mentioned at that time, nor has it ever been

---

[24] Rolland suggests this in his *Musiciens d'autrefois,* p. 207*n.*

[25] Adam, *Souvenirs d'un musicien* (pp. 208–209). He says that Rousseau's articles
"ne donne presque jamais que ses idées particulières," and that the articles "Plain-chant"
and "Contre-point" "fourmillent d'erreurs." He does acknowledge that the articles on
aesthetics contain "des pensées élevées et aperçus ingénieux."

[26] Trahard, in *Les Maîtres de la sensibilité française,* states that Rousseau made mistakes
in judgment concerning polyphony, sonata form, the string quartet, etc. III, 193.

[27] "Il [Rousseau] s'est cru un génie musical, et il n'a eu que des intuitions." *Ibid.,* III,
193.

[28] Rousseau, *Œuvres,* V, 578–579.   [29] Rousseau, *Œuvres,* VI, 346, note 1.

established that such a person existed. The simple truth is that until it can definitely be shown that Rousseau did not compose the *Devin,* as well as *Les Muses galantes, Pygmalion,* and other works, it is safe to accept his own argument as final.[30]

Rousseau's correspondence teems with proof of his knowledge of music. In 1732, when visiting the Abbé Blanchard, he sang a duo with Duroncel,[31] and the Abbé found that the young Rousseau had a marvelous talent for composition.[32] In 1735 he told his father that he intends to practice music, which he claims he knew fairly well.[33] An observer said that Rousseau's new system of notation showed "a man well-versed in the theory of music."[34] When Blainville published his *Nouveau Mode de musique* (1751), Rousseau wrote a letter of criticism to the *Mercure* in which he shows that he perfectly understood the theoretician's work.[35] Blainville answered this letter in the *Mercure* for November, 1751, praising Rousseau's criticism.[36] Boswell asked

[30] Rousseau states that his *Dictionnaire* was sufficient proof of his knowledge of music. V, 584, and VI, 217. He argues that the beauties of the *Devin* "sont celles qu'inspirent le goût et la sensibilité. . . . Il n'y a rien dans le *Devin du village* qui passe, quant à la partie scientifique, les principes élémentaires de composition," VI, 220; that Colette in the *Devin* and Julie in *La Nouvelle Héloise* are sisters, VI, 344; and that all his music resembles the *Devin* in that it has a pastoral character, VI, 346.

Toth claims that Rousseau evolved the *Devin* from Duclos' *Les Caractères de la folie; Women and Rococo in France,* pp. 222 and 231. This is interesting in view of the fact that Duclos undertook to have the work presented at court anonymously. Rousseau, V, 579. Yet it was most probably in reference to this aid that Rousseau later said in his dedication to Duclos that the *Devin* "sans vous n'eût point vu le jour."

Istel, *Jean Jacques Rousseau als Komponist seiner lyrischen Scene Pygmalion,* continuing his studies on that subject in "La Partition originale du Pygmalion de J. J. Rousseau," in the *Annales de la Société Jean Jacques Rousseau,* Vol. 1 (1905), 141–172, gave rise to a heated controversy in a succeeding number of that publication: "La Question du Pygmalion de Berlin," "Objections de M. Jansen, M. Malherbe, et repliques de M. Istel," III (1907), 119–155.

[31] "Fameux haute-contre de l'ancien opéra de Lyon," Rousseau, *Correspondance générale, A Mme Warens,* 29 juin, 1732, I, 17.

[32] *Ibid.,* I, 17.   [33] *Ibid., A son père,* I, 30.

[34] *Ibid.,* I, 183n. Probably the Abbé Desfontaines, *Observations sur les écrits modernes,* XXXI, Lettre 462, 1743.

[35] I, 432: ". . . c'est notre ancien mode plagal qui subsiste encore dans le plain-chant. C'est proprement un mode mineur dont le diapason se prendrait . . . d'une dominante à son octave en passant par la tonique." *Ibid.,* II, 2. Compare Fétis: "Ce mode n'était que le plagal du troisième ton du plain-chant ou, si l'on veut, le mode mineur de *la,* dont il avait banni la note sensible, et qu'il faisait procéder de la dominante à la tonique." *Biographie universelle des musiciens.*

[36] *Ibid.,* II, 7: "Je devais un remerciement à M. Rousseau de la lettre délicate et sensée qu'il a bien voulu publier, etc."

Rousseau for musical guidance.[37] The theoretician, Ballière, sent Rousseau a copy of his *Théorie de la musique,* "as a mark of my sincere admiration for your talents and virtues." [38] When Rousseau answered this letter, Ballière wrote that it would have been a great advantage for his theory if he could have published Rousseau's observations.[39] When the much-discussed *Dictionnaire de musique* appeared (1767–1768), even Rousseau's enemies praised it, and Lalande wrote a flattering recension for the *Journal des Savants.*[40] English and Dutch translations of the work appeared almost immediately, 1770 and 1769, respectively. In Germany, Korner recommended it to Schiller. Grossly treated by later compilers of music-lexicons, the unhappy *Dictionnaire* was pillaged by Framery, Guinguené, and Castil-Blaze, the latter copying no less than three hundred and forty-two articles from it as late as 1821. Finally, Fétis, in his *Biographie universelle des musiciens* (1860), praised Rousseau's dictionary.[41]

Still other contemporaries of Rousseau offered convincing proof of his musical learning and talent. Marmontel, in his *Mémoires d'un père,* recalls that as a young man he heard Rousseau play and sing airs from his opera.[42] The comedian De Marignan gave a brilliant and convincing defense of Jean Jacques as composer of the *Devin* and claimed a large share for Rousseau in the operatic revolution.[43] Gluck was of the same opinion in his *Dédicace d'Orphée* (1774) and stated that Rousseau, had he devoted his life to music, would very likely have reformed the French opera.[44] Corancez, who introduced Gluck to Rousseau, reports that the composer was highly pleased by a remark the *philosophe* made regarding the characterization of Pâris and Hélène in the opera of that name. Here is Rousseau's criticism.

---

[37] *Ibid.,* XII, 189.   [38] *Ibid.,* XII, 261.

[39] *Ballière à Rousseau,* 5 mars, 1767, XVI, 350: ". . . je me serais procuré des lecteurs au moyen de votre autorité qui est d'un grand poids en fait de musique."

[40] *Ibid., A. M. Lalande,* mars, 1768, XVIII, 156–157.

[41] See Jansen, *Jean Jacques Rousseau als Musiker,* pp. 288–291.

[42] Marmontel, *Mémoires,* I, 328: "Il travaillait alors [1752] à la musique du *Devin du village,* et il nous chantait au clavecin les airs qu'il avait composés. Nous en étions charmés."

[43] De Marignan, *Eclaircissements donnés à l'auteur du Journal Encyclopédique sur la musique du Devin du village,* p. 30: ". . . il ne faut que lire son *Dictionnaire,* entendre la musique qu'on fait aujourd'hui, et la comparer avec celle qu'on faisait autrefois, pour juger de la révolution favorable qu'il a opérée dans cet art."

[44] Gluck, *Lettre au Mercure de France sur la musique,* février, 1773. Here the composer praises Rousseau's analysis of the *monologue d'Armide,* from Lulli's opera by the same name.

M. Gluck profusely imbued the role of Pâris with all the brilliance and subtlety that music is capable of portraying. Hélène's rôle, on the other hand, is characterized by a certain classical austerity which never leaves her, even when she is declaring her passion for Pâris.

When Corancez told Gluck this, the composer answered: "It would please me very much to have a number of spectators study my work in this spirit."[45] Gluck's answer reveals that Rousseau was capable of musical criticism of the finest grain. How many critics or musicians or even composers were aware of this characterization by means of music in Gluck's operas? And yet the rank amateur Rousseau saw immediately what the world of criticism has taken years to realize.

Rousseau's ability as a composer is again attested in Corancez' pamphlet *J. J. Rousseau,* also taken from articles in the *Journal de Paris.* In it he tells us that Rousseau composed extempore music to his verses. The vitriolic critic Ange Goudar, whom we have seen ridiculing classical revivals in art and operatic reform movements in general, extolled Rousseau's musical learning.[46] The *Mercure* gave an appraisal of Rousseau as theoretician and musician in December, 1778. Even the inimical *Journal de Trévoux,* as we have noted,[47] praised the articles on music by Rousseau in the *Encyclopedia,* and Fréron, the infamous anti-Encyclopedist, spoke of Rousseau's theoretical achievements in the *Année Littéraire.*[48] A recent "table of the works owned, read, or mentioned by Rousseau" lists 664 bibliographical items, of which at least 75 have some specific bearing on various aspects of music. Here we find treatises on acoustics, aesthetics, theory, alongside compositions, criticism, and original sketches. The ancient authors on music are heavily represented, from Bacchius back to Aristoxenus, and medieval scholars such as Jehan de Meuris and Boethius, find their places among the more modern theoreticians Kircher, Mersenne, Rameau, and Tartini.[49] This constant and universal preoccupation with musical practice and

---

[45] *Journal de Paris,* 18 août, 1788.

[46] Ange Goudar, *Le Brigandage de la musique italienne,* pp. 102–103: "M. Jean Jacques Rousseau est aussi un grand théoricien en musique; peut-être n'est-il pas meilleur musicien, mais il a tout ce qu'il faut pour l'être; non seulement il connaît quelques parties, mais encore toutes les parties de cet art, et les embrasse dans toute leur étendue."

[47] See above, chap. viii, note 22.   [48] Fréron, *Année Littéraire,* II, 283.

[49] Marguerite Richebourg, "La Bibliothèque de Jean Jacques Rousseau," II, *Annales de la société J. J. Rousseau,* XXI (1932), 199–250; Table des ouvrages possédés, lus ou mentionnés par Rousseau.

thought revealed in a catalogue of Rousseau's library offers another incontrovertible document testifying to the Encyclopedist's deep love of the art, and furnishes a clue to his musical competency.

But it remained for Julien Tiersot, the modern critic of music, to give the final word on Rousseau's knowledge of music. In a batch of manuscripts known as *Leçons de musique de J. J. Rousseau* Tiersot found that some of the musical examples show a distinct resemblance to the air *Si les galants de la ville,* from the *Devin du village.*[50] These *Leçons,* Tiersot tells us, were mainly a rehash of Rameau's theories and are indicative of the monumental perseverance on the part of the Encyclopedist to master the use of the *basse fondamentale.* Rousseau meticulously follows Rameau's lead, using the *basse fondamentale* even in the examples of measure and rhythm. The upshot of this assiduous labor was, according to Tiersot, that Rousseau carried these ideas farther than had Rameau himself. As a whole, they form the finest criticism and the severest censure of the practice of Rameau's method. Tiersot concludes:

His *Leçons* are essentially the work of a self-taught student. The application to the subject attested in these lessons, however, gives the lie to those who would never see in Rousseau anything more than a simple amateur who was ignorant of the rules of the art because he never made a serious study of them. On the contrary, if it is true that in the practice of writing music Rousseau lacked the guidance of a competent teacher, it is nonetheless certain that no one has made a more profound study of the theory and principles of the art than he did.[51]

This conclusive evidence, submitted by a man whose authority should be unquestioned, would seem sufficient to banish all doubt regarding Rousseau's powers as a composer, theoretician, and critic. Moreover, Tiersot claims, in his *J. J. Rousseau musicien* (1912), that if Rousseau had devoted his life to music, he would have accomplished for the opera what Gluck did.[52] Many years earlier Jansen came forward in Germany with high praise for Rousseau's grasp of musical theory (1884), stating at that time that "all his theoretical writings opened up new vistas when they appeared and offer even now a storehouse of instruction." [53] However, his claims were not taken seriously by the

---

[50] Tiersot, *Leçons de musique de J. J. Rosseau,* "Article III, première page du MS."
[51] *Ibid.,* p. 267. [52] *Ibid.,* p. 212. [53] Jansen, *Jean Jacques Rousseau als Musiker,* p. 2.

French, and it was not until well into the present century, on the occasion of Rousseau's bicentenary, that authoritative musical scholars took up Rousseau's defense. Besides Tiersot, M. Paul Marie Masson admitted, in 1912, that the Encyclopedist knew music "suffisamment." [54]

The remaining contributors on music have not fared as badly as Diderot and Rousseau. On the whole, they have not been received as badly by scholars as the editor and the so-called musical oracle of the *Encyclopedia*. D'Alembert's rehandling of Rameau's theories, in the *Eléments*, served to establish his reputation. He also was frequently appointed by the *Académie des Sciences* to examine and report on works of a theoretical nature, such as Rameau's *Démonstration du principe* . . . ,[55] and Lacassagne's *Traité général des éléments du chant*.[56] Grimm left a mine of musical criticism in the *Correspondance littéraire* [57] and marveled at the precocity of the young Mozart when that genius was but seven years of age.[58] Cahusac, concerning whom a biography is sadly lacking, was the author of the *Traité de la danse,* which contains much good musical criticism, and wrote libretti for Rameau.[59] Marmontel collaborated with Piccini in that composer's strife with Gluck.[60] In a sense, these men have been considered professionally interested in one or more aspects of the opera or of music in general, and as such they have not had to suffer the harsh fate of their more illustrious collaborators.

The ideal critic of music is, after all, an amateur. These amateur critics, Romain Rolland said of the Encyclopedists, formed interesting and important judgments on music.

Besides, even if they were not particularly qualified in the field of music, the sincere judgment of such intelligent and artistic men would always have to be taken into account. If they are not given a hearing, then whom shall we listen to? It would be a joke if music rejected the opinions of anyone who was not a professional musician.[61]

[54] Masson, "Les Idées de Rousseau sur la musique."
[55] *Extrait des registres de l'Académie Royale des Sciences du 10 décembre, 1749.*
[56] *Ibid., 9 juillet, 1766.* The *secrétaire perpétuel* shared the appointment with D'Alembert.
[57] See Kretzschmar, *Die Correspondance littéraire als Musikgeschichtliche Quelle.*
[58] Grimm, ed., *Correspondance Littéraire,* V, 410.
[59] Principally, the *Fête de l'hymen et de l'amour,* 1748, *Naïs,* 1749, *Zaïs,* 1748, and *Zoroastre,* 1749.
[60] Marmontel wrote the libretti for *Roland,* 1778, *Atys,* 1780, *Didon,* 1783, and *Pénélope,* 1785. He also wrote the books for Grétry's famous operas, *Le Huron,* 1768, *Lucile,* 1769, *Sylvain,* 1771, *L'Ami de la maison,* 1773, *Zémir et Azor,* 1773.
[61] Rolland, *Musiciens d'autrefois,* p. 210.

And the one incontrovertible fact is that these men exercised a tremendous influence upon the music of their time. Hellouin bitterly cedes this point in his *Essai de critique de la critique musicale.*

We can truthfully say that, given the number of documents accumulated in these circumstances (the Bouffons' War, the Gluck affair, etc.) and given the relative value and the influence exerted by these documents, only then was a critical method inaugurated that could deal with the material of the art of music. They formed the first school of musical criticism. I am speaking here of the appearance upon the scene and of the action of those *philosophes* known as Encyclopedists, especially D'Alembert, Rousseau, Diderot, and Grimm.[62]

In combating Rolland's defense of the Encyclopedists, as expressed in the article "Gluck" (1904), Hellouin devotes four pages to a superficial study of the four main Encyclopedists and concludes that they were all ignorant of the art and science of music. Moreover, he claims that whenever they judged sanely, there was an accomplished musician at their side.[63] However, Hellouin offers no proof of these statements. He accuses the Encyclopedists of treachery in their relations with Rameau, stating that before the arrival of the Bouffons the *philosophes* openly defended Rameau against the Lullistes.[64] Rameau's refusal to join the *Encyclopedia* forfeited the patronage of the *Correspondance littéraire,* as well as that of the Encyclopedists.[65] Rousseau's articles drew Rameau's fire, and the rift between them became public.[66] Then the Encyclopedists began their campaign of hate against Rameau and completely wrecked his reputation.[67] This is the first count upon which Hellouin bases his condemnation of Encyclopedist musical criticism.

Gluck, according to this critic, was a schemer who knew how to solicit Encyclopedist patronage. Having become familiar with their doctrines abroad, the composer came to Paris fully prepared to realize their program.[68] This accounts, Hellouin continues, for the Encyclopedists' assiduous propaganda in his behalf:

In short, we are not afraid to admit that Gluck was the outcome of Encyclopedist thought, and that will more easily explain why the personnel on the staff of the *Encyclopedia* defended him with all the stubbornness they were capable of mustering.[69]

---

[62] Hellouin, *Essai de critique de la critique musicale,* p. 35.
[63] *Ibid.,* pp. 54–55.   [64] *Ibid.,* p. 39.   [65] *Ibid.,* pp. 40–41.
[66] *Ibid.,* pp. 44–45.   [67] *Ibid.,* pp. 46, 57.   [68] *Ibid.,* p. 46.
[69] *Ibid.,* p. 47.

The latter part of this remark is a gross overstatement. Diderot mentions Gluck's name only once in his entire writings, and that in a list of six or seven composers taken at random. D'Alembert says nothing in defense of Gluck; as a matter of fact, he is reported to have said that there was too much noise (*tintamarre*) in Gluck's *Iphigénie*.[70] Rousseau wrote but one note of appreciation to the great composer and the *Fragments d'observations sur l'Alceste italien de M. le Chevalier Gluck*, then quarreled with him. And the article concerning Gluck in the *Correspondance littéraire* was not written by Grimm, who was absent.

Hellouin admits that in supporting Gluck the *philosophes* contributed to an amelioration of the opera, but in so doing they killed French musical tradition, by diverting it from its normal channel of development.

By acclaiming Gluck as victor they undoubtedly contributed to a certain amelioration of the lyrical stage. On the other hand, by refusing to understand Rameau further and in making him a victim, they forced the French school of music off the tracks that tradition had indicated. Notice, too, that they did not desire the reorganization of the French school, but its destruction and the substitution of another. For this reason alone French composers ought to bear a grudge against them. If they pushed us toward progress, they nonetheless forced us at the same time toward a foreign manner.[71]

And this is the second reason for denouncing Encyclopedist influence.

The third and fourth charges are less important, even ridiculous. Hellouin blames the Encyclopedists in the one, for having "created a factitious atmosphere over all Europe, in which Italian singers could easily thrive," [72] and in the other, for having encouraged the development of *opéra-comique* in France. He objects to the latter because it is not French, but Italian. Thus, French musical genius was made imitative by the Encyclopedists. What is more, they caused the French opera to turn into an *opéra-comique sérieux*.[73] In fine, the Encyclopedists

were men who, viewed in a general way, offered the supreme quality of nourishing a deep faith in perfectibility. Looked at in this light, they are men of good will. But exercising as they did a veritable dictatorship of opinion, they unfortunately wanted to extend their sway to the field of

---

[70] Cf. Vicomte d'Haussonville, *Le Salon de Mme Necker*, 1882, I, 180.
[71] Hellouin, *op. cit.*, pp. 63–64. [72] *Ibid.*, p. 65. [73] *Ibid.*, p. 66.

music as well. As a result of their musical incompetence, their effect upon music was nefarious. . . .

There it is, then, the action of these Encyclopedists who had the audacity to set themselves up as critics of music. From the purely technical point of view, their action was essentially a reaction, whose unfortunate effects were indefinitely prolonged. They set up a resistance to the rational musical evolution of all of Europe, and inflicted upon it a cruel delay.[74]

Hellouin's indictment of the Encyclopedists, though completely lacking in scholarly method, establishes that group as an important factor in the history of music. His conclusions, however, cannot be accepted in the light of the evidence offered in these chapters.

In reviewing the century of musical criticism with which this work has been chiefly concerned, we may say that the Encyclopedists were the stanchest representatives of French operatic traditions, traditions which they kept alive more effectively than did the French composers. The three chief tenets set up by the late seventeenth-century critics, namely, that the passion love was the most suitable subject for operatic treatment, that the opera must constantly be dealing with scenes exploring emotional conflicts, and that the *merveilleux* was the opera's most important adjunct, were all subscribed to by the Encyclopedists. On the other hand, the classical critics' contention—Perrault excepted— that the opera was essentially a literary genre which was implausible was transformed by the Encyclopedists to read that the opera was a conglomerate art composed of music, poetry, dance, and allied arts in equal parts and no more implausible than tragedy. The Encyclopedists also adopted and furthered the theories of the early eighteenth-century aestheticians (except Chastellux); namely, that music must imitate nature, that music must paint sentiments, and that music is enhanced declamation. To these six concepts that formed the basis of French musical tradition the *philosophes* remained faithful in their music articles for the *Encyclopedia*. The almost perfect cohesion of the Encyclopedist camp during the Bouffons' Quarrel must also be noted, the only musical quarrel in which they took part, wherein these men contended that the Italians offered a source of rejuvenation for the local opera; in their universal appreciation of Lulli's and Rameau's works; in their attempts to offset Rameau's claims for his theory of music as science, wherein they also

---

[74] *Ibid.*, pp. 66–67.

showed that melody in no way can be said to derive from harmony; and, lastly, in their drive for the reform opera.

The Encyclopedists propagated what was useful and sound in Rameau's harmonic theories and prepared the way for Gluck. Upon these two counts must rest their claim to achievement in the field of music. Otherwise stated, they favored what was best at home—musicology and musical criticism—and taught the French to appreciate the masterpieces of musical composition that were being created abroad, without regard for national barriers or prejudices. None of these men was an eminent musician. Nonetheless they all wrote concerning music, they were all interested in the advancement of this art, and their criticism did not fail to have its desired effect. The Encyclopedists established musical criticism as a literary endeavor and at the same time indicated the road music was to follow. In respect to the opera, at least, they were, as later events in that branch of music proved, most successful music critics. They firmly established the salient principles of music drama for Gluck, Berlioz, and Wagner.

APPENDICES

APPENDIX A

INDEX OF ARTICLES ON MUSIC IN THE *ENCYCLOPEDIA*

For the sake of abbreviation, only the first initial of the more frequent contributors is given; thus Rousseau is designated by R, Diderot by D, Cahusac by C, D'Alembert by A, and the Chevalier de Jaucourt by J. The articles signed Brossard were taken from his *Dictionnaire de musique*. Louis Jacques Goussier, (1722–1799) was called in by D'Alembert for the mechanical and technical aspects of musical instruments. He was later associated with the *Encyclopédie méthodique,* section *Arts et métiers.*—Michaud, *Biographie universelle.*

VOLUME I

Abrégé, 36 (D)
Accolade, 73 (R)
Accompagnateur, Accompagnement, 74 (R)
Accord, 78 (R)
Accord de l'orgue, 79 (D)
Accorder, 80 (R)
Accordoir, 80 (D)
Acoustique, 111 (A)
Adagio, 125 (R)
Aigu, 198 (R)
Aines, Demi-aines, 224 (D)
Air, 237 (R)
Air caracterisé, 754 (J)
Allegro, 281 (R)
Alleluia, 281 (Abbé Mallet)
Allemande, 282 (R)
Ambitus, 321 (R)
Ambrosien, 326 (D)
Ame en Lutherie, iii (D)
Amour, galanterie, 754 (J)
Anche, 439 (D)
Andante, 446 (R)
Angélique, 460 (D)
Antiphonie, 512 (R)
Apotome, 540 (R & A)
Archet, 611 (D)
Archiluth, 615 (D)

Ariette, 651 (R)
Arpège, 701 (R)
Arsis, 713 (R)
Atabale, 796 (D)

VOLUME II

B, 2 (R)
Bagues, 13 (D)
Baguettes à tambour, 14 (D)
Baguettes de tambourin, 14 (D)
Baguettes de tymballes, 14 (D)
Baguettes de tympanon, 14 (D)
Baladin, 23 (C)
Baladoire, 24 (C)
Balancé, 29 (D)
Ballet, 42 (C)
Ballets aux chansons, 46 (C)
Ballets de chevaux, 46 (C)
Ballets de collège, 46 (C)
B mol, 2 (R)
B quarre, 2 (R)
Barres, 90 (R)
Bas, 98 (R)
Bascule du positif, 114 (D)
Bascules brisées, 115 (D)
Basse, 119 (R)
Basse chantante, 119 (R)
Basse continue, 119 (R)

Basse contrainte, 119 (R)
Basse-contre, 120 (C)
Basse de flûte à bec, 120 (D)
Basse de flûte traversière, 120 (D)
Basse des Italiens, 120 (D)
Basse de viole, 120 (D)
Basse de violon, 120 (D)
Basse figurée, 119 (R)
Basse Fondamentale, 119 (R); 120 (A)
Basse-taille, 121 (C)
Basson, 127 (D)
Bâtard, 139 (D)
Bâton, 144 (R)
Batte, 147 (D)
Battements, 148 (D)
Battre la mesure, 155 (R)
Billot, 256 (D)
Biseaux, 262 (D)
Blanc, 271 (D)
Boîtes, 313 (D)
Bombarde, 315 (D)
Bouche, 350 (D)
Bourdon, 369 (D)
Bourrée, 372 (C)
Bourrée, 372 (D)
Boursettes, 374 (D)
Brandon, 397 (C)
Branle, 397 (C)
Branle de St. Elme, 397 (D)
Bretagne, 413 (D)
Brève, 414 (R)
Broderie, 434 (R)
Buffet, 459 (D)
Bulafo, 461 (D)
C, 474 (R)
C, sol, ut, 474 (R)
Cabriole, 495 (D)
Cadence, 513 (R); 514 (A); 515 (D)
Canarie, 587 (D)
Canon, 606 (R)
Cantate, 621 (C); 622 (Abbé Mallet, R)
Cantatille, 622 (R)
Cantique, 623 (Abbé Mallet)
Carpée, 698 (D)
Castagnettes, 748 (D)
Castrati, 756 (A)
Catalisme, 541 (D)
C barré, 474 (R)

VOLUME III

Chaconne, 4 (R, A, C)
Chalumeau, 40 (D)

Changement, 132 (C)
Chanson, 139 (R, C)
Chant, 140 (R); 141 (C)
Chanter, 144 (R, C)
Chanterelle, 145 (D)
Chanteur, chanteuse, 145 (C)
Chape, 160 (D)
Chapeau, 174 (R)
Chapelet, 176 (C)
Char, 184 (C)
Chasse, 230 (D)
Chassis, 232 (D); 233 (C)
Chiffrer, 334 (R)
Chœur, 362 (R, C)
Chœurs, 362 (R, C)
Choréographie, 367 (Goussier)
Choristes, 373 (C)
Chreses, 379 (R)
Chromatique, 387 (R)
Chronomètre, 401 (R)
Ciel, 443 (C)
Cithare, 488 (D)
Clairon, 501 (D)
Clarinette, 505 (D)
Clavecin, 509 (D)
Clavecin oculaire, 511 (D)
Clavicorde, 504 (D)
Clavier, 512 (D)
Clé, 516 (R); 517 (A)
Colachon, 612 (D)
Comédie-ballet, 671 (C)
Compositeur, 769 (R, A)
Composition, 772 (R)
Concert, 803 (C, R)
Concertant, 804 (R)
Concerto, 804 (R)
Concert spirituel, 803 (C)
Conjoint, 871 (R, A)

VOLUME IV

Conservatoire, 42 (D)
Consonance, 50 (R); 51 (A)
Contraint, 119 (Landois)
Contre-basse, 131 (D)
Contre-bisseau, 132 (D)
Contredanse, 133 (C)
Contre-fugue, 134 (Landois)
Contre-partie, 139 (R)
Contre-poids, 139 (C)
Contrepoint, 139 (R)
Contre-sens, 141 (A)

Contre-temps, 142 (D)
Cor, 193 (D)
Cordace, 201 (C)
Cordes, 205 (D)
Cornemuse, 251 (D)
Cornet, 252 (D)
Cornet d'écho, 253 (D)
Cornet de récit, 253 (D)
Corps d'entrée, 268 (C)
Coryphée, 289 (C)
Cotillon, 305 (D)
Coulé, 326 (R)
Couler, 326 (D)
Coulisse, 335 (C)
Coulissoire, 336 (D)
Coupé, 347 (C); 348 (R, D)
Couper, 350 (C)
Couplet, 353 (R)
Courante, 376 (R, C)
Couronne, 395 (R)
Courtaut, 399 (D)
Critique, 490 (Marmontel)
Croche, 498 (R)
Croissant, 509 (D)
Cromorne, 513 (D)
Crotale, 515 (D)
Cycinnis, 586 (C)
Cyclopée, 592 (D)
Cymbale, 593 (Abbé Mallet); 594 (D)
D, 609 (R)
Danse, 623 (C)
Danseur, danseuse, 629 (C)
Danseur, 629 (D)
Débit, 651 (C)
Décaméride, 661 (R)
Déchant, 664 (D)
Déclamation, 680 (Marmontel)
Déclamation, 686 (Duclos)
Déclamation, 691 (C)
Décorateur, 700 (C)
Décoration, 701 (C)
Degré, 767 (R)
Demoiselles d'orgue, 820 (D)
Descendre, 874 (R)
Dessus, 895 (R); 896 (C)
Dessus de flûte, 896 (D)
Dessus de flûte traversière, 896 (D)
Dessus de viole, 896 (D)
Détaché, 900 (R)
Détonner, 904 (R)
Diacoustique, 932 (R)
Dialogue, 937 (R)
Diapason, 943 (R)

Diapason, 943 (Thomas & Goussier)
Diapente, 944 (R)
Diaschisma, 951 (R)
Diasteme, 951 (R)
Diatonique, 954 (R)
Diazeuxis, 954 (R)
Dicorde, 955 (D)
Diésis, 971 (R)
Diezeugmenon, 984 (R)
Diminué, 1010 (R)
Diminution, 1011 (R)
Dioxie, 1016 (R)
Discordant, 1033 (R)
Dis-Diapason, 1036 (R)
Dissonance, 1049 (R); 1050 (A)
Diton, 1067 (R)
Divertissement, 1069 (C)
Dixième, 1090 (R)
Dix-septième, 1095 (R)

VOLUME V

Do, 1 (R)
Doigter, 16 (R)
Dominant, 32 (R); 32 (A)
Dorien, 55 (R)
Double, 78 (R); 79 (C)
Double-croche, 78 (R)
Double-emploi, 79 (A)
Double-fugue, 78–79 (R)
Double-octave, 79 (R)
Doublette, 81 (D)
Douzième, 92 (R)
Duo, 166 (R)
Echelle, 250 (R); 251 (A)
Echellette, 254 (D)
Echo, 265 (R, A)
Echomètre, 265 (D)
Ecole, 335 (A)
Ecurette, 380 (D)
Effort, 410 (C)
Egalité, 415 (C)
Elégiaque, 483 (A)
Emmelie, 570 (C)
Enchantement, 619 (C)
Enchanteur, 619 (C)
Enharmonique, 688 (R, A)
Entailles, 717 (D)
Entailloirs, 717 (D)
Enthousiasme, 719 (C)
Entonner, 725 (R)
Entr'acte, 726 (C)
Entrechat, 728 (C)

Entrée, 730 (C)
Eolien, 739 (R)
Epinette, 803 (D)
Episynaphe, 816 (R)
Epitrite, 822 (R)
Epodes, 823 (C)
Espace, 952 (R)

VOLUME VI

Etendue, 46 (C)
Euouae, 207 (R)
Evuidoir, 214 (D)
Exécution, 234 (C)
Expression, 315 (C)
Extension, 327 (R)
Face, 357 (R)
Facteur, 360 (D)
Fanfare, 401 (R)
Fantaisie, 403 (R)
Fausse-Quinte, 454 (R)
Fausset, 437 (R)
Faux, 442 (R)
Faux-bourdon, 443 (R)
Faux-chassis, 443 (C)
Feinte, 465 (R)
Férie, 464 (C)
Fête, 576, 598 (C)
Fêtes de la cour de France, 580 (C)
Fiches, 677 (D)
Fifre, 744 (D)
Figurant, figurante, 748 (C)
Figure, 783 (R)
Figurer, 783 (R, C)
Filière, 798 (Goussier)
Finale, 811 (R)
Fistule, ou petite flûte, 831 (D)
Flageolet, 834 (D)
Fleuret, 863 (D)
Florence, 876 (J)
Flûte, 892 (J); 899 (D)
Flûte allemande, 899 (D)
Flûte allemande ou traversière, 895 (D)
Flûte d'accord, 895 (D)
Flûte de sacrifice, 895 (D)
Flûte de tambourin ou à trois trous, 901 (D)
Flûte Double, 895 (J)
Flûte douce ou à bec, 899 (D)

VOLUME VII

Fondamental, 54 (D)
Fondamentale, 58 (A)

Fondamentaux, 57 (A)
Fort, 190 (R)
Frappé, 288 (R)
Fredon, 293 (R)
Fredonner, 293 (R)
Frise, 309 (D)
Fugue, 360–361 (R)
Fust d'orgue, 401 (D)
F-ut-fa, 341 (R)
Gai, 423 (R)
Gaillarde, 424 (R)
Gaillarde, pas de, 424 (D)
Galère, 441 (D)
Gamme, 457 (R); 457, 460 (A); 458 (des Brosses)
Gargouillade, 515 (C)
Gavotte, 529 (R)
Genre, 594 (R); 596 (A)
Geste, 651 (C)
Gigue, 661 (A)
Glisse, 706 (D)
Gosier, 747 (D)
Goût, 761 (Voltaire); 762 (Montesquieu); 767 (A)
Goût de chant, 770 (R)
Graduel, 811 (Abbé Mallet)
Grasseyement, 861 (C)
Grasseyer, 862 (C)
Grave ou gravement, 865 (R)
Grégorien, 928 (Abbé Mallet)
Grouppe, 970 (R)
Grue, 971 (C)
Guide, 1005 (R, D)
Guidon, 1006 (R)
Guittare, 1011 (Anonymous)

VOLUME VIII

Harmonie, 50–51 (R)
Harmonie figurée, 51 (R)
Harmonique, 54 (R, A)
Harpe, 56 (Oginski)
Harpègement, 58 (D)
Hautbois, 69 (D)
Haute-contre, 70 (Barthes)
Haute-contre de violon, flûte, 71 (D)
Haute-taille, 71 (R)
Hemiole, 113 (R)
Hemiolien, 113 (R)
Hemiope, 113 (R)
Heptacorde, 138 (J)
Heptaméride, 138 (R)
Hexacorde, 196 (R)
Homophonie, 284 (J)

Hyeroche, 406 (J)
Hyerphrygien, 406 (R)
Hypate, 400 (D)
Hyperboleon, 405 (R)
Hyperdiazeuxie, 406 (R)
Hyperdorien, 406 (R)
Hyper-eolien, 406 (R)
Hyperiastien ou mixolydien aigu, 406 (R)
Hyperionien, 406 (R)
Hyperlydien, 406 (R)
Hypermixolydien, 406 (R)
Hypodiazeuxis, 409 (R)
Hypodorien, 409 (R)
Hypoeolien, 409 (R)
Hyposynaphe, 413 (R)
Hyptoides, 400 (D)
Iastien, 468 (R)
Jetté, 528 (D)
Jetté en chasse, 528 (D)
Jeux, 540 (D)
Imitation, 569 (D)
Instruments, 803 (D)
Intermède, 831 (D)
Intervalle, 838 (R)
Intonation, 844 (D)
Ionien, 876 (R)
Irrégulier, 909 (R)

VOLUME IX

Juste, 87 (R)
La, 143 (R)
Languette, 274 (D)
Largo, 294 (R)
Larigot, 294 (D)
Laye, 327 (D)
Légèrement, 352 (R)
Lentement, 385 (R)
Lepsis, 396 (R)
Levée, 438 (R)
Liaison, 455 (R)
Lichanos, 484 (R)
Liées, 488 (R)
Ligature, 519 (R)
Ligne, 526 (R)
Limma, 543 (R)
Litierse, 593 (D)
Longue, 688 (D)
Longuet, 688 (D)
Loure, 705 (D)
Lourer, 705 (R)
Luth, 756 (D)
Luthérien, 757 (J)
Lydien, 774 (D)

Lyre, 778 (J)
Lyrique, 779 (D)
Magade, 844 (J)
Majeure, 870 (R)
Main harmonique, 875 (R)

VOLUME X

Mandore, 14 (J)
Manicorde ou clavicorde, 31 (D)
Manicordion, 31 (D)
Maxime, 215 (D)
Médiante, 293 (R)
Mélodie, 319 (R)
Mélopée, 322 (R)
Menuet, 346 (R, D)
Mèse, 397 (R)
Meson, 398 (R)
Mesure, 410 (R)
Metromètre, 471 (D)
Mi, 484 (R)
Mineur, 546 (R)
Minime, 552 (R)
Mixis, 585 (R)
Mixo-lydien, 585 (D)
Mixte ou mêlé, 588 (D)
Mode, 595 (R)
Mode, 598 (A)
Modulation, 602 (R)
Mol, 625 (D)
Monocorde, 666 (D)
Monter, 685 (D)
Montre de seize pieds, 696 (D)
Motet, 765 (R)
Motif, 766 (Grimm)
Mouvement, 841 (R, D); 842 (D)
Muances, 845 (R)
Musette, 895 (Goussier)
Musette, 897 (D)
Musicien, 898 (R)
Musique, 898 (R)
Musique des Hébreux, 903 (J)
Musique, prix de, 903 (J)
Musique, effet de, 903 (Barthes)

VOLUME XI

Nablum, 3 (J)
Naples, 17 (J)
Nasard, 32 (D)
Nature, la belle, 42 (J)
Naturel, 47 (R)
Nechiloth, 69 (J)

Neginoth, 74 (J)
Nenies, 91 (D)
Nete, 107 (R)
Neuvième, 121 (D)
Noire, 190 (R)
Noter, 251 (R)
Notes, 248 (R)
Note sensible, 251 (R, A)
Nourrir les sons, 261 (D)
O, 296 (R)
Obligé, 305 (R)
Octave, 339 (R)
Octavier, 340 (R)
Octavine, 340 (J)
Odeum, 348 (R)
Œuvre, 411 (R)
Offertoire, 412 (Abbé Mallet)
Office, 413 (D)
Olivette, 451 (D)
Ombrager, 460 (D)
Ondulation, 476 (A)
Onzième, 491 (R)
Opéra, 494 (J); 496 (R)
Opéra-comique, 495 (J)
Opéra des bamboches, 495 (J)
Opéra Italien, 496 (J)
Oratoire, 575 (R)
Orchesographie, 577 (D)
Orchestre, 578 (J)
Oreilles, 623 (D)
Organiser, 629 (J)
Organiste, 629 (D)
Organo, 630 (J)
Orgue, 634 (Thomas & Goussier)
Orphée, 661 (J)
Ouies, 709 (J)
Ouverture, 721 (R)
Ouverture de jambes, 722 (D)
P, 733 (R)
Pandore, 815 (D)
Pantomime, 827 (J)
Paradiazeuxis, 889 (D)
Paramèse, 916 (R)
Paramète, 917 (R)
Paraphonie, 920 (R)
Paraphoniste, 920 (R)
Par-dessus de viole, 932 (D)
Parfait, 940 (R)

VOLUME XII

Paroles, 77 (R)
Partie, 105 (R)

Partition, 107 (R); 107 (Goussier)
Parypate, 109 (D)
Pas, 110 (D)
Passacaille, 114 (R)
Passage, 121 (R)
Passe-mèze, 123 (D)
Passe-par-tout, 124 (D)
Passe-pied, 124 (R)
Pastorale, 159 (D)
Pathétique, 170 (R)
Patrons, 185 (D)
Patte, 188 (J)
Pattes, 188 (D)
Pause, 208 (R)
Pavane, 192 (J, D)
Pédale, clavier de, 235 (Goussier)
Pédale de bombarde, 235 (Goussier)
Pédale de clairon, 235 (Goussier)
Pédale de huit, 235 (Goussier)
Pédale de quarte, 235 (Goussier)
Pédale de trompette, 235 (Goussier)
Pentacorde, 314 (D)
Pentatonon, 317 (D)
Péonien épibate, 319 (D)
Péonique, 319 (D)
Perce, 325 (D)
Perce-à-main, 325 (D)
Perce-bourdon, 325 (D)
Perfidie, 352 (R)
Petteia, 474 (R)
Phantastique, 486 (R)
Phonique, 523 (A)
Phrase, 529 (R)
Phrygien, 531 (R)
Pie, 565 (D)
Pièce, 565 (D)
Pièce d'addition, 568 (D)
Pièce gravée, 568 (D)
Piffaro, 610 (D)
Pilotes, 625 (D)
Pioches, 646 (D)
Piqué, 649 (R)
Pirouette, 655 (D)
Pirouetté, 655 (D)
Plagal, 678 (R)
Plaque, 728 (D)
Plectrum, 755 (J)
Plein-chant, 756 (R)
Plein-jeu, 756 (J)
Poche, 810 (D)
Poème lyrique, 823 (Grimm)
Poésie, 837 (J)

Poésie lyrique, 839 (J)
Poignées, 863 (D)
Point, 873 (R)
Pointe à gratter, 878 (D)
Portée, 144 (R)

VOLUME XIII

Porte-vent, 143 (D)
Porte-vent de plomb, 143 (D)
Position, 161 (R, D)
Pouls, 320 (Anonymous)
Prélude, 287 (R)
Préluder, 287 (R)
Préparer, 300 (R)
Presse, 320 (D)
Prestant, 332 (D)
Presto, 333 (R)
Prix de musique, 392 (J)
Prologue, 443 (D)
Proslambanomenos, 497 (R)
Psalmodier, 537 (R)
Psalterion, 537 (D)
Pyrrhique, 607 (J)
Quadruple-croche, 648 (R)
Quart de soupir, 672 (R)
Quart de ton, 672 (R)
Quarte, 676 (R)
Quarte de nazard, 676 (D)
Quatuor, 695 (R)
Queue, 706 (R); 707 (J)
Quinque, 716 (R)
Quintadiner, 120 (D)
Quinte, 721 (R)
Quinte de flûte à bec, 721 (D)
Quinte de flûte traversière, 721 (D)
Quinte de violon, 721 (D)
Quinte-fausse, 721 (R)
Quinzième, 724 (R)
Rabat, 733 (D)
Rasettes, 814 (D)
Re, 836 (R)
Rebattement, 840 (Brossard)
Rebec, 840 (J)
Rebube, 842 (D)
Rebute, 843 (J)
Recherche, 849 (R)
Récit, 854 (R)
Récitant, 854 (R)
Récitatif, 854 (R)
Redoublé, 876 (R)
Refrain, 900 (J)

VOLUME XIV

Registre de clavecin, 19 (D)
Registres dormants, 20 (D)
Registres mobiles, 19 (D)
Règle de l'octave, 22 (R)
Régulier, 42 (J)
Relation, 63 (R)
Renversement, 122 (R)
Renvoi, 123 (R)
Repercussion, 131 (R)
Répétition, 133 (R)
Replique, 136 (R)
Repos, 139 (R)
Reprise, 147 (R)
Résonance, 181 (R)
Ressorts, 191 (D)
Rester, 193 (R)
Rhythme, 267 (R)
Rhythmique, 269 (R)
Rhythmopeia, 269 (R)
Ricercata, 271 (J)
Rigaudon, 289 (R); 290 (D)
Riom, 295 (J)
Ritournelle, 302 (R)
Rivoltato, canto, 306 (J)
Ronde, 358 (R)
Rosoir, 374 (D)
Roulade, 409 (R)
Sacquebute, 474 (J)
Saillie, 517 (D)
Saltarella, 581 (Brossard)
Sambuque, 595 (J)
Sandale, 609 (D)
Saquebute, 641 (D)
Sarabande, 642 (D)
Saut, 725 (R, D)
Sautereau, 726 (D)
Sauver, 730 (R)
Savonne, 722 (J)
Scheme, 761 (J)
Schisma, 765 (R)
Schoemion, 769 (J)
Scie à main, 786 (D)
Seconde, 858 (D)
Semi, 943 (R)
Semi-brève, 943 (R)
Semicon, 943 (J)
Semi-ton, 946 (R)

VOLUME XV

Sensations, 34 (D)
Septième, 72 (R, A)

Sérénade, 81 (R)
Serinette, 96 (D)
Serpent, 110 (D)
Sesqui, 126 (R)
Sextuple, 139 (R)
Si, 147 (D)
Sicilienne, 166 (D)
Sifflet, 182 (D)
Sifflet de Pan, 182 (D)
Signes, 189 (R)
Silence, 192 (R)
Sillet, 196 (D)
Sissonne, 229 (D)
Sistre, 229 (J)
Sixte, 235 (R)
Soave, 247 (J)
Sol, 309 (R)
Solfier, 319 (R)
Solo, 326 (R)
Sommier de clavecin, 336 (D)
Sommier de grand orgue, 337 (D)
Sommier de positif, 337 (D)
Son, 343 (A); 344 (D); 345 (R)
Sonate, 348 (R)
Sons Harmoniques, 347 (R)
Soufflets de l'orgue, 395 (D)
Soupir, 411 (R)
Sourdeline, 413 (J)
Sourdine, 413 (D)
Sous-dominante, 417 (A)
Soutenir, 422 (R)
Spectacles, 446 (J)
Spiccato, staccato, 461 (R)
Spondaula, 480 (R)
Spondiasme, 480 (J)
Stentato, 509 (J)
Stretto, 546 (J)
Style, 556 (R)
Sujet, 645 (R)
Supposition, 679 (R)
Surnuméraire, 693 (R)
Suspension, 700 (R)
Syllabe, 719 (R)
Symphonie, 740 (J)
Synaphe, 745 (R)
Synaulie, 746 (R)
Syncope, 747 (R)
Synnemenon, 754 (R)
Synnemenon diatonos, 754 (R)
Syntonique, 764 (R)
Syntonolydien, 764 (R)
Syrinx, 774 (J)
Système, 780 (R)

T, 783 (R)
Tablature, 797 (R)
Tacet, 812 (R)
Taille, 856 (R)
Taille de hautbois, 856 (D)
Taille de violon, 856 (D)
Talons, 869 (D)
Tamboula, 874 (Le Romain)
Tambour, 874 (J); 875 (D); 877 (J)
Tambourin, 877 (R); 877 (D)
Tampon, 880 (D)
Tam-tam, 831 (D)
Tasseau, 935 (J)
Tastatura, 935 (J)
Tasto, 935 (J)

VOLUME XVI

Tempérament, 56 (R)
Tempo di gavotta, di menuetto, 90 (J)
Temps, 121 (R)
Tendrement, 131 (R)
Tenue, 142 (R)
Tête, 208 (D)
Têtières, 208 (D)
Tetracorde, 208 (R)
Tetradiapason, 209 (R)
Tetratonon, 212 (R)
Texte, 216 (R)
Theorbe, 252 (D)
Thesis, 275 (R)
Tierce, 321 (R, D)
Tierce de Picardie, 321 (R)
Tierce double, 321 (D)
Tirade, 339 (R)
Toccata, 367 (J)
Tombé, 401 (D)
Ton, 404 (R); 405 (D)
Tonique, 408 (R)
Tons de l'église, 404 (R)
Tordion, 422 (D)
Touche, 445 (D)
Tourelle, 473 (D)
Tournebout, 427 (J)
Tourniquet, 484 (D)
Tous, 497 (D)
Trace-sautereau, 504 (D)
Tragédie, 513 (J)
Transition, 554 (R)
Translation, 556 (R)
Transposition, 561 (R)
Travailler, 569 (R)
Traversière à bec, 571 (D)

Treizième, 578 (R)
Tremblant doux, 578 (D)
Tremblant fort, 579 (D)
Tremblement, 584 (R)
Triade, 609 (R)
Trigonon, 642 (J)
Trihemiton, 642 (R)
Trio, 651 (R)
Triple, 657 (R)
Triplé, 658 (R)
Trite, 663 (R)
Triton, 665 (R)
Trombone, 692 (J)
Trompette, 694 (D, J); 696 (D)
Trompette harmonieuse, 695 (D)
Trompette marine, 695 (D)
Troubadours, 711 (D)
Trouvères, 718 (J)
Tubes, 733 (D)
Tutti, 767 (J)
Tuyau, 770 (J)
Tymbre, 775 (R)
Tympano, 777 (J)
Tympanon des Hébreux, 777 (J)
Unisson, 386 (R)
Ut, 556 (R)

V, 789 (R)
Valeur des notes, 818 (R)
Variations, 845 (R)
Vaudeville, 861 (J)

VOLUME XVII

Veroli, J. Sulpitius, 84 (J)
Verres, musique des, 156 (D)
Vielle, 261 (D)
Vif, 267 (R)
Vilanelle, 272 (R)
Viole, 310 (J)
Viole, basse de, 311 (D)
Violon, 317 (D)
Violons, roi des, 321 (J)
Virtuose, 330 (D)
Vite, 359 (R)
Vocale, 409 (R)
Voix, 428 (J); 436 (R)
Voix angélique, 438 (D)
Voix humaine, 438 (D)
Vraisemblance, 484 (J)
Vuide, 574 (R)
Xroa, 657 (J)
Za, 685 (R)

SUPPLEMENT

The most frequent contributor to these four volumes was Castillon fils, designated by the initials CF. Marmontel was a major contributor in the Supplement; accordingly, we have thought the letter M. sufficient to identify his articles. The articles by Rousseau were taken from his *Dictionnaire de musique,* and those signed Sulzer from this philosopher's *Allgemeine Theorie der Schoenen Künste;* it is now known that J.A.P. Schulze was responsible for most of the articles on music in this work from S–Z and that J. P. Kirnberger wrote many of the music articles from A–R. See Sulzer's *Vorrede* and Riemann, *Dictionnaire,* article "Sulzer."

VOLUME I

A, 1 (CF)
Abréviation, 45 (CF)
Abub, 75 (CF)
Académie de musique, 92 (R)
Accent, 106 (Sulzer); 108, 110 (R, CF)
Accent double, 110 (CF)
Accent musical, 109 (CF)
Accents, 110 (R); (CF)
Accents ecclésiastiques, 110 (CF)
Acciacatura, 112 (CF)
Accident, accidentel, 112 (R)

Accompagnement, 115 (M)
Accompagnement sans chiffres, 116 (CF)
Accompagner, 117 (R)
Accord, 117 (CF); 118 (R, Sultzer)
Accord dissonant, 118 (R)
Accord parfait, 119 (Sulzer)
Accordeur, 120 (R)
Accordo, 120 (CF)
Accordoir, 120 (CF)
Acroama, 153 (CF)
Acte, 155 (R)
Acte de cadence, 155 (R)
Acteur, actrice, 155 (R)

Adonidie, 173 (CF)
Adonie, 172 (CF)
Affettuoso, 182 (R)
Agogé, 211 (R)
Agrément, 213 (R); (CF); (Sulzer)
Air, 237 (M)
Ajustées, 241 (CF)
Alla breve, 287 (R, CF)
Alla cappella, 287 (CF)
Alla francese, 287 (CF)
Alla polacca, 287 (CF)
Alla semi-breve, 287 (CF)
Alla zoppa, 287 (R)
All'ottavo, 287 (CF)
Al segno, 324 (R)
Altambor, 324 (CF)
Alto-basso, 329 (CF)
Amabile, 331 (R)
Amateur, 336 (R)
Ambitus, 340 (R)
Amoroso, 369 (R)
Ampeira, 370 (CF)
Anacamptos, 380 (R)
Anaclétique, 380 (CF)
Anacrousis, 380 (CF)
Anapera, 390 (CF)
Angloise, 430 (CF)
Anonner, 447 (R)
Anticipation, 451 (CF)
Anticiper, 452 (CF)
Antiphonier, 462 (R)
Apodipne, 484 (CF)
Apollon, 484 (CF)
Apothète, 490 (CF)
Appréciable, 492 (R)
Appuyé, 498 (CF)
Apycni, 498 (R)
Araine, 512 (CF)
Arbitrio, 518 (R)
Arc, 528 (CF)
Archi-viole de lyre, 540 (CF)
Arco, 541 (R)
Ardavalis, 541 (CF)
Aria, 553 (Sulzer)
Arioso, 557 (R)
Aristoxéniens, 558 (R)
Armer la clef, 561 (R)
Arpeggio, 566 (CF)
Arsis et thesis, 585 (CF)
Art, 585 (M); 587 (Sulzer)
Ascarus, 627 (CF)
Ascior, 628 (CF)
Aspiration, 653 (CF)

Assai, 653 (R)
Assonance, 656 (CF)
A tempo giusto, 667 (CF)
Athena, 669 (CF)
Atropus, 682 (CF)
Atzeberoscim, 694 (CF)
Aubade, 698 (R)
Authentique, 724 (CF, R)
Axamenta, 727 (CF)
B, 740 (CF)
Balafo, 758 (CF)
Balancement, 761 (CF)
Ballade, 762 (CF)
Ballet, 763 (Sulzer); 764 (R)
Bandereau, 790 (CF)
Barbare, 804 (R)
Barbarisme, 804 (CF)
Barbiton, 806 (CF)
Barcarolle, 806 (R)
Baripycni, 808 (CF)
Baroque, 813 (R)
Barre, 814 (CF); 814 (R)
Barrure, 818 (CF)
Baryton, 819 (R, CF)
Bas, 819 (R)
Bassanello, 824 (CF)
Basse, 824 (Sulzer)
Basse-de hautbois, 825 (CF)
Basse de Nomhorne, 825 (CF)
Basse de viole, 825 (CF)
Basse-double, 825 (CF)
Battement, 828 (R, CF)
Battements, 829 (R)
Batterie, 829 (R)
Batteur de mesures, 830 (R)
Bebisatio, 842 (CF)
Bedon de Biscaye, 842 (CF)
Bémol double, 870 (CF)
Bémoliser, 870 (R)
Béotien, 879 (CF)
Bergamasque, 881 (CF)
Bergeries, 881 (M)
Bi, 886 (R)
Bis, 903 (CF)
Bis-chrome, 903 (R)

VOLUME II

Bobisatio, 1 (CF)
Bocal, 1 (CF)
Bombarde, 11 (CF)

Bombo, 11 (CF)
Bombyx, 11 (CF)
Bonbalon, 11 (CF)
Boule, 39 (CF)
Bourdon, 41 (R, CF)
Bourrée, 41 (R)
Boutade, 43 (R)
Brailler, 50 (R)
Branches, 51 (CF)
Branle, 51 (R)
Bref, 52 (CF)
Bruit, 72 (R)
Brunette, 74 (CF)
Buonaccordo, 80 (CF)
Burbelin, 84 (CF)
C, 88 (R); (CF)
Cachée, 90 (CF)
Cadence, 96 (CF, R)
Cadencé, 96 (R)
Cadenza, 96 (R)
Calabis, 110 (CF)
Caladrone, 111 (CF)
Calique, 140 (CF)
Callinique, 142 (CF)
Calyce, 147 (CF)
Camergo, 148 (CF)
Canarder, 196 (R)
Cannevas, 201 (M)
Canon, 201 (R, CF)
Canoniquement, 213 (CF)
Cantabile, 214 (R)
Canto, 216 (R)
Capacité, 224 (CF)
Capion, 224 (CF)
Capital, 224 (CF)
Caractères de musique, 233 (R)
Carillon, 240 (R)
Carillonner, 240 (CF)
Carillonneur, 240 (CF)
Carnyx, 244 (CF)
Cartelle, 254 (R)
Castrato, 267 (R, Courtépée)
Catabaucalèse, 268 (R)
Catachoreusis, 268 (CF)
Catachrèse, 268 (CF)
Catacoimèse, 268 (CF)
Catakeleusme, 269 (CF)
Cataphonique, 270 (R)
Catapleon, 270 (CF)
Catastome, 270 (CF)
Catatropa, 270 (CF)
Cavatine, 275 (R)
Centoniser, 287 (R)

Céon, 288 (CF)
Cépion, 290 (CF)
Cérodetos, 299 (CF)
Cervelat, 300 (CF)
Césure, 301 (CF)
Chaine de trillo, 302 (CF)
Chalemie, 309 (CF)
Chalil, 310 (CF)
Chanson, 319 (M)
Chansonnette, 320 (CF)
Chansonnier, 320 (CF)
Chant, 320 (M)
Chant ambrosien, 323 (R)
Chant-en-ison, 323 (R)
Chant grégorien, 323 (R)
Chant sur le livre, 323 (R)
Chapelle, 324 (CF)
Charge, 329 (CF)
Charonde, 369 (CF)
Chasse, 372 (R)
Chatzotzeroth, 374 (CF)
Chausser, 381 (CF)
Chevrotter, 397 (R)
Chitarrone, 403 (CF)
Chiterna, 403 (CF)
Chitonée, 403 (CF)
Chœur, 404 (M)
Chœur d'opéra, 405 (M)
Chorieon, 406 (CF)
Chorion, 407 (R)
Chorique, 407 (CF)
Chorodidascale, 407 (Anonymous)
Chorus, 408 (R); 408 (CF)
Chrome, 425 (CF)
Chrotta, 425 (CF)
Chute, 426 (CF)
Circolomezzo, 431 (CF)
Circonvolution, 431 (R)
Cistre, 444 (CF)
Citharistiqué, 446 (R)
Citharoide, 446 (CF)
Citole, 447 (CF)
Claquebois, 450 (CF)
Clarinette, 450 (CF)
Clavecin à roue, 457 (CF)
Clavecin brisé, 457 (CF)
Clavecin vertical, 457 (CF)
Clavicorde, 457 (CF)
Clavier, 458 (R)
Clef petite, 459 (CF)
Clepsiambe, 465 (D)
Clepsiangos, 465 (CF)
Clepsydre, 466 (CF)

Climax, 467 (CF)
Cloaca, 467 (CF)
Codon, 488 (CF)
Collobis, 506 (CF)
Comarcios, 514 (CF)
Comma, 526 (Anonymous)
Commencement, 526 (Sulzer)
Compair, 532 (R)
Composé, 534 (R)
Composer, 535 (R)
Compositeur, 535 (CF)
Composition, 535 (R)
Comus, 535 (CF)
Concert spirituel, 536 (M)
Concours, 537 (R)
Conjointes, 547 (R)
Connexe, 548 (D)
Consonance, 554 (Sulzer); 556 (CF)
Consonant, 556 (R)
Consonante, 556 (R)
Contraste, 570 (R)
Contre-chant, 571 (R)
Contre-danse, 575 (R, Anonymous)
Contre-point, 576 (CF)
Contre-temps, 585 (R)
Contre-tenor, 571 (R)
Copiate, 589 (R)
Cor, 595 (CF, R)
Corde à violon, 598 (La Lande)
Corde sonore, 599 (R)
Cornemuse, 607 (CF)
Cornet à bouquin, 608 (CF)
Corps de voix, 612 (R)
Corps sonore, 612 (R)
Coup, 641 (CF)
Couper, 641 (R); (CF)
Crab, 649 (CF)
Cradias, 649 (CF)
Crematien, 650 (CF)
Crembala, 650 (CF)
Crescendo, 651 (CF, Anonymous)
Crier, 652 (R)
Crisme, 475 (CF)
Croche pointée, 655 (CF)
Croches liées, 655 (CF)
Croches séparées, 655 (CF)
Crochet, 655 (R)
Crome, 656 (R)
Cromorne, 656 (R)
Croque-note, 656 (R)
Crouma, 656 (CF)
Crusithyre, 662 (CF)
Cuclien, 664 (CF)

Curéticon, 666 (CF)
Cymbalum, 667 (CF)
Cynura, 667 (CF)
Cytharistérienne, 674 (CF)
D, 677 (R, CF)
Da capo, 677 (R)
Dactile, 677 (CF)
Dactylique, 677 (R)
Daphnéphonique, 684 (CF)
Déclamation, 687 (R)
Déduction, 687 (R)
Déios, 689 (CF)
Démancher, 691 (R)
Dembes, 691 (CF)
Demi-baton, 691 (CF)
Demi-dessus, 691 (CF)
Demi-mesure, 691 (R)
Demi-pause, 691 (R)
Demi-temps, 691 (R)
Dessiner, 705 (R)
Détaché, 705 (CF)
Détonner, 707 (R)
Deux-quarts, 708 (CF)
Diacommatique, 708 (R)
Diagramme, 709 (CF)
Diaphonie, 713 (R)
Diaptose, 717 (R)
Diaschisma, 717 (R)
Diatesseron, 718 (R)
Diatonique, 719 (R)
Diaule, 719 (CF)
Diazeuxis, 719 (R)
Dichorde, 719 (CF)
Dièse, 719 (R); 720 (CF)
Diéser, 720 (R)
Diopi, 723 (CF)
Diphtongue, 723 (CF)
Direct, 723 (R)
Discant, 723 (R)
Disdiapason, 724 (R)
Disjoint, 724 (R)
Disjonction, 724 (R)
Dissonance, 726 (R); 727 (CF, Anony-
    mous)
Dissonance majeure, 730 (R)
Dissonance mineure, 730 (R)
Dissonner, 730 (R)
Dix-huitième, 731 (R)
Dix-neuvième, 731 (R)
Dodecacorde, 731 (R)
Dorien, 734 (R); 735 (CF)
Double, 738 (R)
Double-corde, 738 (R)

Double-crochet, 738 (R)
Double-octave, 738 (R)
Doubler, 738 (R)
Double-triple, 738 (R)
Dramatique, 741 (R)
Duo, 743 (M); 744 (R, CF)
Duplication, 745 (R)
Dur, 745 (Sulzer); 746 (R)
Ecbole, 748 (R)
Echalotte, 748 (CF)
Echellette, 751 (CF)
Eclisses, 764 (CF)
Eclyse, 764 (R)
Ecmete, 764 (R)
Egal, 775 (R)
Egersis, 778 (CF)
Elégiaque, 784 (CF)
Elégie, 784 (R)
Eléphantine, 784 (CF)
Elévation, 784 (R)
Eliue, 785 (R)
Ellipse, 790 (CF)
Elyme, 792 (CF)
Embaterie, 800 (CF)
Embaterienne, 800 (CF)
Embaukis, 799 (CF)
Emmèle, 803 (R)
Emmélie, 803 (D, CF)
Endématie, 804 (R)
Endosimon, 804 (CF)
En harmonie, 806 (CF)
Enkeleustique, 806 (CF)
Ennéacorde, 806 (CF)
Ensemble, 807 (R)
Entr'acte, 811 (CF, R)
Eolien, 813 (R)
Epiaulie, 818 (R)
Epibomie, 818 (CF)
Epicinion, 818 (R)
Epicytharisme, 818 (CF)
Epigeneum, 820 (D)
Epigonium, 820 (CF)
Epilème, 820 (R)
Epilogue, 820 (CF)
Epimylie, 820 (CF)
Epinette, 820 (Anonymous)
Epiodie, 824 (CF)
Epiphallus, 824 (CF)
Epipompentica, 825 (CF)
Epiproslambanomène, 825 (CF)
Episynaphe, 826 (R)
Epocha, 813 (CF)
Eporcheia, 813 (CF)

Eptaphone, 832 (R)
Epythimbien, 832 (CF)
Equisonance, 848 (R)
Etendue, 882 (R)
Eudromé, 906 (R)
Euouae, 908 (R)
Eupholimme, 908 (CF)
Euthia, 909 (R)
Eviter, 907 (R)
Evolution, 908 (CF)
Exécutant, 910 (R)
Exécuter, 910 (R)
Exécution, 911 (R)
Expressif, 918 (D)
Expression, 921 (Sulzer); 922 (CF, R);
   924 (CF)

VOLUME III

F, 1 (CF)
Fa feint, 1 (CF)
Fabarius, 1 (CF)
Fagot, 2 (C)
Faucet, 8 (D)
Fa-ut, 9 (CF)
Faux-accord, 9 (CF)
Faux-bourdon, 9 (CF)
Fi, 34 (R)
Fides, 38 (CF)
Fidicula, 38 (CF)
Figura bombilaus, 44 (CF)
Figura corta, 44 (CF)
Figura suspirans, 44 (CF)
Figure, 44 (CF)
Filer un son, 45 (CF)
Fixe, 46 (D)
Flatté, 47 (R)
Flûte, 58, 62 (CF)
Flûte de peau, 62 (CF)
Flûte traversière, 62 (CF)
Flûte Tyrrhénienne, 63 (CF)
Foible, 74 (R)
Folies d'Espagne, 81 (CF)
Fondamental, 83 (CF)
Fondement, 83 (CF)
Forcer la voix, 87 (R)
Forte, 86 (R)
Forte-piano, 87 (R)
Fourniture, 109 (CF)
Fragments, 115 (R)
Frappé, 136 (R, CF)
Fugue, 152 (R, CF)
Fugue renversée, 152 (R)

Fuse, 155 (CF)
Fusée, 155 (R)
G, 165 (R)
Gaiement, 166 (CF)
Ginglarus, 225 (CF)
Gingras, 225 (CF)
Gingros, 226 (CF)
Glossocome, 238 (CF)
Glotte, 238 (CF)
Gong, 243 (CF)
Gongom, 244 (CF)
Goût, 247 (R); 248 (CF)
Gracieusement, 248 (CF)
Grande clef, 253 (CF)
Gré-contraire, 254 (CF)
Gros-fa, 269 (R)
Grouppe, 274 (CF)
Guidon, 277 (CF)
Guittare, 278 (CF)
Guittare, de Wanhecke, 278 (D)
Gymnopédie, 284 (R)
H, 285 (CF)
Harmatias, 300 (R, CF)
Harmodie, 300 (CF)
Harmonie, 300 (R); 302 (CF)
Harmonieux, 309 (R)
Harmoniques, 309 (R)
Harmoniste, 309 (R)
Harmonomètre, 309 (R)
Harpe-double, 309 (CF)
Haut-dessus, 312 (R)
Hautes, 312 (CF)
Helicon, 319 (CF)
Hemediton, 322 (R)
Hemiole, 322 (CF)
Hemiope, 322 (CF)
Hesychastique, 368 (CF)
Hexarmonien, 370 (R)
Hieracien, 371 (CF)
Hippothore, 429 (CF)
Hormius, 455 (CF)
Hymée, 481 (R)
Hymne, 481 (R)
Hymne de Castor, 482 (CF)
Hypate-hypaton, 482 (R)
Hypate-meson, 482 (R)
Hyperboléien, 482 (R)
Hyper-hypate, 483 (CF)
Hypermèse, 483 (CF)
Hypertonide, 483 (CF)
Hypothéâtrale, 487 (CF)
Hypotrète, 487 (CF)
Hyppophorbe, 488 (CF)

Iambe, 498 (CF)
Iambique, 498 (R)
Iambyce, 498 (CF)
Idéal, 514 (Chastellux)
Idouthos, 519 (CF)
Imitation, 568 (R, CF)
Imparfait, 569 (R)
Improviser, 569 (R)
Incomposé, 570 (R)
Indigitamenta, 586 (CF)
Inharmonique, 601 (CF)
Instrumental, 618 (R)
Instrumentale, 618 (Anonymous)
Intense, 624 (R)
Intonation, 638 (R)
Iobacchus, 645 (CF)
Ionien, 647 (R); (CF)
Ithomée, 672 (CF)
Ithymbe, 672 (CF)
Jambides, 498 (CF)
Jeu, 551 (R)
Joueur, 654 (R)
Jule, 675 (CF)
Juste, 678 (R)
Kas, 683 (CF)
Kassuto, 683 (CF)
Keren, 684 (CF)
Kerenna, 685 (CF)
Kinnor, 686 (CF)
Kyrie, 691 (CF)
Lamentabile, 701 (CF)
Lapa, 705 (CF)
Large, 706 (R)
Larghetto, 706 (R)
Layette, 719 (CF)
Lemme, 721 (R)
Lento, 722 (CF)
Lettres de la gamme, 733 (CF)
Libitum, 739 (CF)
Licence, 741 (R)
Linonasme, 760 (CF)
Lituus, 764 (CF)
Livre ouvert, 766 (R)
Locrien, 768 (CF)
Longo, 776 (CF)
Longue, 776 (CF)
Lotine, 784 (CF)
Lucernates, 810 (CF)
Lumière, 811 (CF)
Luth, 815 (CF)
Luthier, 815 (R)
Lydien, 817 (CF)
Lydienne, 817 (CF)

Lyra di braccio, 820 (CF)
Lyrique, 820 (M)
Lyrodie, 827 (CF)
Lysiode, 828 (CF)
Lytière, 828 (CF)
Ma, 829 (R)
Machicotage, 829 (R)
Machul, 829 (CF)
Madrigal, 830 (R)
Maestoso, 830 (CF)
Magade, 830 (CF)
Magadiser, 830 (R)
Magasin, 830 (R)
Magraphe, 832 (CF)
Maître à chanter, 835 (R)
Maître de musique, 835 (R)
Manche, 838 (CF)
Marche, 846 (CF)
Marcher, 847 (R)
Marimba, 850 (CF)
Martellement, 858 (CF)
Mascrokitha, 859 (CF)
Matroum, 868 (CF)
Médium, 890 (R)
Mélange, 891 (R)
Mélététinus, 891 (CF)
Mélodie, 895 (R)
Mélodieux, 896 (R)
Mélos, 896 (R)
Menestrel, 897 (CF)
Meniambe, 897 (CF)
Merveilleux, 906 (M)
Mésocope, 910 (CF)
Mésoide, 910 (R)
Mésopycni, 910 (R)
Messanza, 910 (CF)
Mesure, 911 (Sulzer); 916 (CF); (R)
Metacatatropa, 916 (CF)
Metarcha, 916 (CF)
Métrique, 917 (R)
Metzilothaim, 918 (CF)
Milieu, 939 (CF)
Miloina, 939 (CF)
Minnim, 939 (CF)
Mistichanza composa, 939 (CF)
Mnaanim, 940 (CF)
Mobile, 940 (R)
Moderato, 941 (CF)
Modéré, 941 (R)
Moduler, 941 (R)
Mœurs, 953 (R)
Mol, 954 (R)
Monaule, 954 (CF)

Monocorde, 954 (CF)
Monodie, 954 (R)
Monologue, 954 (R)
Mothon, 964 (CF)
Mouvement, 970 (R)
Musical, 982 (R)
Musicalement, 982 (R)
Musique, 982 (R, CF)
Mygdonienne, 983 (CF)
Mylothros, 983 (CF)

VOLUME IV

Nable, 2 (CF)
Naturel, 22 (R)
Neniaton, 25 (CF)
Neume, 35 (R)
Neuvième, 36 (CF)
Nicolo, 45 (CF)
Nkamba, 53 (CF)
Noel, 55 (R)
Nœuds, 56 (D)
Nomion, 59 (R)
Nomique, 59 (R)
Notes de goût, 60 (R)
Note sensible, 60 (CF)
Nsambi, 71 (CF)
Nunine, 72 (R)
Octacorde, 81 (R)
Octave, 86 (R, CF)
Ode, 87 (R)
Odontisme, 100 (CF)
Oeteline, 120 (CF)
Offertoire, 123 (CF)
Olamba, 125 (CF)
Olmous, 127 (CF)
Olophryme, 127 (CF)
Omphalos, 148 (CF)
Opéra, 152 (M); 158 (R); 162 (CF)
Orchestre, 166 (R)
Oreille, 175 (R)
Organiser, 183 (R)
Orgue, 183 (CF)
Orphéaron, 190 (CF)
Orphéon, 190 (CF)
Orthien, 191 (R)
Oxipcni, 216 (R)
Paléomagade, 219 (CF)
Pandure, 230 (CF)
Pantaléon, 231 (CF)
Pantomime, 231 (R); (M)
Papier reglé, 233 (R)

Paraénien, 234 (CF)
Paratrète, 238 (CF)
Parhypate, 239 (R)
Pariambe, 239 (CF)
Pariambides, 239 (CF)
Parodie, 240 (R)
Paroenie, 241 (CF)
Parténienne, 242 (CF)
Partition, 245 (R)
Passage, 245 (CF)
Pastorale, 256 (R)
Pastorelle, 256 (R)
Pat-gong, 256 (CF)
Pathétique, 256 (R)
Pause, 262 (CF)
Pauser, 262 (R)
Pavane, 258 (CF)
Pectis, 273 (CF)
Peira, 273 (CF)
Pelyx, 276 (CF)
Penorcon, 282 (CF)
Pentacontacorde, 283 (CF)
Pentacorde, 282 (CF); (R)
Périélèse, 299 (R)
Périphères, 300 (R)
Petteia, 312 (CF)
Phœnix, 343 (CF)
Phorbeion, 343 (CF)
Phorminge, 343 (CF)
Photinge, 343 (CF)
Phrase, 344 (R)
Phraser, 344 (CF)
Phrygien, 344 (R)
Phryné, 344 (CF)
Pi, 365 (CF)
Pièce, 366 (R)
Pied, 370 (R)
Pincé, 375 (R)
Piqué, 384 (R)
Pithautique, 387 (CF)
Pizzicato, 387 (R)
Plein-jeu, 414 (R)
Plique, 415 (R)
Pointer, 452 (R)
Polemicon, 470 (CF)
Polonaise, 471 (CF)
Polymnastie, 471 (R)
Polyphtongue, 472 (CF)
Ponctuer, 502 (R, CF)
Port-de-voix, 512 (R, CF)
Port-de-voix-jetté, 512 (R)
Positif, 515 (CF)
Præcentorienne, 525 (CF)

Préparation, 527 (CF)
Prima intenzione, 533 (R)
Prise, 533 (R)
Proaulion, 533 (CF)
Progression, 535 (R)
Prologue, 535 (M); 538 (R)
Proportion, 538 (R)
Proprement, 539 (R)
Propreté, 539 (R)
Prosodiaque, 540 (R)
Prosodie, 540 (R, CF); 541 (M)
Protésis, 542 (R)
Psalmodie, 550 (CF)
Psithyre, 550 (CF)
Puérile, 551 (CF)
Pycni, 554 (R)
Pycnos, 554 (CF)
Pythagoriciens, 556 (R)
Pythien, 556 (CF)
Pythique, 556 (CF)
Quantité, 558 (R)
Quarrée à queue, 558 (CF)
Quarte, 558 (CF)
Quarter, 558 (R)
Quatorzième, 559 (R)
Quatuor, 559 (CF)
Quilando, 559 (CF)
Quinque, 559 (CF)
Quinte, 559 (CF); 560 (R)
Quinter, 560 (R)
Rabana, 563 (CF)
Racler, 563 (CF)
Racleur, 564 (CF)
Ranz-des-vaches, air Suisse, 573 (R)
Rapport, 574 (CF)
Ravalement, 577 (R)
Récitatif, 583 (M); 586 (Sulzer); 589 (CF, R)
Récitatif accompagné, 590 (R)
Récitatif mesuré, 590 (R)
Récitatif obligé, 590 (R)
Récitation, 591 (R)
Réciter, 591 (R)
Redoubler, 592 (CF)
Réduction, 593 (R, CF)
Régale, 593 (CF)
Régale à vent, 593 (CF)
Règle de l'octave, 593 (CF)
Régler le papier, 595 (R)
Régleur, 595 (R)
Réglure, 595 (R)
Relatifs, 603 (CF)
Renforcer, 606 (R, CF)

Rentrer, 606 (R)
Renversé, 606 (R)
Renversement, 606 (R)
Répons, 606 (R)
Réponse, 606 (R)
Resserrer, 623 (R)
Retradien, 640 (CF)
Rhythme, 643 (Sulzer)
Ripieno, 651 (R)
Rolle, 666 (R)
Romance, 675 (R)
Rondian, 678 (R)
Rongos, 679 (CF)
Rosalie, 679 (CF)
Rote, 682 (CF)
Roulade, 684 (R, CF)
Roulement, 685 (CF)
S, 691 (R)
Salto, 715 (CF)
Sambuque, 716 (CF)
Sarrane, 739 (CF)
Sauter, 750 (R)
Sauvement, 751 (CF)
Scène, 751 (R)
Schalisehim, 753 (CF)
Schnakade, 754 (CF)
Schryari, 754 (CF)
Scindaphe, 754 (CF)
Sciophar, 755 (CF)
Seconde, 758 (CF)
Segue, 763 (CF)
Semaine, 765 (La Lande)
Semanterion, 766 (CF)
Semi-canto, 770 (CF)
Semi-crome, 770 (CF)
Semi-tonique, 773 (R)
Sensibilité, 779 (R, D)
Septième, 780 (CF)
Serré, 783 (R)
Sicymotyrbe, 789 (CF)
Simicon, 792 (CF)
Simple, 794 (R)
Sixte, 801 (CF)
Solfier, 805 (R); 806 (CF)
Son fixe, 810 (R)
Sonner, 810 (R)
Sonore, 810 (R)
Sophiste, 810 (CF)
Sostenuto, 811 (CF)
Sotto voce, 812 (R)
Souffleur, 812 (CF)
Sourdine, 818 (R)
Sous-médiante, 818 (R); 819 (CF)

Spadix, 819 (CF)
Sphécisme, 823 (CF)
Sphragis, 824 (CF)
Spondaique, 826 (CF)
Spondalies, 826 (CF)
Spondéasme, 828 (R)
Spondée, 826 (CF)
Stable, 826 (R)
Staccato, 826 (D)
Stasimon, 829 (CF)
Strumstrum, 832 (CF)
Su-dominante, 840 (CF)
Suite, 844 (R)
Sumphoneia, 846 (CF)
Supérius, 847 (CF)
Super-sus, 847 (R)
Supposition, 847 (CF)
Suraigues, 847 (R)
Surdastrum, 847 (CF)
Suspension, 850 (CF)
Su-tonique, 857 (CF)
Syllabe, 857 (CF)
Symphoniaste, 857 (R)
Symphonie, 857 (CF)
Synaulie, 857 (R, CF)
Syntonique, 857 (R, CF)
Syrigmalien, 858 (CF)
Syrigmon, 858 (CF)
Syringe, 859 (CF)
Système, 859 (R, CF)
T, 878 (CF)
Ta, 878 (R)
Table, 924 (CF)
Tableau, 924 (R)
Taille, 925 (R)
Tambour, 929 (CF)
Tambourin, 930 (CF)
Tapon, 930 (CF)
Tastosolo, 930 (CF)
Tataboang, 930 (CF)
Té, 931 (R)
Télestérien, 931 (CF)
Tempo giusto, 931 (CF)
Tenedius, 934 (R)
Teneur, 934 (R)
Tenor, 934 (R)
Teponatzle, 934 (CF)
Teretisme, 934 (CF)
Terpandrien, 934 (CF)
Tetracome, 936 (CF)
Thé, 936 (R)
Théracien, 937 (CF)
Tho, 941 (R)

Thrénétique, 941 (CF)
Thripodiphorique, 941 (CF)
Thuraire, 941 (CF)
Tifa, 947 (CF)
Tirade, 947 (CF)
Tityrine, 948 (CF)
Tlounpounpan, 948 (CF)
Toccate, 948 (CF)
Ton de quart, 948 (R)
Tong, 948 (CF)
Toph, 952 (CF)
Tournebout, 952 (CF)
Tragique, 965 (CF)
Transition, 966 (CF)
Transposer, 976 (R)
Tre, 976 (CF)
Tremamento, longo, 976 (CF)
Tremolo, 976 (CF)
Triade enharmonique, 976 (CF)
Tricorde, 977 (CF)
Trigone, 977 (CF)
Trilletto, 977 (CF)
Trillo, 977 (CF)
Triple, 977 (CF)
Triplum, 977 (R)
Tripos, 977 (CF)
Triton, 977 (CF)

Tro, 977 (CF)
Trombe, 979 (CF)
Trompette, 979 (CF)
Tympanischisa, 982 (CF)
Tzeltzelim, 982 (CF)
Ugab, 988 (CF)
Unisson, 989 (R, CF)
Univoque, 994 (R)
Upinge, 996 (R)
V, 983 (CF)
Vénitienne, 983 (CF)
Ventre, 983 (R)
Vers, 984 (M)
Vibration, 988 (R)
Viole, 988 (R)
Viole bâtarde, 988 (CF)
Viole d'amour, 988 (CF)
Violon, 988 (CF)
Virginale, 988 (CF)
Virgule, 989 (R)
Virile, 989 (CF)
Vocale, 994 (R)
Volume, 995 (R)
Vraisemblance, 996 (M)
Ypoptère, 1004 (CF)
Zygie, 1004 (CF)

AUTHORITIES ON MUSIC QUOTED IN THE
ENCYCLOPEDIA

Agostini, Leonardo, Le gemme antiche figurate. 2 vols. Rome, Appresso dell'autore, 1657–1669.

Albrecht, J. W., Tractatus physicus de effectibus musices in corpus animatum. Leipzig, Martin, 1734.

Alembert, Jean d', Eléments de musique. Lyons, Bruyset, 1762.

Anglebert, Jean Henri d', Principes de l'accompagnement, in Pièces de clavecin. Paris, 1689.

Bacchius, Isagoge musicæ artis, in Mersenne, Harmonie universelle. Paris, F. Morellum, 1623.

Baglivi, Giorgio, Opera omnia medico-pratica et anatomica. Paris and Lyons, Rigaud, 1704.

Ballière de Laisement, Charles L. D., Théorie de la musique. Paris, Didot le Jeune, 1764.

Banchieri, Adriano, Cartella, ovvero regole utilissime a quelli che desiderano imparare il canto figurato. Venice, Vincenti, 1601.

Bartholin, Caspari, De tibiis veterum. Venice, Monetæ, 1677.

Batteux, Abbé, Les Beaux-Arts réduits à un même principe. Paris, Durand, 1746.

Belleforest, François de, La Cosmographie universelle. Paris, M. Sonnius, 1575.

Bernouilli, Daniel, "Réflexions et éclaircissements sur les nouvelles vibrations des cordes," *Mémoires de l'Académie des Sciences de Berlin,* Vol. IX, 1755.

—— "Sur le mélange de plusieurs espèces de vibrations," *Mémoires de l'Académie des Sciences de Berlin,* Vol. IX, 1755.

Bethizy, J. L., Exposition de la théorie et de la pratique de la musique. Paris, M. Lambert, 1754.

Bonnet, Jacques and Pierre Bourdelot, Histoire de la danse sacrée et profane. Paris, D'Houry fils, 1723.

Bononcini, Giovanni Maria, Il pratico musico. Venice, G. Sala, 1678.

Bontempi, Giovanni Andrea, Nova quatuor vocibus componendi methodus. Dresden, Seyffert, 1660.

—— Historia musica. Perugia, Constantini, 1695.

Boyle, Robert, Essay on Languid Motion. London, Davis, 1685.

Brossard, Sebastien, Dictionnaire de musique. Paris, Ballard, 1703.

Burette, Pierre Jean, "Dissertation où l'on fait voir que les merveilleux effets attribués à la musique des anciens ne prouvent point qu'elle fût aussi parfaite que la nôtre," Mémoires de l'Académie des Inscriptions et Belles-Lettres, Vol. V, 1729.

Calliachius, Nicolaus, De ludis scenicis. Padua, J. Manfre, 1714.

Callieres, François de, Mots à la mode. Paris, C. Barbin, 1692.

Calmet, Augustin, Commentaire littéral sur tous les livres de l'Ancien et du Nouveau Testament. 22 vols. Paris, P. Emery, 1707–1716.

Campion, François, Traité d'accompagnement. Paris, 1716.

Capella, Martianus, Satyricon. Lyons, C. Raphelengium, 1599.

Chardin, Jean, Journal de voyage en Perse et aux Indes Orientales. London, M. Pitt, 1686.

Chastellux, François de, Essai sur l'union de la poésie et de la musique. Paris, Merlin, 1765.

Delair, Denis, Traité d'accompagnement pour le théorbe. Paris, 1690.

Derham, William, "Experiments and Observations on the Motion of Sound," Philosophical Transactions of the Royal Society of London, Vol. XXVI, No. 313 (1707).

—— "Vibrations of Pendulums," ibid., Vol. XXXIX, No. 440 (1736).

Descartes, René, Compendium musicæ. Rotterdam, Zijill et Ackersdijk, 1650.

Diemerbroeck, Isbrandus de, Opera omnia anatomica et medica. Utrecht, 1685.

Dodart, Denis, "Mémoire sur les causes de la voix de l'homme et de ses différents tons," 1703; being an unpublished paper read at the Académie des Sciences et Arts, Nov. 13, 1700.

Doni, Antonio Francesco, Dialogo sopra la musica. 1541.

Doni, Giovanni Battista, Compendio del trattato dei generi e dei modi della musica. Rome, A. Fei, 1635.

Du Bos, J. B., Réflexions critiques sur la poésie et la peinture. 2 vols. Paris, Mariette, 1719.

Du Chesne, André, Les Antiquités et recherches des villes de France. Paris, J. Petit-Pas, 1609.

Du Halde, J. B., Description géographique, historique, chronologique, politique et physique de l'Empire de la Chine. Paris, P. G. Le Mercier, 1735.

Dumas, Louis, L'Art de la musique. Paris, l'auteur, 1753.

Euler, Leonhardt, Tentamen novæ theoriæ musicæ. Petersburg, Ex typographia Academiæ scientiarum, 1739.

Euler, Leonhardt, "Du véritable caractère de la musique moderne," *Mémoires de l'Académie Royale de Berlin,* 1764.

Fauchet, Claude, Recueil de l'origine de la langue et de la poésie française. Paris, Patisson, 1581.

Ferrein, Antoine, Lettre sur le nouveau système de la voix et sur les artères lymphatiques. E. J. Bertin, s.l., 1748.

Feuillet, Raoul Auger, Choréographie; ou, L'art de décrire la danse par caractères, figures, et signes démonstratifs. Paris, Brunet, 1699.

Fontenelle, Bernard le Bouyer de, Histoire du théâtre français, in Œuvres (Paris, M. Brunet, 1742), Vol. III.

Froger, François, Relation d'un voyage fait en 1695, 1696, et 1697 aux côtes d'Afrique . . . Paris, 1698.

Furetière, Antoine, Dictionnaire universel. Amsterdam, Desbordes, 1685.

Galilei, Vincenzo, Dialogo della musica antica e della moderna. Florence, Marescotti, 1581.

Gaudentius, Introductio harmonica. Amsterdam, 1652.

Gerson, Jean Charlier de, De laude musices. Antwerp, 1706.

Glareanus, Henricus Loricus, Dodecachordon. Basel, Wonnegger, 1559.

Haller, Albrecht von, Elementa physiologiae corporis humani. 8 vols., Lausanne, Bousquet, 1757–1766, Vol. III, "Respiratio, Vox."

Holder, William, A Theory of the Natural Grounds and Principles of Harmony. London, 1694.

Hotteterre, Jacques, Principes de la flûte traversière. Paris, Ballard, 1707.

Huygens, Christian, Novus cyclus harmonicus. The Hague, 1698.

—— Cosmotheros. The Hague, 1698. French translation by Dufour under the title La Pluralité des mondes.

Jamard, Recherches sur la théorie de la musique. Paris, Jombert, 1769.

Kepler, Johannes, Harmonices mundi. Linz, G. Tampachii, 1619.

Kircher, Athanasius, Musurgia universalis. 2 vols. Rome, Corbelletti, 1650.

—— Phonurgia nova. Kempten, R. Dreherr, 1673.

Lebeuf, Jean, Traité historique et pratique sur le chant ecclésiastique. Paris, J. B. Herissant, 1741.

Levens, Abrégè des règles de l'harmonie. Bordeaux, 1743.

Loulié, Etienne, Eléments ou principes de musique. Paris, Ballard, 1696.

—— Nouveau système de musique. Paris, Ballard, 1698.

—— "Chronomètres," & "Sonomètres," *Mémoires de l'Académie des Sciences de Berlin,* 1699 and 1701.

Malcolm, Alexander, A Treatise of Musick. Edinburgh, 1721.

Massieu, Guillaume, Histoire de la poésie française. Paris, Prault fils, 1739.

Mattheson, Johann, Grosse General-Bass Schule. Hamburg, Kissner, 1731.

Mei, Girolamo, Discorso sopra la musica antica e moderna. Venice, 1602.

Ménestrier, Claude François, Des ballets anciens et modernes. Paris, R. Guignard, 1682.

Mersenne, Marin, Harmonie universelle. Paris, S. Cramoisy, 1636–1637.

Meursius, Johannes, Orchestra, sive de saltationibus veterum. Lyons, G. Basson, 1618.

Montfaucon, Bernard de, L'Antiquité expliquée. Paris, La Compagnie des libraires, 1716.

Moreri, Louis, Dictionnaire historique. Lyons, Girin et Riviere, 1674.

Morhof, Daniel Georg, Epistola de scypho vitreo per certum vocis sonum rupto. Kilonii, J. Reuman, 1672.

Nauze, Louis Jouard de la, "Les Chansons de l'ancienne Grèce," *Mémoires de l'Académie des Inscriptions et des Belles-Lettres,* Vol. IX (1732).

Newton, Isaac, Philosophiæ naturalis principia mathematica. London, 1687.

Parran, Antoine, Traité de la musique théorique et pratique. Paris, Ballard, 1639.

Penna, Lorenzo, Li Primi Alberi musicali. Venice, G. Sala, 1678.

Prætorius, Michael, Syntagma musicum. 3 vols. Wittenberg, 1614–1620.

Printz, Wolfgang Kaspar, Musica modulatoria vocalis. Schweidnitz, 1678.

—— Historische Beschreibung der edlen Sing- und Klingkunst. Dresden, J. C. Mieth, 1690.

Quantz, Johann Joachim, Essai d'une méthode pour apprendre à jouer de la flûte traversière. Berlin, Voss, 1752.

Rameau, Jean Philippe, for all published writings on music, *vide infra,* Bibliography.

Rameau, P., Le Maître à danser. Paris, Villette, 1725.

Riccoboni, L., Traité de la réformation des théâtres. 1743.

Roberts, Francis, "On the Defects and Musical Notes of the Trumpet and Trumpet Marine," *Phil. Trans.,* Vol. XVII, (1692).

—— "Concerning the Distance of Fixed Stars," *Philosophical Transactions,* Vol. XVIII, No. 209 (1694).

Rollin, Charles, Histoire ancienne. Paris, Etienne, 1731–1738, Vol. IV. Polybe et la musique.

Romieu, J. B., "Nouvelle découverte des sons harmoniques graves," *Mémoires de l'Académie des Sciences et Lettres.* Montpellier, 1752.

Rousseau, Jean, Traité de la viole. Paris, Ballard, 1687.

Roussier, Pierre Joseph, Mémoire sur la musique des anciens. Paris, Lacombe, 1770.

Saint Lambert, Michel de, Les Principes du clavecin. Paris, 1697.

Salinas, Francisco, De musica. Salamanca, Gastius, 1577.

Salmon, Thomas, Essay to the Advancement of Music by casting away all Cliffs and uniting all sorts of Music. London, 1672.

Sauveur, Joseph, "Table générale des systèmes tempérés de musique," *Mémoires de l'Académie des Sciences,* 1711.

Serre, J. A., Essai sur les principes de l'harmonie. Paris, Prault fils, 1753.

Souhaitty, Jean Jacques, Nouveaux éléments du chant. 1677.

Spon, Jacob, Miscellanea eruditæ antiquitatis. Lyons, 1685.

Sulzer, J. G., Allgemeine Theorie der schœnen Künste. 5 vols. Leipzig, Weidmannsche, 1792–99.

Tabourot, Jehan, Orchesographie. Lengres, Des Preyz, 1588.

Tartini, Giuseppe, Trattato di musica seconda la vera scienza dell'armonia. Padua, 1754.

—— Principles and Power of Harmony. London, 1771. Contains an account of Tartini's Treatise of Music, edited by B. Stillingfleet.

Tosi, P. F., Opinioni dei cantori antichi e moderni. Bologna, 1723.

Vatri, René, "L'Origine et les progrès de la tragédie," Mémoires de l'Académie des Inscriptions et des Belles-Lettres, Vol. XV.

—— "Avantages que la tragédie ancienne retirait de ses chœurs," Mémoires de l'Académie des Inscriptions et des Belles-Lettres, Vol. VIII.

Vossius, I., De poematum cantu. Oxford, 1673.

Walker, "Some Experiments and Observations concerning Sounds," Philosophical Transactions, Vol. XX, No. 247 (1698).

Wallis, John, "Trembling of Consonant Strings," Philosophical Transactions, Vol. XII (1677).

—— "Division of the Monochord," Philosophical Transactions, Vol. XX (1698).

Walther, J. G., Musikalisches Lexicon; oder, Musikalische Bibliothek. Leipzig, 1732.

BIBLIOGRAPHY

BIBLIOGRAPHY

Abert, Hermann, J. G. Noverre und sein Einfluss auf die dramatische Ballett-komposition. Berlin, 1908.

Adam, Adolphe, "Rousseau musicien," in Souvenirs d'un musicien (Paris, 1853), pp. 177–215.

Addison, Joseph, The Spectator. Oxford, 1886.

Alembert, Jean d', "Compte rendu de la démonstration du principe de l'harmonie de Rameau, extrait des registres de l'Académie Royale des Sciences du 10 décembre, 1749" (with Mairan and Nicole), in Rameau, Démonstration du principe de l'harmonie.

—— Eléments de musique . . . éclaircis, développés et augmentés. Lyons, 1762.

—— Eléments de musique théorique et pratique suivant les principes de M. Rameau. Paris, 1752.

—— Fragments sur l'opéra, 1752, in his Œuvres et correspondance inédites, ed. by Henry, Paris, 1887.

—— "Lettre à M. Rameau pour prouver que le corps sonore ne nous donne pas et ne peut nous donner par lui-même aucune idée des proportions," Mercure, Mar. 1762.

—— Œuvres complètes. 18 vols. Paris, 1805.

—— Œuvres et correspondance inédites, ed. by Charles Henry. Paris, 1887.

—— Réflexions sur la musique en général et sur la nôtre en particulier, 1773, in his Œuvres et correspondance inédites, ed. by Henry. Paris, 1887.

—— Réflexions sur la théorie de la musique, 1777, in his Œuvres et correspondance inédites, ed. by Henry. Paris, 1887.

Algarotti, Francesco, Saggio sopra l'opera in musica. 2d ed. Leghorn, 1763.

—— Opere. 10 vols. Cremona, 1778–1784.

André, Yves Marie, Essai sur le beau, où l'on examine en quoi consiste précisément le beau dans le physique, dans le moral, dans les ouvrages de l'esprit, et dans la musique. Paris, 1741.

Annales de la Société J. J. Rousseau, 29 vols. Geneva, Jullien, 1905–1943.

Arnaud, François, "Essai sur le mélodrame: ou drame lyrique," in Variétés Littéraires, III (1768), 23–30.

—— Lettre sur la musique à M. le comte de Caylus. Paris (?), 1754.

—— Œuvres complètes. 3 vols. Paris, 1808.

—— La Soirée perdue à l'Opéra. Paris, 1776.

Arnaud, François, ed., "Lettre de M. Sulzer à un de ses amis où il expose le plan de son dictionnaire sur les arts et les sciences," *Variétés Littéraires, Œuvres*, III (1768).

—— ed., "Lettre sur Il Teatro alla moda," *Variétés Littéraires,* I (1768).

Arnold, T. F., The Art of Accompaniment from a Thorough Bass as Practised in the 17th and 18th Centuries. Oxford, 1931.

Arteaga, Stefano, Le rivoluzioni del teatro musicale italiano dalla sua origine fino al presente. Venice, 1785.

Aubert, Jean Louis, Réfutation suivie et détaillée des principes de M. Rousseau. Paris, 1754.

Avison, Charles, An Essay on Musical Expression. London, 1752.

Bassi, Antonio Benedetto, Lettre adressée à la Société olympique de Paris à l'occasion de l'opéra bouffon italien de Versailles. Paris, 1787.

Bâton, Charles, Examen de la lettre de M. Rousseau sur la musique française. Paris, 1753.

Batteux, Abbé, Les Beaux-Arts réduits à un même principe. Paris, 1746.

Bauer, Heinrich, J. F. Marmontel als Literarkritiker. Dresden, 1937.

Beaumarchais, P. A. C. de, Discours préliminaire à l'opéra de Tarare. Paris, 1787.

Berlioz, Hector, Les Grotesques de la musique. Paris, 1871.

Bianchi, Giovanni Antonio, De i vizj e de i defetti del moderno teatro, e del modo di corregergli e d'emendarli. Rome, 1753.

Billy, André, Diderot. Paris, Editions de la France, 1932.

—— "Diderot chez ses amis," in *Les Œuvres Libres,* 1932, No. 128, pp. 267–310.

Blainville, Charles Henri, L'Esprit de l'art musical. Geneva, 1754.

Blanchet, Jean, L'Art ou les principes philosophiques du chant. Paris, 1756.

Bobillier, Mlle (*pseud.,* Michel Brenet), Les Concerts en France sous l'ancien régime. Paris, 1900.

Boileau, N., Œuvres. 4 vols. Paris, Langlois, 1830.

Boissy, La Frivolité. Paris, 1753.

Bollioud de Mermet, L., De la corruption du goût dans la musique française. Lyons, 1746.

Bonneval, de, Apologie de la musique et des musiciens français contre M. Rousseau. Paris, 1753.

Boyer, Pascal, Lettre à M. Diderot sur le projet de l'unité de clef dans la musique. Paris, 1767.

Bricaire de la Dixmérie, Nicolas, Lettres sur l'état présent de nos spectacles. Paris, 1765.

Brijon, C. R., Réflexions sur la musique. Paris, 1763.

Briqueville, Eugène de, L'Abbé Arnaud et la réforme de l'opéra au XVIIIième siècle. Avignon, 1881.

Brosses, Charles de, Lettres familières écrites d'Italie. 2 vols. Paris, 1858.
—— Lettres inédites. Paris, 1929.
Brunetière, F., Etudes critiques; VIIième série. 5th ed. Paris, 1901.
—— Manuel de l'histoire de la littérature française. 2d ed. Paris, 1899. VIième
  époque: "Les Commencements de l'opéra français."
Burney, Charles, The Present State of Music in France and Italy. London,
  1771.
—— The Present State of Music in Germany, the Netherlands and United
  Provinces. 2 vols. London, 1773.
Cahusac, Louis de, La Danse ancienne et moderne; ou, Traité historique de
  la danse. 3 vols. Paris, 1754.
Calsabigi, Raniero di, Lettre à l'auteur du *Mercure,* Paris, août, 1784.
—— Risposta che ritrovò nella gran città di Napoli alla critica ragionatissima
  delle poesie drammatiche del Cavaliere di Calsabigi. Venice, 1790.
Campbell, T. M., "Wagner—Nietzsche, to January, 1872," *P.M.L.A.,* LVI,
  No. 2 (June, 1941), 544–577.
Carlez, Jules, Framery, littérateur-musicien. Caen, 1895.
—— Grimm et la musique de son temps. Caen, 1872.
Casanova, J., Mémoires. 8 vols. Paris, 1880.
Castel, Louis Bertrand, Lettre d'un académicien de Bordeaux sur le fonds de
  la musique. Paris, 1754.
—— Réponse critique d'un académicien de Rouen à l'académicien de Bor-
  deaux sur le plus profond de la musique. Paris, 1754.
Caux de Cappeval, N. de, Apologie du goût français relativement à l'opéra;
  poème, avec un discours apologétique, et des adieux aux Bouffons. Paris.
  1755.
Caveirac, Abbé de, Lettre d'un visigoth à M. Fréron, sur sa dispute har-
  monique avec M. Rosseau. Paris, 1754.
Cazes, André, Grimm et les encyclopédistes. Paris, 1935.
Cazotte, Jacques, La Guerre de l'opéra; lettre écrite à une dame en province
  par quelqu'un qui n'est ni d'un coin ni de l'autre. Paris, 1753.
—— Observations sur la lettre de J. J. Rousseau au sujet de la musique fran-
  çaise. Paris, 1753.
Chabanon, Michel P. G. de, Eloge de Rameau. Paris, 1764.
—— Observations sur la musique. Paris, 1779.
Chastellux, François Jean de, Essai sur l'union de la poésie et de la musique.
  Paris, 1765.
Chevrier, François Antoine, Constitution du patriarche de l'opéra. Paris, 1754.
—— Observations sur le théâtre, dans lesquelles on examine avec impartialité
  l'état actuel des spectacles à Paris. Paris, 1755.
—— Le Retour du goût. Paris, 1754.
Collé, Charles, Journal et mémoires. 3 vols. Paris, 1868.

Condillac, Etienne, Traité des sensations. Paris, 1754.

Corancez, Olivier de, "Lettre sur Gluck," *Journal de Paris,* 18, 21, 24, août, 1788.

—— Jean Jacques Rousseau. Paris, 1798.

Coste d'Arnobat, C. P., Doutes d'un pyrronien proposés amicalement à J. J. Rousseau. Paris, 1753.

Cucuel, Georges, Les Créateurs de l'opéra-comique français. Paris, 1914.

—— "La Critique musicale dans les revues du dix-huitième siècle," *L'Année Musicale,* VIII (1912), 127–203.

—— La Popelinière et la musique de chambre au dix-huitième siècle. Paris, 1913.

Dacier, André, Poétique d'Aristote. Paris, 1692.

Dacier, Emile, L'Opéra au dix-huitième siècle, les premières représentations du Dardanus de Rameau," November–December, 1739, Paris, 1903.

Dandré-Bardon, L'Impartialité de la musique, épître à J. J. Rousseau, Paris, 1754.

Desfontaines, Abbé, Observations sur les écrits modernes. Paris, 1735.

Desnoiresterres, Gustave, La Musique française au dix-huitième siècle; Gluck et Piccini. Paris, 1872.

Diderot, Denis, Correspondance inédite. 2 vols. Paris, 1931.

—— Lettres à Sophie Volland. 3 vols. Paris, 1930.

—— Œuvres complètes. 20 vols. Paris, 1875–1879.

Doumic, René, in his Etudes sur la littérature française, L'opéra et la tragédie (1895), Paris, 1896.

Du Bos, J. B., Réflexions critiques sur la poésie et la peinture. 2 vols. Paris, 1719.

Ducros, Louis, Les Encyclopédistes. Paris, 1900.

Durey de Noinville, J. B., Histoire du théâtre de l'opéra en France. Paris, 1753.

—— Histoire du théâtre . . . édition corrigée et augmentée des pièces qui ont été représentées sur le théâtre de l'opéra par les musiciens italiens depuis le premier août 1752 jusqu'à 1754. Paris, 1757.

Du Roullet, François, Lettres sur les drames-opéra. Paris, 1776.

Ecorcheville, Jules, Corneille et la musique. Paris, 1906.

—— De Lulli à Rameau, l'esthétique musicale. Paris, 1906.

Encyclopédie. Paris, Vols. I–II, 1751, Vol. III, 1753, Vol. IV, 1754, Vol. V, 1755, Vol. VI, 1756, Vol. VII, 1757; Neuchâtel, Vols. VIII–XVII, 1765; Amsterdam, Supplement, Vols. I–II, 1776, Vols. III–IV, 1777; Paris and Amsterdam, Tables, Vols. I–II, 1780; Paris, Le Breton, David, Briasson, Durand, Planches, Vol. I, 1762, Vols. II–III, 1763, Vol. IV, 1765, Vol. V, 1767, Vol. VI, 1768, Vol. VII, 1769; Paris, Vols. VIII–IX, 1771, Vols. X–XI, 1772; Paris & Amsterdam, Supplement, 1777.

Encyclopédie de la musique et dictionnaire du conservatoire. Paris, Delagrave. Part II, Vol. I: Lucien Chevaillier, "Esthétique"; Vol. III: Lionel de la Laurencie, "La Musique française de Lulli à Gluck."

Epinay, Louise Florence d', Mémoires. 2 vols. Paris, 1865.

Estève, Pierre, L'Esprit des beaux-arts. 2 vols. Paris, 1753.

Euler, L., Tentamen novæ theoriæ musicæ. Petersburg, 1739.

Eximeno, Antonio, Dell' origine e delle regole della musica, colla storia del suo progresso, decadenza e rinnovazione. Rome, 1774.

Fénelon, François de, Lettre sur les occupations de l'Académie Française. 3 vols. Paris, 1835.

Fétis, F. J., Biographie universelle des musiciens. Paris, Firmin-Didot, 1865; 2d ed., 1866–1880.

Foliot, Mme (*pseud.*) Ce que l'on doit dire. Paris, 1753.

Font, A., Essai sur Favart et les origines de la comédie mêlée de chant. Toulouse, 1894.

Forkel, Johann Nicolaus, Allgemeine Litteratur der Musik. Leipzig, 1792.

—— Musikalisch-kritische Bibliothek. 3 vols. Gotha, 1778–1779.

Framery, Nicolas Etienne, Encyclopédie méthodique, Musique (with Guinguené & Momigny). Paris, Vol. I, 1791; Vol. II, 1818.

—— Lettre à l'auteur du Mercure, septembre, 1776.

—— ed., Journal de musique, historique, théorique, et pratique, sur la musique ancienne et moderne, dramatique et instrumentale chez toutes les nations. Paris, 1770.

—— ed., L'Année Littéraire, 1754–1790.

Frederick II, Lettre au public par main de maître. The Hague, 1753.

Fréron, Elie C., Lettres sur la musique française en réponse à celle de J. J. Rousseau. Paris, 1754.

—— Suite des lettres. Paris, 1754.

Gaiffe, F., Le Drame français au dix-huitième siècle. Paris, 1910.

Garcin, Laurent, Traité du mélodrame; ou, Réflexions sur la musique dramatique. Paris, 1772.

Gastoué, A., and others, La Musique française du moyen âge à la Révolution. Paris, 1934.

Goudar, Ange, Le Brigandage de la musique italienne. 1777.

—— Remarques sur la musique et la danse. Venice, 1773.

——Supplément aux remarques . . . Venice, 1773.

Grétry, A. E. M., De la vérité, 3 vols. Paris, 1801.

—— Mémoires; ou, Essais sur la musique, 3 vols. Paris, 1795.

—— "Réflexions d'un solitaire," *Mercure de France,* Nov.–Dec., 1913.

Grimm, Friedrich Melchior, "Lettre à M. Raynal sur Omphale," 1752, in his Correspondance littéraire, XVI, 309–312.

—— "Le Petit Prophète de Boemischbroda," 1753, in his Correspondance littéraire, XVI, 313–336.

Grimm, Friedrich Melchior, ed. Correspondance littéraire, 16 vols. Paris, 1877–82.

—— "Lettre sur Omphale," 1752, in his Correspondance littéraire, XVI, 282–309.

Gros, Etienne, "Les Origines de la tragédie lyrique et la place des tragédies en machines dans l'évolution du théâtre vers l'opéra," Revue d'Histoire Littéraire, avril-juin, 1928.

—— Phillippe Quinault. Paris, 1926.

Guiet, René, "L'Evolution d'un genre: livret d'opéra en France de Gluck à la Révolution," Smith College Studies in Modern Languages, Vol. XVIII (October, 1936–July, 1937).

Haussonville, Vicomte d', Le Salon de Mme Necker. 2 vols. Paris, 1882.

Hazard, Paul, La Crise de la conscience européenne. 3 vols. Paris, 1935.

Hellouin, Frédéric, Essai de critique de la critique musicale. Paris, 1906.

Hertel, Johann Wilhelm, Sammlung musikalischen Schriften grösstentheils aus den Werken der Italienen und Franzosen übersetzt. Leipzig, 1757–1758.

Hirschberg, Eugen, Die Encyklopädisten und die französische Oper im 18. Jahrhundert. Leipzig, 1903.

Holbach, Paul H. D. d', Lettre à une dame d'un certain âge sur l'état présent de l'opéra. Paris, 1752.

Istel, Edgar, J. J. Rousseau als Komponist seiner lyrischen Scene Pygmalion. Leipzig, 1901.

Jansen, A., Jean Jacques Rousseau als Musiker. Berlin, 1884.

Jourdan, J. B., Le Correcteur des bouffons à l'écolier de Prague. Paris, 1752.

—— Seconde Lettre du correcteur . . . contenant quelques observations sur l'opéra de Titon, le Jaloux corrigé, et Le Devin de village. Paris, 1752.

Journal de musique, par une société d'amateurs, Paris, 1773–1777.

Journal de musique et des théâtres de tous les pays, par une société de musiciens et de gens de lettres. Paris, 1804.

Journal de Paris.

Journal de Trévoux.

Jullien, Adolphe, La Musique et les philosophes aux dix-huitième siècle. Paris, 1873.

—— La Ville et la cour au dix-huitième siècle. Paris, 1881.

Kretzschmar, H., "Die Correspondance littéraire als musikgeschichtliche Quelle," in Jahrbuch Peters für 1903.

La Borde, J. B. de, Essai sur la musique ancienne et moderne. 4 vols. Paris, 1780.

—— Mémoire sur les proportions musicales. Paris, 1781.

La Bruyère, Jean de, Les Caractères. Paris, Hachette, 1868.

Lacassagne, Joseph, Traité général des éléments du chant. Paris, 1766.

Lacépède, B. G. E. de, La Poétique de la musique. 2 vols. Paris, 1785.

La Fontaine, J. de, Œuvres, Les Grands Ecrivains de la France. Paris, 1883.

La Harpe, J. F. de, Cours de littérature. 16 vols. Paris, Depelafol, 1825.

—— "Gluck," in *Journal de Politique et de Littérature,* 1777.

La Laurencie, Lionel de, "Les Bouffons," Société Internationale de Musique. Paris, 1912.

—— Contribution à l'histoire de la symphonie française vers 1750. Paris, 1911.

—— Les Créateurs de l'opéra français. Paris, Alcan, 1921.

—— Le Goût musical en France. Paris, 1905.

La Martinière, de, Introduction générale à l'étude des sciences et des belles-lettres. Berlin, 1756.

La Morlière, J. R. de, Lettre d'un sage à un homme très respectable et dont il a besoin. Paris, 1754.

Landowska, Wanda, Les Allemands et la musique française au dix-huitième siècle. Poitiers, 1911.

—— Musique ancienne; le mépris pour les anciens, la force de la sonorité, le style, l'interprétation, les virtuoses, les mécènes de la musique. Paris, 1909.

Láng, P. H., Music in Western Civilization. New York, Norton, 1941.

Lanson, Gustave, Esquisse d'une histoire de la tragédie française. New York, 1920.

Laugier, Marc Antoine, Apologie de la musique française contre M. Rousseau. Paris, 1754.

—— Sentiments d'un harmonophile sur différents ouvrages de musique. Paris, 1756.

Lavoix, H., Histoire de l'instrumentation depuis le seizième siècle à nos jours. Paris, 1878.

Leblond, Gaspard Michel, ed., Mémoires pour servir à l'histoire de la révolution opérée dans la musique par M. le Chevalier Gluck. Paris, 1782.

Lecerf de la Viéville, J. L., Comparaison de la musique italienne et de la musique française. Brussels, 1704.

Lefebure, L. F. H., Bévues, erreurs et méprises de différents auteurs célèbres en matière musicale. Paris, 1789.

Le Gras, J., Diderot et l'Encyclópedie. Amiens, 1928.

Leo, Werner, Diderot als Kunstphilosoph. Königsberg, 1918.

Lespinasse, Julie de, Lettres. 2 vols. Paris, Longchamps, 1811.

Lessing, E., Sammtliche Schriften. Schink ed. 32 vols. Leipzig, 1825.

Levinson, Andrei, Meister des Balletts; translated from the Russian by R. von Walther. Potsdam, 1923.

Lindemann, Frido, Die Operntexte Quinaults vom literarischen Standpunkte aus Betrachtet. Leipzig, 1904.

Malebranche, Nicolas, Recherche de la vérité. 2 vols. Paris, 1935.

Malherbe, C., "Un Précurseur de Gluck, le comte Algarotti," *Revue Musicale,* 1902.

Marcello, Benedetto, Il teatro alla moda, o sia metodo sicuro e facile per ben comporre ed eseguire l'opere italiane in musica. Venice, 17——.

Marignan, de, Eclaircissements données à l'auteur du *Journal Encyclopédique* sur la musique du *Devin de village*. Paris, 1781.

Marin, F. L. C., Ce qu'on a dit, ce qu'on a voulu dire, lettre à Mme Foliot. 1752.

Marmontel, J. F., Essai sur les révolutions de la musique en France. 1777.

—— Mémoires d'un père. 4 vols. Paris, 1804.

—— Poétique française. 2 vols. Paris, 1763.

Marpurg, F. W., Historisch-kritische Beyträge zur Aufnahme der Musik. 5 vols. Berlin, 1754–1760.

Marsan, J., La Pastorale dramatique en France à la fin du XVIIième et au commencement du XVIIIième siècle. Paris, 1905.

Masson, P. M., "Lullistes et Ramistes," *Année Musicale* (Paris), 1911.

—— "Musique italienne et musique française, la première querelle," *Rivista Musicale Italiana* (Torino), Vol. XIX, fasc. 3 (1912).

—— "Les Idées de Rousseau sur la musique," *Société Internationale de Musique*. Paris, 1912.

—— L'Opéra de Rameau. Paris, 1930.

Mercure de France, Paris, 1724–1791.

Metastasio, P., Opere. 6 vols. London, 1813.

Michaud, L. G., ed., Biographie universelle. Paris, 1880.

Mirabeau, H. G. R. de, Le Lecteur y mettra le titre. London, 1777.

Molière, Œuvres complètes; ed. by Despois & Mesnard. 9 vols. Paris, 1873–1912.

Moline, Pierre Louis, Conversation entre Lulli, Rameau et Orphée aux Champs-Elysées. Paris, 1774.

Monin, H., "Les Œuvres posthumes et la musique de Jean Jacques Rousseau," Revue d'Histoire Littéraire. Paris, 1915.

Montesquieu, Lettres Persanes. Paris, 1721.

Morand, Pierre de, Justification de la musique française. The Hague, 1754.

Mornet, Daniel, La Pensée française au dix-huitième siècle. 5th ed. Paris, 1938.

Naves, Raymond, Voltaire et *l'Encyclopédie*. Paris, 1938.

Newman, Ernest, Gluck and the Opera. London, 1895.

Niedeken, Hans, J. G. Noverre, sein Leben und seine Beziehungen zur Musik. Halle, 1914. Inaugural-Dissertation.

Nougaret, P. J. B., De l'art du théâtre en général. Paris, 1769.

Noverre, J. G., Lettres sur les arts imitateurs. 2 vols. Paris, 1807.

Nuitter et Thoinan, Les Origines de l'opéra français. Paris, 1886.

Patu et Portelance, Les Adieux du goût. Paris, 1754.

Perrault, Charles, Critique de l'opéra; ou, Examen de la tragédie intitulée *Alceste, ou le Triomphe d'Alcide*: Paris, 1674.

—— "Le Siècle de Louis le grand," Paris, 1687.

Perrault, Charles, Parallèle des anciens et des modernes. 4 vols. Paris, 1688–1697.

Pidansat, M. F. Mairobert de, Les Prophéties du grand prophète Monet. Paris, 1753.

—— Réponse du coin du roi au coin de la reine. 2d ed. Paris, 1753.

Pougin, Arthur, J. J. Rousseau musicien. Paris, 1901.

Poulet-Malassis, La Querelle des Bouffons. Paris, 1876.

Prod'homme, J. G., "Pierre de Jélyotte," *Internazional Musik Gesellschaft,* Vol. III (1901–1902).

—— "Diderot et la musique," *Internazional Musik Gesellschaft,* Vol. VIII, avril, 1914.

—— "Les Dernières représentations du *Devin de village,*" *Revue Musicale,* Vol. VII (1926).

Prunières, Henry, Le Ballet de cour en France avant Benserade et Lulli. Paris, 1914.

—— "La Fontaine et Lulli," *Revue Musicale,* Vol. VIII, août, 1921.

—— "Lecerf de la Viéville et l'esthétique musicale classique au dix-huitième siècle," *Société Internationale de Musique,* June, 1908.

—— Lully. Paris, 1927.

—— Nouvelle Histoire de la musique. Paris, 1936.

—— L'Opéra italien en France avant Lulli, Paris, 1913.

Quadrio, Francesco Saverio, Della storia e della ragione d'ogni poesia. 6 vols. Bologna, 1739–1752.

Quatremère de Quincy, A. C., "De la nature des opéras-bouffons italiens, et de l'union de la comédie et de la musique dans ces poèmes," *L'Esprit des Journaux,* Vol. IX (1789).

—— Dissertation sur les opéras-bouffons italiens. 1789.

Quinault, Philippe, Œuvres. 5 vols. Paris, 1715.

Racine, Jean, Poésies, avec une étude sur Racine et la musique par Gustave Samazeuilh. Paris, 1936.

Raguenet, François, Défense du paralèle. Paris, 1705.

—— Paralèle des Italiens et des Français en ce qui regarde la musique et les opéras. Paris, 1702.

Rameau, Jean Philippe, Code de musique pratique. Paris, 1760.

—— "Controverse sur le même sujet," in his Code de musique pratique.

—— Démonstration du principe de l'harmonie servant de base à tout l'art musical. Paris, 1750.

—— Erreurs sur la musique dans *l'Encyclopédie.* Paris, 1755.

—— Génération harmonique; ou, Traité de musique théorique et pratique. Paris, 1737.

—— "Lettre à M. D'Alembert sur ses opinions en musique insérées dans les articles Fondamental et Gamme de *l'Encyclopédie,*" in his Code de musique pratique.

Rameau, Jean Philippe, "Lettre au *Mercure* sur la musique," *Mercure,* May, 1752.

—— "Lettre aux philosophes concernant le corps sonore et la sympathie des tons," *Mémoires de Trévoux,* août, 1761.

—— Nouveau Système de musique théorique. Paris, 1726.

—— Nouvelles Réflexions sur la démonstration du principe de l'harmonie. Paris, 1752.

—— "Nouvelles Réflexions sur le principe sonore," in his Code de musique pratique.

—— Observations sur notre instinct pour la musique et sur son principe. Paris, 1754.

—— "Origines des sciences," in his Code de musique pratique.

—— Réponse à MM. les éditeurs de *l'Encyclopédie.* Paris, 1757.

—— Suite des erreurs. Paris, 1756.

—— Traité de l'harmonie réduite à ses principes naturels. Paris, 1722.

Récy, René de, "Rameau et les Encyclopédistes," *Revue des Deux-Mondes* (Paris), July, 1886.

Rémond de Saint-Mard, Toussaint, Réflexions sur l'opéra. The Hague, 1741.

Richebourg, L., Contribution à l'histoire de la querelle des Bouffons. Paris, 1937.

Richebourg, Marguerite, "La Bibliothèque de J. J. Rousseau," in Annales de la Société J. J. Rousseau, XXI, 199–250.

Riedel, F. J., Ueber die Musik des Ritters C. von Gluck. Vienna, 1775.

Riemann, Hugo, Dictionnaire de musique. Paris, 1931.

—— Geschichte der Musiktheorie. 2d ed. Berlin, 1920.

Robineau, Lettre d'un parisien contenant quelques réflexions sur celle de J. J. Rousseau. Paris, 1754.

Rochemont, de, Réflexions d'un patriote sur l'opéra français et sur l'opéra italien. Lausanne, 1754.

Rolland, Romain, "Gluck," *Revue de Paris,* June 15, 1904.

—— Musiciens d'autrefois. 10th ed. Paris, 1927.

—— Les Origines du théâtre lyrique moderne, histoire de l'opéra en Europe avant Lulli et Scarlatti. Paris, 1895.

—— Voyage musical au pays du passé. Paris, 1919.

Rousseau, Jean Jacques, Correspondance générale, ed. by Dufour. 20 vols. Paris, 1924–1934.

—— Lettre sur le drame musical en France et en Italie," in A. Jansen, J. J. Rousseau als Musiker.

—— Œuvres complètes. Paris, 1792. Ecrits sur la musique, Vols. XIX–XXII.

—— Œuvres complètes. 8 vols. Paris, 1856–58.

Ruhlière, C. C. de, Jugement de l'orchestre de l'opéra. Paris, 1753.

Sachs, Curt, Eine Weltgeschichte des Tanzes. Berlin, 1933.

Saint-Evremond, Charles de, Œuvres. 7 vols. London, 1725.

Saint-Lambert, J. F. de, "Lettre à M. le Baron d'Holbach sur l'opéra," in *Variétés littéraires,* Vol. III.

Saunier de Beaumont, Lettre sur la musique. Paris, 1743.

Scherer, E., "Melchior Grimm," *Revue des Deux Mondes,* 15 Oct., 1885.

Schopenhauer, Arthur, "Die Welt als Wille und Vorstellung," in Sämmtliche werke, vols. II–III, Leipzig, 1937–1939.

Serre, J. A., Observations sur les principes de l'harmonie, occasionnées par quelques écrits modernes sur ce sujet, et particulièrement par l'article Fondamental de M. D'Alembert dans l'Encyclopédie. Geneva, 1763.

Silin, Charles, Benserade and His Ballets de cour. Baltimore, Md., 1940.

Suard, J. B., "Lettre écrite de l'autre monde par l'Abbé des Fontaines à M. Fréron," in Recueil des mémoires.

—— Mémoires et correspondance. Paris, 1858.

Sulzer, J. G., Allgemeine Theorie der schoenen Künste. 5 vols. Leipzig, 1792–1799.

—— "Lettre à un de ses amis," in Arnaud, François, *Variétés Littéraires,* Vol. III.

Tiersot, Julien, Gluck. Paris, 1919.

—— J. J. Rousseau musicien. Paris, 1912.

—— "Les Leçons de musique de J. J. Rousseau," Vol. XIV (1912–1913).

—— Lettres de musiciens écrites en français du XV au XXième siècles. Turin, 1924.

—— La Musique dans la comédie de Molière. Paris, 1922.

Toth, Karl, Woman and Rococo in France. London, 1931.

Trahard, P., Les Maîtres de la sensibilité française. 4 vols. Paris, 1933.

Travenol, Louis, Arrêt du conseil d'état d'Apollon en faveur de l'orchestre de l'opéra contre J. J. Rousseau. Paris, 1753.

—— Histoire du théâtre de l'Académie Royale de Musique. Paris, 1757.

—— La Galerie de l'Académie Royale de Musique. Paris, 1754.

Vander, Straeten, E., Voltaire musicien. Paris, 1878.

Variétés Littéraires, ed. by Arnaud and Suard. 4 vols. Paris, 1768.

Varnum, Fanny, Le Chevalier de Chastellux. Paris, 1936.

Villeneuve, Lettre sur le méchanisme de l'opéra italien. Paris.

Voltaire, F. M. A. de, Questions sur *l'Encyclopédie.* 9 vols. [Paris], 1770–1772.

Wagner, Richard, "Das Kunstwerk der Zukunft," in his Gesammelte Schriften und Dichtungen, Leipzig, 1871–1883, Vol. III.

—— "Oper und Drama," in his Gesammelte Schriften und Dichtungen, Leipzig, 1871–1883, Vol. IV.

Yzo, Lettre sur celle de J. J. Rousseau sur la musique, in Recueil de mémoires, 1753.

ANONYMOUS WORKS

L'Anti-Scurra, ou préservatif contre les Bouffons italiens, in Recueil de mémoires.

L'Apologie du sublime bon mot, in Recueil de mémoires.

Déclaration du public au sujet des contestations qui se sont élevées sur la musique, in Recueil de mémoires.

Dissertations sur la musique française et italienne par M. L'A . . . P . . . Amsterdam, 1754.

"Epître aux bouffonistes," in Recueil de mémoires.

Lettre critique et historique sur la musique française et la musique italienne, et sur les Bouffons à Mme D., in Recueil de mémoires.

Lettre de MM. du coin du roi à MM. du coin de la reine sur la nouvelle pièce intitulée la Servante Maîtresse. Paris, 1753.

Nouvelle Lettre à M. Rousseau sur celle qui parut de il y a quelques mois. Paris, 1754.

La Paix de l'opéra, in Recueil de mémoires.

Réflexions lyriques, in Recueil de mémoires.

"La Réforme de l'opéra, poème," in Recueil de mémoires.

Relation véritable et intéressante du combat des fourches caudines livré à la Place Maubert au sujet des Bouffons, in Recueil de mémoires.

Remarques au sujet de la lettre de M. Grimm sur Omphale, Paris, 1752, in Recueil de mémoires.

COLLECTION OF PAMPHLETS

Recueil de mémoires, dissertations, lettres, et autres ouvrages critiques, historiques et littéraires, pour servir de supplément aux Mémoires de l'Académie Royale des Sciences et celle des Inscriptions et Belles-Lettres, Vol. CCCXXXIV.

INDEX

INDEX

Académie des Sciences approved Rameau's thesis, 104; appointed D'Alembert to report on works of theoretical nature, 164
Académie Royale de Musique, 117
Accent, 44; index to good melodic composition, 45
Accords fondamentaux, 110
Acoustics, geometrical justification for Rameau's theories, 102; material offered Rameau by physicists lost upon him, 111
Acting, emphasis placed on singing in detriment to, 18
Action ballet, 55, 74, 76, 82
Adam, Adolphe, 159
Addison, Joseph, 10*n*
Aestheticians, reaction to French rage for music, 13; measure music in terms of classical standards, 14; Encyclopedists adopted theories of, 167
Affections, doctrine of, adhered to by Encyclopedists, 61 ff.; *see also* Emotions; Passions
Alceste (Gluck), 81, 118, 120, 121; post-Encyclopedist critics object to, 132
Alcidiane (Benserade), 76
Alembert, Jean d'; 33, 41, 130, 135, 140, 165; quoted, 34; on musical imitation, 62; at loss for definite aesthetic of music, 63; music qualified as *contre-sens,* 64; on flute sonata, 65; final decision on Bouffons' Quarrel, 100; controversy with Rameau, 101-12; edition of Rameau's theory, 101; tributes to Rameau, 102, 105, 108; effort to keep Rameau from going astray, 102; criticism of Rameau's theory, 103; accused of treachery, 104, 105, 106; attack on French music, 106; Grimm's defense of, 109; tradition of music, 118; gave currency to Rameau's ideas, 133; called a traitor to Rameau's theories, 155; taken to task for errors in harmony, 155; praise of, 157; Rousseau's errors corrected in articles by, 159; reception by scholars, 164; criticism of Gluck, 166
Alexandrian, retained by Quinault for recitative, 8; not to be employed in opera, 38

Algarotti, Count Francesco, 113, 127; Calsabigi's principles culled from, 114; influence upon Gluck, 117; libretto constructed on model of Racine's *Iphigénie:* attitude toward opera, 128
Allegorical creations, bizarre, 51, 52
Allemands et la musique française . . . Les (Landowska), 156
Allgemeine Litteratur der Musik (Forkel), 136
Allgemeine Theorie der schoenen Künste (Sulzer), 80, 134
Allgemeine Theorie des Denkens und Empfindens (Eberhard), 136
Amadis (Lulli-Quinault), 48, 53
Amours déguisés, 76
André, Yves Marie, 14, 17; attempt to restate aesthetic values, 15
Andromède (Corneille), 3
Année Littéraire, 162
"Anti-scurra . . . , L'" (Caux de Cappeval), 92
Apologie du sublime bon mot, L', 93
Appendices, 169-208
Aria, *da capo aria,* 35, 39, 41*n;* broken line preferable, 38; how opera, differs from song: need for repetition of parts of, 39; overemphasis on, brought singer into prominence, 40; should represent an emotional crisis, 41; French resisted introduction of form into opera, 42; opera based on recitative and, but half an opera, 44; in French opera, 52; *see also* Melody
Ariadne (Benda), 137
Ariettes, introduction of Italian, changed course of English opera, 144
Aristotle, theory of purging emotions, 130
Aristoxenus, 162
Armide (Gluck), 120; Quinault's text and some of Lulli's music used in resetting, 113
Armide (Lulli-Quinault), 27, 51, 91, 93; reset by Gluck, 113
Arnaud, François, 129, 134, 135; Encyclopedist bias, 141; as music critic, 142

Arrêt rendu à l'amphithéâtre de l'Opéra (Diderot), 91, 102

Art-as-an-imitation-of-nature thesis, 14 f., 36, 61 ff., 99, 135

Artaserse (Metastasio), 37

Arteaga, Stefano, 112; compendium of virtues and abuses of Italian opera, 129; quoted, 130*n*; traces decline in Italian opera to *philosophes*, 131; dissatisfied with French and Italian forms of opera, 132

Arteserse (Vinci), 99

Arts which imitate nothing, 66

Assoucy, d,' Charles Coypeau, 3

Attilio Regolo (Metastasio), 37*n*

Au petit prophète de Boehmischbroda et au grand prophète Monet (Diderot), 93, 97

Avison, Charles, 138

Bacchius Senex, Greek musicographer, 162

Bach, C. P. E., 151

Bach, Johann Sebastian, 111, 156

Ballet, 23 ff.; use in opera, 53; dramatic tendency, 74; costumes, 74; in reign of Louis XIV, 76; highest expression of, 76; main defect, 77; tenets, 78; Rousseau opposed to, 79; revolution in, 80; how it came to take place of lyrical tragedy, 141; *see also* Dance

Ballet comique de la royne, Le, 74

Ballet de cour, 23, 26, 74

Ballet des prospérités, Le (Benserade), 76

Ballet des sauvages in Gluck's *Iphigénie en Tauride*, 83

Ballet en action, or *poème-ballet*, 55, 74, 76, 82

Ballet master, 82

Ballet pantomime, singer expected to complement music by means of, 55, 58; Grimm's proposal, 59; Diderot set stage for modern, 74; result of coöperation of dance, music, and mime, 79; transformation of old figure dances into, 80; revived by Noverre, 80, 81; how first was born, 81; Noverre's development of, 82 ff.; ridiculed, 145

Ballière de Laisement, C.L.D., 161

Barberinis, especially Cardinals Antonio and Francesco Barberini, 3

Barbier, Francisco A., 90

Baron, actor, 58

Baroni, Leonora, 3

Basse fondamentale, discovery of, 107; Ra-

meau's new method of accompaniment, 157*n*; Rousseau's effort to master, 163

Bassi, Antonio B., 133

Bastien et Bastienne (Mozart), 137

Bâton, Charles, 97

Bâton, noise of, 71

Batteux, Abbé, 14, 16, 17

Beaumarchais, P.A.C. de, tried to bring libretto up to level of Salieri's music, 147

Beauty, three categories defined, 15; Sulzer's theory of the beautiful and the useful, 135

Beaux-Arts réduits à un même principe, Les (Batteux), 16

Belton et Elisa (Noverre), 81

Bemerkungen zu Diderot's Versuch über die Malerei (Goethe), 136

Bemetzrieder, Anton, 72*n*, 136, 158

Benda, Georg, 137

Benserade, court ballet, 23, 24, 74, 76

Bergonce de Botta, 22

Berlioz, Hector, 156; Encyclopedists established principles of music drama for, 168

Bianchi, Giovanni A., 134

Bibliothèque de Neuchâtel, 106

Billy, André, 157

Biographie universelle des musiciens (Fétis), 161

Birds, song of, 67

Blainville, Charles H., 157, 158, 160; answer to Rousseau, 98

Blanchard, Abbé, 160

Blanchet, Jean, 145, 146, 148*n*

Boehmischbroda, little prophet of, 90 f.

Boethius, Anicius M., 162

Boileau, N., 49, 153; protest against new mixed genre in opera, 4; Quinault's harshest critic, 5; praise of Lulli, 6; opinion of the opera, 7, 9, 48; Quinault vindicated at expense of: taken to task by Cahusac, 27; prejudiced viewpoint, 28

Bollioud de Mermet, L., 19; quoted, 71*n*

Bouffons' Quarrel over respective excellence of Italian and French music, 89; responsibility for, laid at door of Encyclopedists, 92; won by Rousseau, 95 ff.; ended, 97; postlude, 98; Rameau's animosity to Encyclopedists grew out of, 102; cohesion of Encyclopedist camp during, 167

Bouffons' troup, 36, 89, 144; did not create a revolution in French opera, 100; touched off powder-keg of Encyclopedist's animosity, 113; French music freed from shackles as result of, 114; selections from Italian operas in repertory, 115

Bourgeois gentilhomme, Le (Molière), 76

Boyer, Pascal, 148n, 158

Bricaire de la Dixmérie, N., 148n

Brijon, C. R., 143

Brosses, Charles de, 19

Brunetière, F., 8n

Burney, Charles, 137, 158; quoted, 118n, 138

Caffarelli, singer, 39, 40

Cahusac, Louis de, 4n, 41, 48, 156, 158; quoted, 22-31 *passim*, 33, 34, 70; authority on the ballet, 23; best page of musical history written in eighteenth-century France, 30; based claims for excellence of French opera upon *merveilleux*, 50; saw in opera a vehicle for dances, 53; ón music of the entr'acte: his wants for the opera summed up, 55; counseled speeding up delivery, 58; suggestions for improvement of chorus, 59; theory of music, 63, 65; felt that Lulli's music played traitor to Quinault's text, 63, 64; attacks on dance routine, 74; articles on the dance, 75 ff.; collaboration with Rameau, 75, 77; on action ballet, 76; collaboration with Rameau, 77; Noverre's praise for articles on the dance, 84; part in *Le Devin du village*, 159; musical criticism, 164

Calsabigi, Raniero di, Gluck's librettist, 113, 118, 127; guided reform-opera with principles culled from Algarotti, 114; libretti criticized by Arteaga, 132; defense of Gluck's operas and his own libretti, 134;

Campra, André, 19, 24n, 27

—— A. H. de La Motte and, 76

Caproli, Carlo, 3

Capua, Rinaldo da, 91

Caractères de la folie, Les (Duclos), 160n

Carraccioli, Neapolitan ambassador, 121

Casanova, J., 38n

Castel, L. B., 90

Castil-Blaze, François H. J., 161

Castillon fils, author of articles on music, 33

Castor et Pollux (Rameau), 149

Catherine de Medici brought Italian fêtes to France, 22 f.

Caux de Cappeval, N. de, poems against the Queen's Corner, 92

Cavalli, Francesco, 3

Cazotte, Jacques, 90, 97; defense of French music, 92

Ce qu'on a dit, ce qu'on a voulu dire (attributed to Marin), 90

Chabanon, Michel P. G. de, quoted, 20n; animosity to the *Encyclopedia*, 145; on function of music, 146

Chaconnes, 79

Chambers' *Cyclopedia*, 21

Chant périodique, 42

Charles VI, Emperor, 41

Chastelleux, François J. de, 135, 167; questions validity of Rousseau's doctrine, 66; apology for instrumental music, 67

Chevaillier, Lucien, 157

Chords, classification of fundamental, 110

Chorus, suggestions for improvement of, 59

Church opposed opera as a source of vice, 6n

Cinq mémoires sur différents sujets de mathématiques (Diderot), 157

Clairon, Mlle, actress, 115n

Classical imitation, sarcasm leveled against, 145

Classicism, disintegration of French, 4

Coin de la reine, 90; poems against, 92

Coin du roi, 90; seized upon Rousseau's "opera" to confound opposition, 95; insistence on *status quo* in French opera, 100

Colbert, J. B., 30

Collé, Charles, 111, 158; part in *Le Devin du village*, 159

Comédie Française 98

Comedy, French: little more than a vehicle for *la galanterie*, 7

Comedy ballet, 26; Lulli's, 23; Molière's, *see* Molière, comedy ballet

Comic-opera singers, Italian, *see* Bouffons

Comparaison de la musique italienne et de la musique française (Lecerf de la Viéville), 13

Composer, relationship of poet and, 11; given credit for creation of opera, 27; melody neglected by French, 45; literary orientation, 56; counseled to study language prosody, 59; glaring defects of Italian, 99; considered creator of opera, 153

Composition, aesthetic theory of, based up-
on examination of French works, 33;
Cahusac's compromise between Lulli and
Rameau type operas, 59; *see also* Music;
Opera
Concerto, Brijon's concept of, 144
Concerts spirituels, 69, 157*n*
Condillac, Etienne, 140
Conductor, poor location: entirely taken up
with singers, 71
Consolations des misères de ma vie, Les
(Rousseau), 159
"Consonance" (Rousseau), 104
Corancez, Oliver de, 154*n*, 161
Corelli, Arcangelo, unacquainted with reci-
tative and aria-type opera, 41
Corneille, 3, 4, 11, 113, 149; conces-
sions to love in plays of, 7; could never
be set to music, 17; effect of plays,
29
*Correcteur des Bouffons à l'écolier de
Prague, Le* (Jourdan), 92
Correspondance littéraire (ed. Grimm),
122, 127, 164, 166, 165
Coryphées, or dance choruses, 82
Costumes of ballet, 74
Counterpoint, 129
Cours de littérature (La Harpe), 151
Court ballet, 23, 26, 74
Court *fêtes,* evolution, 26; paved way for
opera, 26*n*
Criticism of music, before the Encyclopedia,
3-20; seventeenth century, 3-18; one of
most significant statements in history of,
11*n*; eighteenth century, 13 ff.; basis of
Encyclopedists' claim to significance in
field of, 89; influence of the *Encyclopedia*
on, 125-68; post-Encyclopedist, in
France, 149-54; established as a literary
endeavor, 168; *see also* Opera, criticism
"Criticism of Music in the Encyclopedia,"
1-85
Critics, music: misunderstood music of
instruments, 61; Encyclopedist, self-
taught in art of music, 141; course followed in France, 1670–1770, 153; the
ideal, an amateur, 164; *see also* Encyclopedists
Critique de l'opéra . . . (Perrault), 12
Cunning Man, The, adaptation of Rousseau's *Devin,* 138
Cyclopedia, Chambers', 21

Da capo aria, 35, 39, 41*n*, 99
Dacier, André, quoted, 4*n*, 5*n*
Dance, 74-85; principal object of, 16; as an
element in opera, 26, 53 ff.; Cahusac
stanchest champion of, 53, 54; Marmontel's defense of, 54; must imitate nature,
75, 78; must "paint," 75; should derive
from fabric of ballet, 79; Diderot's appraisal, 79; Noverre's innovations, 80;
Noverre's two categories, 82; Gluck insisted on as essential part of opera, 118;
see also Ballet
Dance choruses, 82
Dancers in French opera, 26; in the ballet,
83
Dancing pantomine, *see* Ballet pantomine
Dardanus (Rameau), 20
Dauvergne, Antoine, 117
Declamation, music conceived as, and result
of, enhanced, 6, 17, 18; basis of Lulli's
operas, 28; in the Lulli-Quinault opera
and in the Rameau opera, 29; principal
element, 33; the basis of recitative, 34, 35;
two types, 35; melody can never be based
on theatrical, 44; revision of, 58; Diderot
sought to enlarge sphere of, 114; natural
as opposed to classical, 115
Déclamation chantante, 28
Déclamation notée, see Recitative
*Déclaration du public au sujet des con-
testations qui se sont élevées sur la
musique,* 92
Dédicace d'Orphée (Gluck), 161
De Gamaches, physicist, 111
De I vizi e de I defetti del moderno teatro
(Bianchi), 134
De la liberté de la musique (Alembert), 100
De l'art du théâtre en générale (Nougaret),
149
Della storia e della ragione d'ogni poesia
(Quadrio), 134
*Dell' origine e delle regole della mu-
sica* . . . (Eximeno), 133
Démonstration du principe de l'harmonie
(Rameau), 104, 164
Descartes, Rameau a disciple of, 102; Ra-
meau misunderstood, 111
Destouches, Philippe N., 19, 27, 89
Devin du village, Le (Rousseau), 94, 99,
137, 163; Gluck's compliment to, 121;
translated by Mylius and Schink, 136;
adaptation of, given at the Drury Lane,
138; a model of *opéra-bouffon,* 149;

controversy about: facts according to Rousseau, 159

Dictionnaire de musique (Rousseau), 52, 106, 134, 136, 151, 160n; reception: translations, 161

Diderot, Denis, 54n, 129, 136, 137, 165; appreciation of instrumental music, 61, 68; theory of music, 61; critic of instrumental music, 71 ff.; quoted, 72, 116, 119; set stage for ballet pantomime, 74; an innovator of revitalized ballet, 79; appraisal of dancing art, 79; Noverre's praise of, 84; part in Bouffons' Quarrel, 91, 93; plea for saner criticism, 93; praise of Rameau, 101; effort to keep Rameau from going astray, 102; defense of *Encyclopedia* in Rameau controversy, 108; Grimm's defense of, 109; reform campaign, 113 ff.; prepared the French for Gluck, 114; influence upon Gluck, 114, 117; visions of ideal opera, 115; insisted that music must take upper hand in opera, 116; Gluck's greatest debt to, 119; prerequisites demanded in poet-composer: relations to reform opera, 120; challenge to construct a libretto on model of Racine's play, 128; mastery of matters musical, 138; influence, 142; placed among the sophists, 152; differences of opinion regarding musical criticism, 155; study of music, 157; gained earliest renown as a mathematician, 158; accepted as authority on matters musical, 158; confided section on music to Rousseau care, 159; slight mention of Gluck, 166

Discours préliminaire (Alembert), 62, 108

Divertissements, Quinault's imitation of meter of love songs from, of Molière's comedy ballets, 8; of Lulli's operas, 23, 28; of Quinault's, 23, 24, 25; in the lyrical tragedy and the lyrical ballet, 25; growing importance, 26; in Lulli-Quinault operas, 29, 53 f., 57; in Rameau operas, 29; an integral part of action, 53 ff.; ideal, 53; insistence of the *style galant* on, 57; fixed dances of *ballet de cour* held sway in, 74; highest expression of ballet, 76; Rameau's talents hampered by prevailing mode of, 113; *see also* Ballets; Machines

Donna superba, La (Capua), 91

Double aria, *see* Duet

Drack, translator, 138

Drama, influence of, at an end, 34; distinguished from opera, 35 ff.; Greek, 51; successful opera must be based on good, 153; *see also* Tragedy

Dramatist, difference between art of, and that of opera poet, 37

Dramaturgy, 9

Dresden opera orchestra, 70

Du Bois, J. B., 14, 17

Duclos, Charles Pinot, 160n

Duet, or double aria, 38; as dialogue, 41

Dumesnil, Mlle, actress, 58, 115n

Duni, Egidio R., 114, 158

Duroncel, singer, 160

Du Roullet, François, 113, 118, 127; engaged Gluck to write a French opera, 117; libretto modeled on Racine's *Iphigénie*, 119, 128; document on cause and effect of Gluck reform, 123; go-between for Encyclopedists in their relations with Gluck, 140

Eberhard, Johann A., 136

Eckardt, Johann Gottfried, 157n

Ecorcheville, Jules, quoted, 6n

Eléments de musique . . . (Alembert), 101, 104, 105, 109, 133; put into German, 112; clearest approach to Rameau's theories found in, 112; translated by Marpurg, 135; errors in harmony, 155; influence, 157; served to establish author's reputation, 164

Eloge de Rameau (Chabanon), 145

Emotions, introduction of love into opera, 7, 12, 167; purpose of art to express, 16; music makes direct appeal to, 17; words could never adequately express, 18; representation of, 61 ff.; opera must deal with conflict of, 167; *see also* Passions

Enchantement, element of, in *merveilleux,* 48 ff.

Encyclopedia, Diderot's articles on instruments, 71 ff.; influence on Noverre, 80, 81, 82, 84; raw material for arguments in Bouffons' Quarrel, 89; first official act as an organ of musical criticism, 89; one of prime achievements, 94; loss of popularity, 100; Rameau refused to do articles on music, 102; influence on criticism of music, 125-68; nefarious influence on opera attacked, 133; articles on music from Sulzer's dictionary in-

Encyclopedia (*Continued*)
cluded in Supplement, 135; post-
Encyclopedist criticism of music in
France, 149-54; few works as roundly
abused as music articles, 155; faults in
Rousseau's articles held up as a reflection on, 159
"Encyclopédie" (Diderot), flayed by La
Harpe, 152
Encyclopédie du conservatoire, 157
Encyclopédie méthodique, 151
Encyclopedists, turned to Italy for guidance, 20; source of material for their
polemics and reform campaign, 21; division of opinion concerning the *merveilleux,* 53; unwilling to admit that French
did not have a national opera, 56; suggested reforms of the opera, 57-60;
espoused imitation-of-nature theory and
view that instrumental music must
"paint," 61 ff.; interest in technical progress of instrumental music, 68; controversy fomented by, 89 ff. (*see also*
Bouffons' Quarrel); classical reproof of
activity of, 92; indictment against, as
geometers, 94, 95; insistence on *status
quo* in French opera, 99; Rameau
owed much to: his ungenerous and hostile attitude, 112; influence upon Gluck,
117; accused of fostering a realistic theory of imitation, 118*n*; influence upon
Algarotti, 128; decline in Italian opera
attributed to, 131; position concerning
Lulli-Quinault operas, 153; greatness of
their victorious revolution, 153; scored
by Landowska, 156; charge most frequently made against, 157; Hellouin's
indictment of, 165 ff.; accused of killing
French musical tradition, 166; stanchest
representatives of French operatic tradition, 167; claim to achievement,
168
*Encyklopädisten und die französische Oper
. . . Die* (Hirschberg), 156
England, propagandists for the Encyclopedists in, 137
Ensemble, French music precludes, 71
Entr'acte, music of, should continue illusion of spectacle, 55
Entretiens sur le fils naturel (Diderot), 74,
79
"Epître aux Bouffonistes" (Caux de Cappeval), 92

Ernelinde (Philidor), 115*n*, 158
Erreurs sur la musique dans l'Encyclopédie
(Rameau), 102, 104, 116; an attack on
Rousseau, 106; Rousseau's answer, 107
Esprit de l'art musical, L' (Blainville), 98
Esprit des beaux-arts, L' (Estève), 16
Essai de critique de la critique musicale
(Hellouin), 156, 165
Essay on Musical Expression (Avison), 138
Estève, Pierre, 14, 16, 17
Europe galante, L' (La Motte and Campra),
24*n*, 76
Examen d'Andromède (Corneille), 11
*Examen de deux principes avancés par M.
Rameau . . . .* (Rousseau), 107
Eximeno, Antonio, 112, 133
Expert, Henri, 157

Fâcheux, Les (Molière), 76
Facial expression, 55
Feelings, *see* Emotions; Passions
Fel, Mlle, singer, 30, 91
Fénelon, François de, 4, 49, 153; quoted,
7; attitude toward music, 6
Fêtes, a prime factor in development of
opera, 21, 22; taken to France, 22 f.;
popularity at court, 23; first efforts at
national opera in France partook nature
of, 47; seventeenth-century, 76
Fêtes de Bacchus et de l'amour, 76
Fêtes de l'hymen de l'amour (Rameau and
Cahusac), 77
Fétis, F. J., 151, 161; quoted, 160*n*
Film, music of the, 9
Filtz, Anton, 157*n*
First violin, musicians of orchestra directed
by, 71
Flute, 65
"Fondamentale" (Alembert), 103
Fontenelle, Bernard Le B. de, 9, 66, 129
Forkel, Johann N., 136
*Fragments d'observations sur l'Alceste . . .
de M. . . . Gluck* (Rousseau), 121,
166
Framery, Nicolas E., 151, 153, 161
France, made music-conscious by Lulli, 13;
influence of *Encyclopedia,* 140-48; *see
also* Language, French; Music, French;
Opera, French
French, the: traditional in artistic tastes:
asked to awaken from their musical
lethargy, 33; eye for color, 59
Fréron, Elie C., 90, 97, 162

Gabrieli, singer, 39, 40
Galeazzo, Duke of Milan, 22
Galiani, Abbé, 127
"Gamme" (Alembert), 104
Garcin, Laurent, 148n
Garrick, David, 81
Gastoué, A., and others, 157
Gavottes, 79
Geminiani, Francesco, 138
Génération harmonique (Rameau), 101
Geometry, effort to separate music from, 14; Rameau's geometrical justification for his acoustical theories, 102, 109; abuse of, in music, 104
Germany, influence of Encyclopedia, 134 ff.
Gesamtkunstwerk (Wagner), 136
Geschichte der Abderiten (Wieland), 136
Gestures, 55
Gilbert, Gabriel, 29
Gluck, Christoph Willibald Chevalier von, 11, 128, 136, 151; idea for pantomimic dancing used by Noverre in collaboration with, 59; ballet-pantomime first used in his Alceste, 81; portion of reform opera owing to Noverre, 83; reform-opera, 89, 113-23; decision to turn from opera seria to tragédie lyrique, 113; Diderot's influence, 114, 117; gave music full sway in opera, 116; subscribed in toto to French tenets, 117; chose Paris for unfolding his reform opera, 117; quoted, 119; debt to Diderot: influence of Encyclopedists, 119; five great operas, 120; praise of Rousseau, 121; set Algarotti's Iphigénie to music, 128; criticized by Arteaga, 132; monographs on, 135; Roullet his go-between with Encyclopedists, 140; Arnaud's campaign in favor of reform opera, 141; realized all Arnaud's demands: what he did for opera summed up, 142; reforms claimed for, accomplished before his advent on scene, 143; attacked by La Harpe, 152; realized all ideals of Encyclopedists: put music in its proper place, 153; confidence in Rousseau's musical knowledge, 161; criticized by Hellouin, defended by Encyclopedists, 165; way prepared for, 168; Encyclopedists established principles of music drama for, 168
Gluck-Piccini Quarrel, 120; Arnaud's activity, 141; collaboration between Marmontel and Piccini, 164

Gods, Greek: upon the stage, 48 ff.
Goethe, Wolfgang von, 136
Goudar, Ange, 144, 146, 162; quoted, 145
Goudar, Sara, 145
Goussier, L. J., 72n
Grands ballets, Benserade's, 76
Grande Encyclopédie, La, 72
Grand opéra, earliest use of term, 25
Gregorian chant, 145
Grétry, A. E. M., 114, 153, 154n, 158; theory of music, 64; quoted, 142
Grimm, Friederich M., 33, 37, 38, 41, 71, 128, 129, 130, 137, 164, 165, 166; quoted, 35; definition of opera, 36; on need for repetition, 39; saw evils that Italian insistence on melody lead to, 40; defense of song in opera, 49; saw soul of French opera in merveilleux, 50; what he objected to in merveilleux, 50 ff.; ideas concerning ballets and divertissements, 54; on development of opera in Italy and France, 57; proposed pantomimic dancing with singers in orchestra pit, 59; on instrumental music, 65; on extracting ballet from the opera, 77; analysis of French ballets, 78; banished songs from opera, proscribed minuets, gavottes, and chaconnes from ballet, 79; attack on French music, 89 ff., 100; upheld Italian supremacy in verse and music, 90; Rameau's operas lauded by, 102, 110; defense of D'Alembert and Diderot in Rameau controversy, 109; influence in spreading Encyclopedist ideas, 127; Rousseau's errors corrected in articles by, 159
Gris de lin, Le, 76
Grosse General-Bass Schule (Mattheson), 111
Guerre de l'Opéra . . . , La (Cazotte), 92
Guinguené, music lexicographer, 161

Handbuch bei dem Generalbasse (Marpurg), 111
Handel changed course of English opera, 144
Harmony, as principal feature of operatic composition, 32; melody not outgrowth of, 43, 103, 107, 168; effect of Rameau's works on, 101; his theory of, 102, 103, 106; Rameau a master of, 108; danger of submerging theory in so-called sci-

Harmony (*Continued*)
  entific system, 109; first impetus toward
  doctrine of functional, 110; Rousseau's
  effort to popularize Rameau's theory, 112
Hasse, composer, 40, 41, 151
Hellouin, F., 156; indictment of Ency-
  clopedists, 165 ff.
Hercules amoureux (Benserade), 76
Herder, J. G. von, 136
Hertel, Johann W., 136
Hiller, J. A., 114, 137
Hirschberg, Eugen, 156
*Historisch-kritische Beyträge zur Auf-
  nahme der Musik* (Marpurg), 135
History of Music (Burney), 137
Holbach, Paul H. T. d', 90; part in *Le
  Devin du village,* 159
"Holzhacker," 71

"Idylle en musique" (St. Evremond), 8
Imitation-of-nature thesis, 14 f., 36, 99;
  attempt to force music into, 61 ff.; re-
  bellion against, 135
Instincts, theory of art based on, 16
Instrumental music, 61-73; apogee waited
  upon perfection of professional musicians, 31, 69; badly understood by critics,
  61; "peindre les sentiments" function,
  64; Rousseau an enemy of, 65; inferior
  to vocal, 65; tendency to condemn, 66;
  Encyclopedists' interest in technical progress, 68; progress dependent upon advance in manufacture of instruments,
  69; why French are incapable of having,
  96; failed to imitate nature successfully,
  131; must have a definite subject in
  mind, 144; *see also* Orchestra
Instruments, musical: endowed with human sentiments, 61; progress of music
  dependent upon advance in manufacture
  and playing of, 69; Diderot's three main
  groups, 72
Interpretation, musical: material of, 15
Iphigénie en Aulide (Gluck), 118n, 119,
  120, 128, 152, 166
Iphigénie en Aulide (Racine), as fit subject
  for musical treatment, 116; Dr. Burney's
  view, 118n; Diderot's analysis of scene
  from, 119; Du Roullet's version, 119,
  128, 152; Diderot's challenge to construct a libretto on model of, 128; Algarotti's libretto constructed on model of,
  set to music by Gluck, 128

Iphigénie en Tauride (Gluck), 83, 120
Istel, Edgar, 160n
Italians, supremacy in verse and music, 90
Italy, French turn to, for guidance, 20;
  influence of *Encyclopedia,* 127 ff.

Jaloux sans rival, Le (Noverre), 84
Jansen, A., 116n, 136; points of compari-
  son between Rousseau and Wagner, 137;
  praise for Rousseau, 163
Jaucourt, Chevalier de, 30, 41, 46, 48;
  quoted, 22, 23, 29; defense of song in
  opera, 49; definition of music, 68
Jélyotte, singer, 30, 91, 156
J. J. Rousseau (Corancez), 162
J. J. Rousseau musicien (Tiersot), 163
Jommelli, Niccoló, 59, 113, 114, 122
Jourdan, J. B., 90, 92, 95
Journal de Musique, 151
Journal de Paris, 118, 162
Journal de Politique et de Littérature, 152
Journal des Savants, 136, 161
Journal de Trévoux, 162; excerpt, 107n
Journal historique (Collé), 111
Jugement de l'orchestre de l'Opéra (Ruh-
  lière), 94
Jullien, Adolphe, 155
Justification de la musique française . . .
  (Morand), 97

King's Corner, *see Coin du roi*
Kircher, Athanasius, 162
Kirnberger, Johann P., 111, 134
Korner, Christian G., 161
Kunst des reinen Satzes, Das (Kirnberger),
  111
Kunstwerk der Zukunft, Das (Wagner),
  137

La Borde, J. B. de, 148n, 158
La Bruyère, Jean de, 4, 49, 153; quoted,
  8n; conception of the opera, 10, 48
Lacassagne, Joseph, 144, 146, 148n, 158n,
  164
Lacépède, B. G. E. de, divorced music from
  words, 150
La Cour, Mathon de, 151
La Harpe, J. F. de, 153; criticism of *Alceste,*
  132; enemy of the *Encyclopedia,* 151
Lalande, Michel R. de, 27, 161
La Laurencie, Lionel de, quoted, 5
La Martinière, de, essayist, 19
La Motte-Houdard, *ballet lyrique,* 24 ff.;

ballet de cour had renaissance in work of, 74
—— and Campra, 24n, 76
Landowska, Wanda, 156
Láng, Professor, 113, 114; quoted, 110
Language, degree of accent in, determines its musical adaptibility, 45; *see also* Words
—— French: capable of aria in Italian manner, 42; why, does not lend itself to musical adaptation, 45, 96, 98, 140; impossible to adapt to Italian music, 142
—— Italian: lends itself to musical adaptation, 45, 128
Lavoix, H., 69
Lecerf de la Viéville, J. L., 13
Leçons de clavecin (Diderot), 157
Leçons de musique de J. J. Rousseau, 163
Lecteur y mettra le titre, Le (Mirabeau), 150
Lefebure, Louis F. H., 154n, 155
Leo, composer, 32, 40
Leroquais, musicologist, 157
Lespinasse, Julie de, 148n
Lessing, E., 136
Lettre adressée à la société olympique de Paris (Bassi), 133
"Lettre à La Harpe" (Gluck), excerpt, 119
Lettre à M. D'Alembert . . . (Rameau), 104, 105
Lettre à M. Grimm . . . (Rousseau), 90, 107
Lettre à M. le B . . . d'H . . . sur l'opéra (Saint-Lambert), 140
Lettre à M. Rameau (Alembert), 104
Lettre au Mercure (Gluck), 121
Lettre à un de ses amis . . . (Sulzer), 134
Lettre à une dame . . . sur l'état . . . de l'opéra en Arcadie . . . (Holbach), 90
Lettre au Père Martini (Arnaud), 142
Lettre au sujet des observations du . . . Chastellux . . . (Diderot), 116
Lettre écrite . . . par l'abbé D.F. à M.F. (Suard), 92
Lettres sur les arts imitateurs (Noverre), 80
Lettre sur Iphigénie en Tauride (Arnaud), 142
Lettre sur la musique française (Rousseau), 95, 98, 136, 137; main objection to, 97; much attacked but little refuted, 100
Lettre sur les drames opéra (Du Roullet), 123
"Lettre sur Omphale" (Grimm), 89, 102

Liberté de la musique, La (Alembert), 102, 129
Librettist, relationship of composer and poet, 11; first writers for operatic stage in France, 29; must write with an eye to melodic adaptation: difference between dramatist's art and that of, 37; should be a musician, 38; given credit for much of success of eighteenth-century composers, 40; Gluck's, 113, 118; underestimation of power of musical expression, 119; must observe technique of dramatic writing, 131; composer should be inspired by, 133
Libretto, opera: Quinault's, 8; a vehicle for musical expression, 16; must limit itself to scant vocabulary: a new genre, 18; sacrificed to the music in France, 29, 32; before Corneille and Racine, 29; sacrificed to singer in Italy, 32; first to introduce historical characters into, 52; Italian music for French, 60; reform of the Italian, 113; Diderot insisted on value of a good, 115; written for composer, 116; overemphasis of role of, 131
Literati, reaction to French rage for music, 13
Literature, opera criticized as, 4 ff.
Lombardy claimed as place of origin of opera, 22
Louis XIV, ballets given during reign of, 76
Love, introduction of, into opera, 7, 12; most suitable subject for operatic treatment, 167
Lulli, 3-20 *passim,* 45, 91, 93; composing music for Molière's comedy ballets, 3; most violent critics spared, 5, 19; Boileau's praise of, 6; made the French music-conscious, 13; interpreted whole of scene, 17; reason for decline in popularity, 19; real creator of French opera, 23; *déclamation notée,* 28, 29; recitative brought to perfection by, 28; orchestra and singers, 29; a Florentine, comparable to other Italian composers, 30; a despot in his theater, 31, 69; type of melody used, 35; Marmontel claims unacquainted with recitative and aria-type opera, 41; could not allow extensive use of *divertissement,* 54; orchestral music: drilling of orchestra, 69; overtures, 70; an exception to ordinary run of French composers, 98; compared with Rameau,

Lulli (*Continued*)
108; operas not best sort of composition, 116; Gluck certain of conquering old guard defenders of, 118; cardinal point in his conception of *tragédie lyrique*, 143; tradition that music embellishes words, 146; praised at expense of Quinault, 153; universal appreciation of works, 167

Lulli-Quinault operas, 4-20 *passim*, 26, 27, 59; critics' protest against mixed genre, 4; probably introduced Quinault to technique of song writing, 8; time given to *déclamation* and to *divertissement*, 29; Rameau operas based on, 32, 57; Encyclopedists' attitude toward, 32; contain models of *divertissement*, 53 f.; Encyclopedists sought to change local opera by patching old creations, 58; Cahusac felt that music played traitor to text, 63, 64; influence of *ballet de cour*, 74; contemporary opinion of, 153

Lyric ballet, 25, 26

Lyrical tragedy, *see* Tragédie lyrique

Lyrico-dramatic spectacle proposed, 60

Machines, 3, 10, 47, 52

Magic, element of, in *le merveilleux*, 48 ff.

Mairan, physicist, 111

Maîtres de la sensibilité française, Les (Trahard), 157

Malebranche, Nicolas, effort to separate music from geometry, 14

Mannheim school, 156*n*

Marcello, Benedetto, 113

Mariage forcé, Le (Molière), 76

Marie de' Medici, 74

Marignan, de, 161

Marin, F. L. C., 90

Marmontel, F. J., 33, 41, 47, 48, 75, 115*n*, 153, 161; quoted, 42, 53, 56; defense of *le merveilleux*, 50; defense of the dance, 54; on role of the orchestra, 55; rewrote Quinault's libretti for Piccini, 56; *déclamation simple*, 58; advocated new music for Quinault's texts, 60; on instrumental music, 68; on pantomimic dancing, 79; part in Gluck-Piccini Quarrel, 121, 164; became Piccini's librettist, 121; poem in defense of Piccini's operas, 122

Marpurg, F. W., 111, 112, 114, 135, 136

Marre, Abbé de la, 91*n*

Martelli, Pier J., 113

Masson, Paul Marie, 164

Mattheson, Johann, 111

Maure, Mlle le, singer, 64

Mazarin, introduction of Italian opera to France, 3, 23

Melody, type of declamation used in writing, 34; importance in Italian and French operas, 35; aesthetic of, 36; most effective when prepared by recitative, 37; need for repetition, 39; Italian insistence on, 40; best type created in Italy, 41; knowledge of harmony useless in composition of, 43, 103, 107, 168; passions most satisfactorily expressed in, 43; can never be based on declamation, 44; monotony caused by lack of accent, 45; good, defined by Rousseau, 46; monotony of French, blamed on *merveilleux*, 51; Rousseau's definition, 66; for Rousseau the mainstay of music, 96; Rameau's theory, 106; Rameau a master of, 108; determined by prosody, 142; aim of all music must be, 145 f.; *see also* Aria

Mémoires . . . (Diderot), 102

Mémoires (Grétry), 142

Mémoires d'un père (Marmontel), 161

Ménestrier, Père, 76

Mercure, 89, 117, 128, 151, 160, 162

Mérobert, *see* Pidansat, M. F. M. de

Mersenne, Marin, 162

Merveilleux, le, role, 10; of the Quinault opera, 25; a major aspect of opera, 47 ff., 167; depends for its subjects upon mythology, 48 ff.; soul of French opera in, 50; Rousseau's attack upon, 52; attempt to introduce elements of, into ballet, 76*n*; what led to idea, 141

Metastasio, Pietro, 38*n*, 115, 116*n*; operas, 36*n*, 41; set stage for eighteenth-century Italian opera, 39; host of great composers collaborated with, 40; Vinci's opera based on play by, 99; reform of Italian libretto, 113; plays represent high-point in operatic composition, 131

Meuris, Jehan de, 162

Mime as essential part of opera, 118

Minuets, 79

Molière, 7, 27*n*; his *intermèdes* the only haven of the dance, 76

——— comedy ballets, 17*n*, 23, 24, 25, 57, 76; Lulli composing music for, 3; Quinault's imitation of meter of love songs from *divertissements* of, 8; influence of *ballet de cour*, 75

Moline, Pierre L., 135

Momigny, J. J., 154*n*

Mondonville, composer, 27, 66, 91*n*, 95, 144; motets, 70

Monsigny, Pierre A., 114

Montesquieu, on art of dancing, 75

Monteverdi, composer, 41*n*

Morand, Pierre de, 97

Motif, repetition of, 39

Mouret, Jean Joseph, opera composer, 19, 27

Mozart, 11, 122, 137, 164; gave music full sway in opera, 116

Muguet, singer, 51

Muses galantes, Les (Rousseau), 106, 160

Music, conceived as enhanced declamation, 6; of the film, 9; interdependence of words and, 13, 17, 146; must imitate nature, 14, 16; measured in terms of classical standards, 14; accentuates force of poetry, 15; principal object to express passions and sentiments, 16; seen as a major art, 16; attempt to integrate operatic, into field of artistic endeavor, 17; articles on in the *Encyclopedia*, 21, 89; Cahusac's articles, 23 ff.; all-important element in opera, 29, 30, 31, 32, 45; best page of musical history, 30; prospered under Lulli, 31; perfection waited upon development of professional musicians, 31; first critics to look at opera from view point of, 33; flexible meters, 38; should be an actor, 55; must be dominant element on lyric stage, 56; principal object to "paint," 61, 64, 130; anthropopsychical aspects, 61; Rousseau on aim of, 65; Rousseau's two categories, 66; rescued from tyranny of natural law, 68; conflict over respective excellence of Italian and French, 89 ff.; experimental spirit in, 94; for Rameau the universal principle of all arts and sciences, 102, 107, 109; as science, 103, 105, 106, 157 f. (*see also* Geometry); physical and artistic material is one, 110; power to imitate, 115, 143; the handmaid of poetry, 130; aim must be melody, 145 f.; cannot paint: is not an imitation of nature, 146; beauties of, depend on performance, 147; manner in which, may imitate nature, 150; quarrel between French and Italian, began with Raguenet,

151; important element of opera, 153; *see also* Opera; Orchestra; Singing

—— French: attack against, which culminated in the Bouffons' Quarrel, 89; Rousseau's attack upon, 95 ff.; slow movement due to language, 96; genius of, resided in theatrical declamation, 98; D'Alembert's attack, 106; tenets, 117; made imitative by Encyclopedists, 166; six concepts that formed basis of, 167

—— German: practically unknown in France, 156

—— Italian: for French libretti, 60

Musical theory, Rousseau's esteem for Rameau's accomplishments in field, 107, 108, 110; Rameau's discoveries, 107, 110; *see also* Harmonic theory

Musicians, music's apogee waited upon perfection of professional, 31, 69

Musikalisch-kritische Bibliothek (Forkel), 136

Musique française du moyen âge à la Révolution, La, 157

Mylius and Schink, translators, 136

Mythology, *merveilleux* depends for its subjects upon, 48 ff.; best source of opera plots, 130

Naples opera orchestra, 70

"Natural music," 17

Nature, music must imitate, 14, 16; natural beauty in music exists eternally in, 15; music the result of obedience to laws of, 17

Neveu de Rameau, Le, (Diderot), 115, 136, 156*n*

Nietzsche, F., 143; quoted, 36*n*

Nitocris (Terradellas), 93

Nougaret, Pierre, 149

Nouveau Mode de musique (Blainville), 160

Nouvelle Héloise, La (Rousseau), 160*n*

Noverre, J. G., 78, 79, 148*n*; *ballet en action,* or *poème-ballet,* 55, 74; idea used in collaboration with Gluck, 59; went to Germany to create modern ballet, 77, 81; indebtedness to *Encyclopedia,* 80, 81, 82, 84; revived art of pantomime, 80, 81; divided the dance into two categories, 82; responsible for ballet in Gluck's works: had music written to suit dialogue of ballet, 83; Goudar's sarcasm leveled against, 145

Oboe, 65
Observations sur Alceste (Rousseau), 137
*Observations sur la lettre de J. J. Rous-
seau . . .* (Cazotte), 97
Observations sur la musique (Chabanon),
145
*Observations sur les principes de l'har-
monie . . .* (Serre), 140
Oedipus of Sophocles compared with that
of Corneille, 7
Olivet, d', abbé, 45
On ne s'avise jamais de tout (Sedaine-
Monsigny), 149
Opera, scope for depiction of passions, 9,
41; classical objection to, 10; interdependence of words and music, 13, 17,
146; why successful, are rare: how concept of, differs from tragedy, 18; historical considerations, 21-31; introduction into France, 22; music the all-
important element, 29, 30, 31, 32, 45;
first critics to look at, from view point
of music, 33; distinction between drama
and, 35 ff.; Grimm's definition, 36; need
for repetition of melody and parts of
aria: purpose of melody, 39; should in-
volve scenes of great pathos, 39; became
fixed to suit singer's wishes, 40; highest
form of musical endeavor, 43; Noverre's
conception, 83; Diderot insists that music
must take upper hand, 116; basis for
the new, 116; Algarotti's attitude toward, 128; music the handmaid of
poetry: mythology the best source of
plots, 130; tendency to evaluate on basis
of libretto, 131; ensemble technique of
opera buffa introduced into *opera seria*,
143; Beaumarchais' order of preference,
147; considered from point of view of
literature only, 152; criticized on dramatic grounds, 153; essentially a literary
genre, 167; *see also* Composer; Librettist; Libretto; Instrumental music; Orchestra; Singers; *and under names of
composers and librettists, e.g.* Lulli; Quinault
—— criticism, 32-56; based chiefly on literary and dramatic grounds, 9 ff.; St.
Evremond's, 10, 11; touchstone of
French, 13; of a journalistic turn, 19
—— English: how Handel changed course
of, 144
—— French: development owes first impetus to Mazarin, 3; license for a national, accorded, 3, 23; Lulli's skepticism,
3; critics' protest against new mixed
genre, 4; criticized as literature, 4 ff.;
distinguished from Italian, 4 f., 46, 142;
quarrel over respective merits of Italian
and, 13; revolt of audiences: desire for
more modern compositions, 19; Encyclopedists turned to Italy for guidance,
20; Lulli the real creator: ballet reduced
to minor role, 23; Cahusac's account of
inception of, 30, 31; mid-eighteenth century, 32; tendency to remain fixed drew
Encyclopedists' fire, 32; little distinction
between recitative and melody, 35; con-
cern for vigor of the national, 35; resistance to introduction of aria form, 42;
based on theatrical declamation, 44;
cause of dearth of melody, 45; use of
the spectacular, 48; mythology and the
supernatural should provide soul of,
48 ff.; continued dramatization of Greek
epic: violation of natural laws, 49;
Grimm's diatribe against, 51; aria in,
can only be applied to *air de danses,* 52;
messiah of the new, had to be a foreigner, 56; suggested reforms, 57-60; in
conflict with classical tragedy, 57; *style
galant,* 57, 92; inquiry into causes of
monotony, 58; speedy recitative and
movement advocated, 58; new, to show
even distribution of recitative and melody, 60; *ballet de cour* an immediate ancestor, 74; dance the saving grace, 77;
music and text inseparable, 97; secret of
musical expression in, 98; Bouffons did
not create a revolution in, 100; Rameau
rejuvenated, 108; after Lulli, unchanged
until coming of Rameau, 113; abuses
traced to classical declamation: correctives, 115; Saint-Lambert's grievances,
140; course followed, 1670–1770, 153;
turned into *opéra-comique sérieux,* 166;
three chief tenets, 167
—— Italian: distinguished from French,
4 f., 46, 142; introduced into France, 3;
rejected by St. Evremond, 11; quarrel
over respective merits of French and, 13;
place of origin, 21 f.; took on elements
of the *fêtes,* 22; brought to France, 23;
Neapolitan school, 32; *da capo aria* form,
35; eighteenth-century melody, of recitative and aria type, 40; best type, 41;

highest expression of the art, 42, 43; based on classical Greek tragedy, 49; reason for quick growth, 57; overture, 70; scored by Rochemont, 99; "natural declamation" found in *recitativo* and *aria* of, 115; Arteaga's analysis, 131; flayed by Goudar, 144
—— reform: Gluck's, 89, 113-23; inspired by Frenchmen, 113; Diderot's ideas, 114; articles on, are refinements of Diderot's ideas, 120; way paved by *Encyclopedia*, 122; Arnaud's campaign in favor of, 141
Opéra-ballet, 25, 26; Rameau's, 25, 26, 27, 74, 76
Opera buffa, Italian, 94; texture of, 58; Piccini's *forte*, 120; French disgusted with, 133; Nougaret on, 149; troupe, *see* Bouffons
Opéra-comique, French, 11*n*; spread of new, to foreign lands, 114; encouraged by Encyclopedists, 166
Opera poem, *see* Libretto
Opera poet, *see* Librettist
Oper und Drama (Wagner), 137
Orchestra, role of, 55; better understanding of organization of, 69; opera orchestras in Paris, Dresden, and Naples, 70; poor location of conductor: musicians directed by first violin, 71; over-importance given to, 131
Orchestral music, under Lulli and Rameau, 31; emphasized as principal feature of operatic composition, 32; Lulli's, 69; change wrought in compositions, 70; *see also* Instrumental music; Music
Orfeo (Monteverdi), 41*n*
Orphée (Gluck), 120, 146; priceless compliment to Rousseau in *Dédicace d'*, 121
Ortes, Giammaria, 113
Overture, 70, 129; Gluck's use of, 143

Pantomime, *see* Ballet pantomime
Parallèle des italiens et des français, en ce qui regarde la musique et les opéras (Raguenet), 13
Paride ed Elena (Gluck), 118
Paris, opera the rage of, 13; reception of Gluck's reform-opera, 120; clearing-house for ideas concerning art and literature, 127
Paris opera orchestra, 70
Passions, scope of opera for depiction of, 9, 41; melody represents high point of,

37; most satisfactorily expressed in melody, 43; human voice best equipped to render accents of, 65; expressed in sounds, 138; *see also* Emotions
Peines et les plaisirs de l'amour, Les (Gilbert), 30*n*
Père de famille, Le (Diderot), 84
Pergolesi, composer, 32, 36, 40, 41, 52, 55, 115
Période musicale, 42
Perrault, Charles, 167; quoted, 3, 12, 13; champion of moderns against ancients, 11; criticism of opera, 12; tradition that music embellishes words, 146
Perrin, Abbé, opera poem, 30
—— and Cambert, granted license for a national opera, 3, 23; assembled musicians and singers, 30
Petit Prophète de Bochmischbroda, Le (Grimm), 90 f., 95, 98, 100, 137; Pidansat's parody of, 92
Phaëton (Lulli-Quinault), 63
Phaëton (Racine), 7
Phèdre (Racine), 8*n*
Philidor (François André Danican), 114, 151, 157, 158
Philidor, Anne Danican, founded "concerts spirituels," 69
Philosophes, see Encyclopedists
Piccini, composer, Marmontel rewrote Quinault's libretti for, 56; *opera buffa:* Gluck-Piccini Quarrel, 120, 164; collaboration with Marmontel, 164
Pidansat, Mathieu F. M. de, 91
Pirro, 157
Platée (Rameau), 76, 110
Plato, attitude toward music, 6
Poem, *see* Libretto
Poème-ballet, 55, 78
Poet, *see* Librettist
Poétique de la musique, La (Lacépède), 150
Poetry, tends toward musical expression, 15; great, contains its own music, 17; *see also* Opera poem
Poets, French, could not represent violent passions, 141
Poinsinet, book to *Ernelinde* rewritten by Diderot, 158
"Polemics and Reforms," 87-123
Polymnie (Marmontel), 122
Pomone (Perrin), 29
Popelinière, La, 106
Porpora, Nicola Antonio, 32, 36

Post-Encyclopedist criticism of music in France, 149-54
Principes généraux d'acoustique (Diderot), 157, 158n
Principles of Composition (Rameau), 139
Prod'homme, J. G., 156
Prophéties du grand prophète Monet, Les (Pidansat), 92
Prosody, 44, 47; determines melody, 142; attempt to base musical, upon principles of accentuation, 143
Prunières, Henry, 157
Psyché (Molière), 76
Pygmalion (Mouret), 74
Pygmalion (Rameau), 110
Pygmalion (Rousseau), 136, 137, 159, 160

Quadrio, Francesco S., 113, 134
Queen's Corner, *see Coin de la reine*
Quelques réflexions sur la musique moderne (Framery), 151
Questions sur l'Encyclopédie (Voltaire), 155
Quinault, Philippe, error in terming his operas *tragédies en musique*, 4n; singled out for abuse, 5 ff.; Boileau's invective aimed against, 5 f.; turned to opera libretto: made tragedy a long love duet, 8; Racine's jealousy and emulation of, 8n; Perrault's defense of, 11; *divertissement* of operas, 23, 24, 25; new genre: insufficient use of ballet, 23; *tragédie lyrique: merveilleux* element of opera, 25; forced to curtail role of the dance, 27; growing popularity as a poet: Voltaire's vindication of, 27; Encyclopedists' drive to rehabilitate, 27, 28; Lulli's debt to, 28, 29; verses did not lend themselves to aria type of melody, 42; use of the *divertissement*, 48, 54; great poetic invention, 50; Marmontel rewrote his libretti for Piccini, 56; incorporated the dance into the opera, 76; Arteaga's criticism, 131; wrote ideal type of *tragédie lyrique*, 152; considered the creator of opera, 153

Racine, Jean, 4, 37, 113; asked Boileau's aid in completing *Phaëton*, 7; concessions to love in works of, 7; competition with Quinault, 8n; could never successfully be set to music, 17; plays elevated French dramatic taste, 29; Diderot's analysis of

scene from *Iphigénie*, 119; *see also Iphigénie en Aulide*
Raguenet, François, 13, 151
Rameau, Jean Philippe, theory of harmony, 14n, 43, 139, 153, 157, 158, 162, 164; savagely attacked, 19; opera ballet, 25, 26, 27, 74, 75; time given to declamation in operas, 29; turned opera into vast *fête* or *divertissement*, 29, 48, 59; made music all-important element in opera, 29, 30, 31, 32, 45; principal changes wrought by, 32; reactionary elements in works, 33; influence of Lulli-Quinault, 57; followed public taste in compositions, 69; *style galant* defeated, 92; talents hampered by *divertissements*, 113; operas not best sort of composition, 116; Gluck certain of conquering old guard defenders of, 118; D'Alembert's *Eléments* gave currency to ideas of, 133; Gluck got idea of active chorus from, 143; forced too many notes into *tragédie lyrique*, 144; D'Alembert called a traitor to theories of, 155; Rousseau's praise of, 157n; Rousseau followed in use of *basse fondamentale*, 163; Encyclopedists accused of treachery in relations with, 165; universal appreciation of works, 167; attempts to offset claims for his theory of music as science, 167; the useful and sound in his harmonic theories propagated, 168
——controversy, 101-12; as theorist and composer, 101 ff., 110; refusal to do articles on music for *Encyclopedia*, 102; lauded by Encyclopedists: his animosity to them, 102, 107, 110; discovery of chordal relations: geometrical justification for acoustical theories, 102; quoted, 103, 105; accused D'Alembert of treachery, 104, 105, 106; D'Alembert's praise of, 105; gave French best they were capable of attending to, 106; animosity to Rousseau, 106; theory that melody is to be derived from harmony, 106; popularizers of his theories, 107, 112; rejuvenated opera, 108; D'Alembert defended against accusation of, 109; grossly maltreated Rousseau, 112
Ramler, critic, 136
Raynal, Abbé, 158; quoted, 101n
Recitative, use of Alexandrian for, 8, 38; St. Evremond's objection to, 10; English

and German objection, 10n; or *déclama-tion notée*, of Lulli's operas, 28, 29, 32; declamation the basis of, 34, 35; melody most effective when prepared by, 37; opera based on aria and, but half an opera, 44; defined by Rousseau, 46; Italian, 89

Récy, René de, 155

Réflexions d' un patriote sur l'opéra . . . (Rochemont), 98

"Réflexions lyriques" (Caux de Cappeval), 92

Réflexions sur la musique . . . (Brijon), 143

"Réforme de l'Opéra, La" (Caux de Cappeval), 92

Reform opera, *see* Opera, reform

Remarques sur la musique et la danse (Goudar), 144

Rémond de Saint-Mard, Toussaint, 18

Repetition of melody and parts of aria in opera, 39

Réponse du coin du roi au coin de la reine (Pidansat), 91

Revolutionists as music critics, 149 ff.

Rhetoric, effort to outline a new, for composition of opera, 18

Riccoboni, L., 8

Riedel, F. J., 135

Riemann, Hugo, 111 f., 156n; quoted, 35n, 67n

Risposta che ritrovò . . . alla critica ragionatissima delle poesie drammatiche . . . (Calsabigi), 134

Rivoluzioni del teatro musicale italiano, Le, (Arteaga), 129

Rochemont, de, comparison of Italian and French operas, 98 f.

Roland (Lulli-Quinault), 53, 54

Roland (Piccini), 120, 122

Rolland, Romain, 119, 156; quoted, 164; defense of Encyclopedists, 165

Rome, claimed as place of origin of opera, 22; introduced dancing pantomime, 145

Rossi, Luigi, 3

Rousseau, Jean Jacques, 9, 34, 43, 165; denied that opera existed in France, 35; quoted, 41, 44, 45, 46, 53; theory of melody, 42 ff.; good melody and recitative defined by, 46; saw two distinct problems involved in opera, 47; attack upon the *merveilleux,* 52; saw no place in opera for the dance, 55, 79; criticism

of French opera, 56; criticism of singers' conduct on stage, 58; musical doctrines, 61 ff.; enemy of musical instruments, 65; on overture, 70; on orchestras, 70 f.; articles on music, 89; as composer of an Italian-type *opera buffa,* 94; attack upon French music: won Bouffons' war for Encyclopedists, 95 ff.; main objection to his criticism, 97; Blainville's answer to, 98; *Lettre* much attacked but little refuted, 100; tributes to Rameau, 102, 157n; on geometrical relations of sound, 104; Rameau's animosity to: his attack on, 106; respect for Rameau's authority 106, 112; answer to his attack, 107; Diderot's defense of, in Rameau controversy, 108; grossly maltreated by Rameau, 112; Gluck's praise of, 117, 121; theory that silence could be expressed musically, 119; champion of Encyclopedists: admirer of Gluck's reform opera, 120; repercussions of theories upon German art and thought, 136; points of comparison between Wagner and, 137; adaptation of his *Devin* given at Drury Lane, 138; only poet composer of France, 149; scored by Landowska, 156; considered link between Rameau and Gluck, 157; most violently attacked of all contributors to *Encyclopedia,* 158; facts about *Le Devin,* 159; proof of his knowledge of music, 160; criticism that pleased Gluck: ability as composer: table of works owned, read, or mentioned by, 162; effort to master use of *basse fondamentale,* 163; attitude toward Gluck, 166

Ruhlière, Claude de, 118n; attack against Encyclopedists, 94

Sacre rappresentazioni, 21

Saggio sopra l'opera in musica (Algaratti), 128 f.

St. Evremond, Charles de, 4, 49, 99, 134, 153; quoted, 6, 8, 10, 18n; criticism of opera, 10, 11

Saint-Lambert, F. J. de, intellectual kinship to *philosophes:* list of grievances concerning French opera, 140

Saisons, Les (Benserade), 76

Salieri, Antonio, 147

Sallé, Mlle, dancer, 74

Sammlung musikalischen Schriften . . . (Hertel), 136

"Satire X" (Boileau), excerpt, 5
Saunier de Beaumont, champion of French opera, 19
Savoie, Cardinal de, 76
Savoie, Duchesse de, 76
Scarlatti, composer, 32, 36, 41, 55
Schink and Mylius, translators, 136
Schobert, Johann, 157n
Schopenhauer, Arthur, 36n; quoted, 146
Schulze, J. A. P., 134
Science, music as, 103, 105, 106, 109; see also Geometry
Seconde Lettre du correcteur des Bouffons (Jourdan), 95
Sensations, theory of art based on, 16
Serre, Jean Adam, 140
Setting, musical: critics' underestimation of, 4
Silence expressed musically, 119
Singers, became tyrannical, 40; expected to complement music by means of pantomime, 55, 58; style and delivery: conduct on operatic stage, 58; in orchestra pit to accompany pantomimic dancing, 59; all-important, 131
Singing, tradition that song is enhanced declamation, 17, 18; emphasis placed on, to detriment of acting and declaiming, 18; recitative, 28; under Lulli, 31
Singspiel, development furthered by Le Devin du village, 137
Sonata, 61; Brijon's concept of, 144
Song, defined as exalted speech, 13; how opera aria differs from, 39; no connection between speech and, 45; rationale of, in opera, 49; merveilleux gave plausibility to, 50; French, 96
—— of birds, 67
Sounds, passions expressed in, 138
Sourdéac, Marquis de, 47
Spectacle, use of, 23
Spectacle lyrique, 48
Speech, no connection between song and, 45; see also Language; Words
Stage machinery, 3, 10, 47, 52
Stamitz, Johann W. A., 151, 157n
Style galant, insistence on divertissement, 57; defeated Rameau and the French serious opera, 92
Suard, J. B., 92, 141, 148n
Sulpitius, Johann, creator of operatic form, 22
Sulzer, Johann G., 41, 80, 134

Supernatural, element of, in merveilleux, 48 ff.
Switzerland, postlude to Bouffons' Quarrel appeared in, 98
Symphonie, is instrumental melody, 65; Brijon's concept of, 144

Tartini, Giuseppe, 43, 162
Taste, good, defined, 16
Telemann, Georg Philipp, 156n
Télémaque (Mirabeau), 150
Terradellas or Terradeglias, Domenico, 93, 115
Théâtre Français, 149
Théorie de la musique (Ballière), 161
Thésée (Lulli-Quinault), 53
Tiersot, Julien, quoted, 106, 163
Titon et l'Aurore (Mondonville), 91, 92, 95
Tone, Rameau's discovery of fundamental tone, 110
Torelli, machines, 3
Toth, Karl, 160n
Tourneux, Maurice, 155
Traetta, composer, 59, 113, 115, 122; introduced ensemble technique of opera buffa into opera seria, 143
Tragédie lyrique, or Quinault opera, 25; principal element of the new, 33; chorus, 59; innovations due to: Gluck's decision to turn from opera seria to, 113; interest in German and Italian, 114; ballet came to take place of, 141; achievements of Lulli, Rameau, and Gluck, 143; opéra-bouffon overshadowing, 149; Quinault wrote ideal type, 152
Tragédies en musique, 4n
Tragedy, as a fit subject for musical treatment, 116, 152
—— classical: transformation into opera, 3 ff.; how concept of opera differs from, 18; influence upon French opera, 57
Trahard, P., 159
Traité de la danse (Cahusac), 50, 75, 164
Traité de la prosodie française (Olivet), 45
Traité des sensations (Condillac), 140
Traité général des éléments du chant (Lacassagne) 164
Triomphe de l'amour, Le (Lulli-Quinault), 26, 76
Trois chapitres, Les (Diderot), 95

Ueber die Musik des Ritters von Gluck (Riedel), 135

Useful and the beautiful, Sulzer's theory of, 135

Vandeul, Mme de, Diderot's daughter, 72n
Variétés littéraires (Arnaud), 134
Variétés littéraires (Saint-Lambert), 140, 141
Verità nemica dell' apparenza sollevata dal tempo, La, 76
Vertheidigung der Oper (Ramler), 136
Vinci, composer, 32, 36, 42, 52; opera based on Metastasio's play, 99
Vocal music, voice best equipped to render accents of passion, 65; impossible to the French, 96; best, approaches closest to spoken language, 144; see also Singing; Song
Voisenon, Abbé, 91n
Vols, 52
Voltaire, vindication of Quinault at expense of Boileau, 27; rehabilitated Quinault as opera poet, 153; misquoted Cahusac, 155; contradicted Boileau's judgment of Quinault, 155n

Wagner, Richard, quoted, 136; points of comparison between Rousseau and, 137; Encyclopedists established principles of music drama for, 168
Weisse, Felix, 137
Wieland, Christoph M., 136
Wit put into music, 19
Words, interdependence of music and, 13, 17; could never adequately express emotions, 18; object of, 44; French sacrifice music to, 45; thesaurus of musically adaptable French, 46; singled out for their musical adaptability, 52; see also Language

Yzo, Polemical writer, 97

Zarlino, Gioseffo, 111
Zeno, Apostolo, 41, 52; reform of Italian libretto, 113
Zingara, La (Capua), 91n
Zoroastre (Rameau), 110